Essential Personal Finance

Young people face unprecedented financial challenges: rising student debt, stiff competition for jobs, barriers to home ownership, dwindling state benefits and prospects of a longer working life. Today, students need financial knowledge and skills more than ever before, not just to build their own financial security, but to create the new generation of advisers that can help all citizens navigate the complex world of personal finance.

Essential Personal Finance is a guide to all the key areas of personal finance: budgeting, managing debt, savings and investments, insurance, securing a home and laying the foundations for retirement. It also provides an introduction to some of the essential foundations of a modern undergraduate finance qualification, including:

- The nature of financial institutions, markets and economic policy that shape the opportunities and decisions that individuals face.
- The range of financial assets available to households, the risk-return trade-off, basics of portfolio construction and impact of tax.
- The importance of the efficient market hypothesis and modern portfolio theory in shaping investment strategies and the limitations of these approaches.
- Behavioural finance as a key to understanding factors influencing individual and market perceptions and actions.
- Using financial data to inform investment selection and to create financial management tools that can aid decision-making.
- A comprehensive companion website accompanies the text to enhance students' learning and includes answers to the end-of-chapter questions.

Written by authors who contribute experience as financial advisers, practitioners and academics, *Essential Personal Finance* examines the motivations, methods and theories that underpin financial decision-making, as well as offering useful tips and guidance on money management and financial planning. The result is a compelling combination of an undergraduate textbook aimed at students on personal finance and financial services courses, and a practical guide for young people in building their own financial strength and capability.

Lien Luu is a Chartered and Certified Financial Planner and a fellow of the Chartered Institute of Insurance. She is also a Registered Life Planner and has previously worked as a financial planner helping clients build wealth. Lien is currently an Associate Head of School for Enterprise and Commercial in the School of Economics, Finance and Accounting, Coventry Business School and has taught at universities for more than 15 years.

Jonquil Lowe is an economist and has previously worked as an investment analyst and head of the Money Research Group at Which?. Jonquil is now Senior Lecturer in Economics and Personal Finance at The Open University and also a freelance researcher/author.

Jason Butler is an author of the first and second editions of *The Financial Times Guide to Wealth Management: How to plan, invest and protect your financial assets*. He is also a columnist for *The Financial Times* where, as 'The Wealthman', he writes about personal finance-related issues. Jason also provides expert comments on personal finance to BBC Radio and a range of other publications, media and websites.

Tony Byrne is a financial planner and an ex-accountant. He has been a regular contributor to both national and local press for many years. He has written a regular column for *Money Marketing* for more than 10 years. He is a previous Chairman of The Institute of Financial Planning Northern Home Counties branch.

Essential Personal Finance

A Practical Guide for Students

Lien Luu, Jonquil Lowe, Jason Butler
and Tony Byrne

Routledge
Taylor & Francis Group

LONDON AND NEW YORK

First published 2017
by Routledge
2 Park Square, Milton Park, Abingdon, Oxon OX14 4RN

and by Routledge
711 Third Avenue, New York, NY 10017

Routledge is an imprint of the Taylor & Francis Group, an informa business

British Library Cataloguing in Publication Data
A catalogue record for this book is available from the British Library

Library of Congress Cataloging in Publication Data
Names: Luu, Lien, 1967– author. | Lowe, Jonquil, author. | Butler, Jason
(Financial planner), author.
Title: Essential personal finance: a practical guide for students /
Lien Luu, Jonquil Lowe, Jason Butler and Tony Byrne.
Description: 1 Edition. | New York: Routledge, 2017. | Includes index.
Identifiers: LCCN 2016041399| ISBN 9781138692930 (hardback) |
ISBN 9781138692954 (pbk.) | ISBN 9781315531496 (ebook)
Subjects: LCSH: Finance, Personal.
Classification: LCC HG179.L888 2017 | DDC 332.024–dc23
LC record available at https://lccn.loc.gov/2016041399

ISBN: 978-1-138-69293-0 (hbk)
ISBN: 978-1-138-69295-4 (pbk)
ISBN: 978-1-315-53149-6 (ebk)

Typeset in Gill Sans
by Out of House Publishing

Visit the companion website: www.routledge.com/cw/luu

Printed and bound by CPI Group (UK) Ltd, Croydon, CR0 4YY

Contents

CONTENTS

Figures

Tables

Boxes

Acknowledgements

The publication of this book has only been made possible by the invaluable contribution of many people. First of all, we are delighted to acknowledge our gratitude to the editor, Mr Andy Humphries, for the critical part he played in this project. With his encouragement, guidance, help and support, we obtained the much-needed impetus to turn ideas into a proposal. Then, with his persistent efforts and persuasive skills, he obtained the editorial board's support for the book. We are therefore also greatly indebted to the editorial board for their support for the project.

We are also grateful to our anonymous reviewers who took the time to carefully examine the proposal and make invaluable suggestions on ways to improve the book. We hope they will be pleased with the result.

Hendrik Pontson, a student at Coventry University, worked patiently to help translate ideas into illustrations in Chapters 1, 5, 6, 7 and 12. Laura Johnson, assistant editor, has also been wonderful on this project, cheerfully providing us with direction and guidance on the steps needed to move the project forward. Penny Harper, the copy-editor, has impressed us with her thoroughness and meticulousness and we are grateful for her help.

We give sincere thanks for the help and support we have received and hope that the book will serve as an indispensable addition to the body of literature on personal finance.

Introduction

Essential Personal Finance: A Practical Guide for Students has a twofold aim. First, it is a textbook for students studying personal finance as part of a finance-related undergraduate qualification or for professional exams. Second, it is a practical guide for building the personal wealth that you need in current market-based economies in order to meet your goals and build financial resilience and financial independence.

Unlike most other textbooks in the field, this one is written by a group of practitioners and academics. We have been brought together by our common interest in personal finance and commitment to enhancing financial capability and education. While the chapters in this book collectively provide a comprehensive and complete introduction to the key areas of personal finance, we each bring a different perspective. This is reflected in our various chapters which may be viewed rather as independent articles.

The chapters reveal a high degree of harmony between us on the important tenets and foundations of sound **financial planning**. However, you will also sense our different perceptions about money and sensitivities to aspects, such as risk. This serves to underline how personal finance and financial planning are as much art as science. As you study the text, you may enjoy identifying and debating the tensions between these perspectives as they aid you in forming your own financial views and capabilities.

We wish you well in your studies and, even more importantly, in your future lives and trust that a healthy outlook towards money and sound financial planning will help you to achieve your goals whatever they may be.

Lien Luu
Jonquil Lowe
Jason Butler
Tony Byrne

Part I

Have a vision and a plan

Chapter 1

The necessity of private wealth

Lien Luu

Young people in the UK and many other countries face unprecedented financial challenges – rising student debt, stiff competition for jobs, barriers to home ownership, dwindling state benefits and prospects of a longer working life. Indeed, newspapers frequently speculate that, as a result of the high cost of providing pensions, young people in the UK might never be able to retire. Yet, the UK's formal education system does not adequately prepare young people to deal with these challenges and consequently, personal debt has now reached a record level and people, both young and old, are struggling to meet their personal financial commitments. This chapter explores why you should take control of your personal finances and build a secure future by creating private wealth.

Learning outcomes

By the end of this chapter you will:

- understand the importance of taking control and responsibility for your personal finances;
- be aware of fundamental demographic and social changes in society that necessitate individual responsibility;
- understand the benefits of creating personal wealth and the different methods of wealth accumulation.

1.1 Defining wealth

'To get rich is glorious' is a quote commonly attributed to Deng Xiaoping who became the leader of an impoverished China in 1978. He introduced an ambitious programme of economic reform resulting in a remarkable transformation of the country. In the process, the Chinese were given the state's blessing to embark on a rapid quest for the accumulation of private wealth. More than 30 years later, China has more billionaires than the USA: 568 billionaires in 2016 compared with 535 in the United States, giving China the biggest population of billionaires in the world (Hurun cited in Frank, 2016). Box 1.1 highlights other differences in the wealthy between the two countries.

❖ BOX 1.1 COMPARING THE RICH IN CHINA AND THE USA

China's relatively recent economic rise means that the wealthy tend to be younger and that the rich are more likely than their American counterparts to make their fortunes in property. Key differences are:

America's wealthy have more money. The net wealth of the top 400 in the USA accounts for 15.09 per cent of GDP, while in China it accounts for 7.6 per cent.

America's wealth is distributed more evenly across the country. Wealth in China is more concentrated in coastal areas. These areas have benefited from policies promoting development. The top nine people on Forbes' list of the wealthiest Chinese are from those provinces. In contrast, America's wealthy are spread more evenly throughout the country. Except California and New York, there are not very significant geographical differences.

China's wealthy are younger. Since 1992, China's market economy has grown rapidly, and many of today's wealthy began to get rich then. People around 50 years old make up the largest group; they were around 30 years old in 1992. The average age of China's richest 400 is 49 years old, the average for the USA is 65.

Sources of wealth. China's wealthy made their fortunes from property, while in the USA information technology is an important source of wealth. America's wealthy come from a greater variety of fields: sports, the media, express delivery services and airplane rental. In China, these industries have not made anyone wealthy enough to make the Forbes list. The ability of the internet to create wealth is strong in the USA, but China's wealthy IT moguls got rich through income from the online gaming industry. Of China's wealthy, 129 had operations related to property and their total worth makes up approximately 35 per cent of the total for all 400. Of America's wealthy, 36 people (9 per cent) had operations related to property and their total worth makes up approximately 6.8 per cent of the total for all 400. Thirty of America's wealthiest 400 have operations related to IT, software and the internet, but in China the number is 18.

Source: adapted from ChinaFile (2012).

In the UK, many people may dream of becoming wealthy but may not be active in pursuing wealth as a goal. Other goals such as having fun, travelling, pursuing a successful career and having a good relationship may seem more relevant and important at a young age. Ambivalence towards money and wealth poses another barrier to the pursuit of wealth. Money is a taboo subject, yet most of us have powerful feelings about it. Some people feel guilty about having too much money, while others feel ashamed of not having enough or not making enough money. Some are afraid to deal with money at all fearing that it will corrupt them in some way or make them feel inadequate, while others constantly worry about money, which affects the quality of their lives (Sabri et al., 2006). In the Christian tradition, a modest accumulation of wealth is promoted so that individuals can look after themselves but hoarding excessive wealth is seen as a burden and even a sin (Tycehurst and Roberts, 2015). However, with fundamental social and demographic changes taking place, wealth accumulation is now a necessity if individuals are to take care of themselves.

Wealth has many dimensions and includes both **financial capital** and **human capital**. In financial terms, it refers to the total value of all assets accumulated less the value of any debts held. Assets include money in the bank, savings, investments, property and other forms of financial capital an individual may possess at a particular time. Money, thus, is just one form of wealth.

Wealth is also different from income because it measures the capital value of the **stock** assets at a given point in time, while income represents a regular **flow** of money. However, the two are related because income can be set aside to build wealth and the stock of wealth can produce income (for example, as when money in a savings

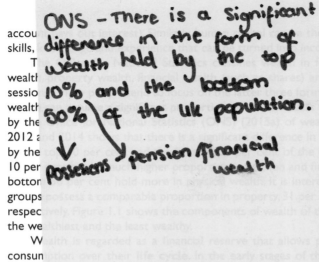

accou... *[handwritten note overlaps]*...ought of as the stock of
skills, ...me through working.

T... ...ur categories: pension
wealt... ...d physical wealth (pos-
sessio... ...s of wealth, but pension
wealt... ...vealth. Indeed, research
by the ... ...th in the UK between
2012 a... ...he form of wealth held
by the ... JK population. The top
10 per ... ...ancial wealth, while the
bottor... ...ting, though, that both
groups ... ...ent versus 34 per cent,
respec...ively...e two different groups,
the we...

[Handwritten note: ONS – There is a significant difference in the form of wealth held by the top 10% and the bottom 50% of the UK population. ↓ possessions ↓ pension financial wealth]

W... ...ople to smooth their
consum...life cycle, savings and
borrowing (or gifts from others) are used to fund education, family formation and
property acquisition. Ideally, income then increases relative to consumption enabling
debts to be reduced and wealth to be accumulated. In the later stages, wealth is used
to maintain consumption in retirement when income from work declines or stops.

In the earlier stages of the life cycle, wealth may consist largely of housing,
housing-related items and functional possessions, such as cars, furniture and other
durable items to meet current consumption needs. As households mature, property
tends to gain in value, and other forms of wealth such as pensions and other savings
become more important. A high level of savings may be expected among older households, since they have had time to accumulate these through employer pension plans
and other savings and investments (Lafrance and LaRochelle-Côté, 2012).

Despite ambivalent attitudes towards wealth, its possession can have a significant impact on the quality of life. Indeed, research suggests that the satisfaction individuals derive from their wealth can have an impact on their economic and consumer
choices, job productivity, physical and mental health, and even marital happiness

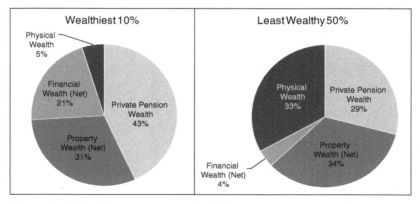

Figure 1.1 Wealth components in the UK
Source: ONS (2015a, p.9).

(Gasiorowska, 2014). This well-being dimension of wealth underlines its importance as a goal.

ACTIVITY 1.1

What is your attitude towards wealth? How do you define wealth in your culture? What kinds of assets do people in your culture hold?

1.1.1 Global uneven distribution of wealth

Wealth is unequally distributed in the world. According to Credit Suisse (2015), the value of the global wealth was worth more than $250 trillion in 2015. A striking point is that the majority (71 per cent) of the world population owns just a small proportion (3 per cent) of global wealth, while a tiny minority (0.7 per cent) owns more than 45 per cent of global wealth – see Figure 1.2. Individuals who have more than $3,210 belong to the wealthiest half of the world's population, those with more than $68,800 belong to the top 10 per cent, while those who have more than $759,900 belong to the top 1 per cent.

The global **average** net-worth is calculated at $52,400 per adult, but this masks regional variations. Switzerland heads the list with average wealth of $567,000, followed by New Zealand ($400,000), Australia ($364,000) and the USA ($353,000). Countries with wealth below $5,000 are heavily concentrated in central Africa and South Asia.

Extreme wealth is also geographically concentrated in certain parts of the world. The USA has the highest concentration of wealth, with 46 per cent of millionaires living there, followed by the UK, Japan, Germany, France and China – see Figure 1.3.

In the UK, wealth is also unequally distributed, with the top 10 per cent owning 45 per cent of the country's £11.1 trillion total household wealth. The least wealthy half of households own just 9 per cent (see Figure 1.4).

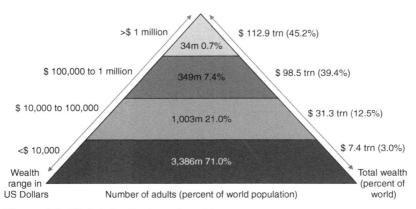

Figure 1.2 Global distribution of wealth
Source: adapted from Credit Suisse (2015, p.24).

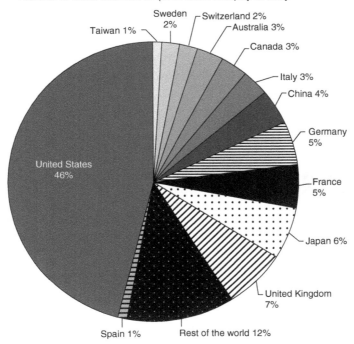

Figure 1.3 Global distribution of millionaires
Source: adapted from Credit Suisse (2015, p.25).

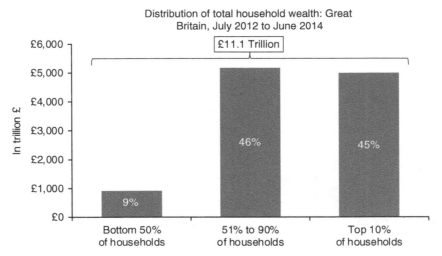

Figure 1.4 Distribution of wealth in the UK
Source: data from ONS (2015a).

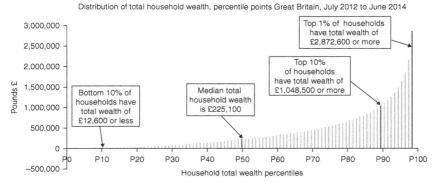

Figure 1.5 Distribution of household wealth in the UK
Source: ONS (2015a, p.3).

Research by the ONS (2015a) shows that the **median** household total wealth in the UK was £225,100. Averages, like the median value, mask the wide disparity between the rich and the poor. The bottom 10 per cent possesses an average wealth of £12,600 while the top 10 per cent have over £1 million each. The top 1 per cent has a staggering average sum of more than £2.8 million each (see Figure 1.5).

1.2 Reasons why it is necessary to create wealth

There are many reasons why it is important for you to accumulate wealth and these can be grouped under **push factors** and **pull factors**. Push factors include demographic and social changes while pull factors include better living standards, better health and longevity. The following will discuss each of these factors in turn.

1.2.1 Push: increasing life expectancy

A worldwide trend of increasing life expectancy means that you will need to have more economic resources to cover a longer life span. For example, in the UK, life expectancy has been increasing by about two years every decade and an average woman born in 2016 can expect to live to 94. Those born in 2066 or later are expected to have an average life expectancy of over 100 (ONS, 2015b).

ACTIVITY 1.2

1. What factors do you think have contributed to the rising life expectancy in the UK and the rest of the world?
2. Suggest which countries are likely to have the highest rate of life expectancy. Suggest reasons why.

[Answers to this Activity are at the end of the chapter.]

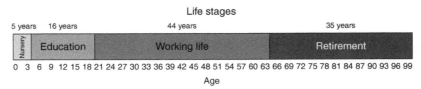

Figure 1.6 Length of working life versus retirement

It is paradoxical that at a time when life expectancy has increased and people are living longer, retirement age has not shifted dramatically. In the USA, for example, the Social Security system allows people to retire early at age 62 if they are willing to take a slight reduction in their monthly pension. Consequently, retirement at age 62 is more common than retirement at age 65. In the UK, individuals are allowed to take money from their private pension funds from the age of 55 (age 50 before 2010) and so, with sufficient money, individuals can retire early. The average number of years spent in retirement has risen as a result.

Figure 1.6 shows the typical life cycle that a university student might experience. Let's assume retirement at 65, the working life would be 44 years. With retirement age still set at 65 in many developed countries, spending between 20 and 35 years in retirement is common. The expansion of education in many countries means that people start working later, thereby reducing the length of time for saving. Individuals, therefore, face a choice: retire later, live on less or build up more wealth.

1.2.2 Push: gap between life expectancy and healthy life expectancy

As people live longer, a gap between life expectancy and a healthy life expectancy may emerge. For example, the number of years spent with illness or disability is increasing, from 10.1 years to 11.5 years for the UK and from 10.6 years to 11.7 years for the USA in 2013 (Noack et al., 2015). As the population ages and the prevalence of age-related illness rises, more resources will be required to pay for the costs. In 2012, the UK spent £144.5 billion or 9.2 per cent of GDP on healthcare, partly as a result of ageing population (Martin, 2014). Statistics collated by Age UK (2016) paint a stark picture. An estimated 4 million older people in the UK (36 per cent of people aged 65–74 and 47 per cent of those aged 75-plus) have a limiting long-standing illness. If nothing is done about age-related diseases, it is estimated that there will be more than 6 million people with a long-term limiting illness or disability by 2030. This may require £5 billion additional expenditure on health and social care by 2018.

Although healthcare is free at the point-of-use in the UK, there might be a waiting list, delays and a lack of choice. Moreover, long-term care is not free. Those with low income and capital may qualify for means-tested state help, but this typically means losing the ability to choose the standard of care you might prefer. With financial resources, you can choose to access better quality healthcare.

In the USA, healthcare poses the greatest uncertainty in retirement, especially as Americans live longer on average than their UK counterparts. Fidelity (2015) projects that a 65-year-old couple retiring in 2015 will need an average of $245,000 to cover medical expenses in retirement. A recent report shows that the amount needed is probably higher, between $280,000 and $318,000 (McGrath, 2016). In China, the greatest concerns among the retired are illness and healthcare costs (French, 2014).

1.2.3 Push: falling birth rates and ageing population

While life expectancy rises, birth rates are falling. The global fertility rate is 2.5 children per woman. This hides regional differences. The total fertility rate in the UK in 2014 was 1.8 children, in comparison to 1.4 in Germany and 1.4 in Japan in 2015 (World Bank, 2015b), which is below the replacement rate of 2.07 deemed necessary to maintain the population (Japantimes, 2015). In Africa, on the other hand, the fertility rate is well above the global average, with 7.27 in Niger, 6.53 in Uganda and 6.06 in Mali (Geoba, 2016).

The combination of declining birth rates and rising life expectancy in some regions produces an ageing population. By 2050, it is estimated that 37 per cent of the European population will be over 60 years old (Euronews, 2015). In China, the proportion aged 60 and over will increase to 19.3 per cent by 2020 and to 43.2 per cent by 2050 (Shi and Xu, 2015). In India, it is estimated that the share of 60 years and over will reach 20 per cent by 2050 (Bloom *et al.*, n.d., p.303). In contrast, only 10 per cent of the population of Africa is projected to be over 60 by 2050 (UN, 2015).

An ageing population exerts a huge strain on the healthcare system and public finances, affecting the government's ability to look after us in old age. In some cultures, children are expected to look after their elders in old age. With declining birth rates and increasing childlessness, this support may no longer be available.

1.2.4 Push: diminishing role of the government in retirement provision

These social and demographic changes have exerted a huge pressure on public finances and European governments have taken measures to curb the welfare bill. In the UK, for example, the government has already taken steps to increase the state pension age. For many years, the state pension age for men was 65 and women 60. But from 2018, both men and women's state pension age will be 65, increasing in stages to 67 between 2026 and 2028. After that, the government will then commission an independent review of the state pension age every five years and the pension age is then expected to rise in line with life expectancy. It is anticipated that those in their early 20s today will have to wait until they are at least 70 before they can take their state pension (This is Money, 2016). Similar measures are being implemented elsewhere. In China, the government will increase standard retirement ages – currently 50 or 55 for women and 60 for men – by five years each (Economist, 2014) and end the one-child policy. However, some in China believe the problem lies in the low birth rates rather than the growth of elderly people (Rui *et al.*, 2015). The same demographic pressures are also putting these countries under strain.

1.2.5 Push: diminishing role of employer

Rising life expectancies and falling birth rates are also posing a huge strain on employer-sponsored pension systems around the world. In response, a number of countries have shifted their retirement schemes from defined benefit (where employers promise an income in retirement) to defined contribution (where income is dependent on contributions and investment performance).This change shifts many of the decisions about financing retirement away from *institutions* – firms and governments – toward *individuals*, imposing on workers the responsibility to save, invest and spend wisely over the life cycle. Individuals now face many risks: under-saving, failure to invest wisely and running out of money due to longevity risk (Lusardi and Mitchell, 2011).

In the UK, in the 1990s, it was common for companies to offer employees a defined benefit scheme (also known as final salary).With increasing life expectancy and regulatory burdens, only one of the FTSE 100 companies is now offering a defined benefit scheme. Individuals now must take responsibility for their income in retirement because under defined contribution schemes, contributions will have a direct impact on the level of income received in retirement.With state pension uncertain and employers no longer promising retirement income, individuals must look after themselves.

1.2.6 Push: diminishing role of the family

The need for individuals to take greater responsibility is also necessitated by the changing family structure. In the past, many generations lived under the same roof, with the younger generations providing pastoral care for the elderly. However, partly as a result of increasing longevity, increasing trend of non-marriages and childlessness, many people now live alone. In 2014, for example, 28 per cent of 26.7 million households in the UK contained only one person (ONS, 2014).A similar trend is observed in the USA. In 1970, only 17 per cent of the US population was living alone. By 2012, the proportion of single-person households had increased to 27.4 per cent (Ibtimes, 2013). In China, single-person households are also on the rise. From 2000 to 2010, the number of single-person households doubled. A report attributes this to the growing number of unmarried and old people who live alone. In 2010, the number of such one-person households with the member aged between 30 and 80 stood at 43.2 per cent.The percentage of one-person households with the member over 80 years of age stood at 40 per cent in 2010 (CNTV, 2014). Without an extended family to look after them and the state role decreasing, individuals will need resources to pay for services when their ability to look after themselves diminishes.

1.2.7 Pull: relationship between health and wealth

Besides these push factors, there are good pull reasons why individuals should build sufficient resources. One important reason is the link between health and wealth.As we all know, there is a close relationship between money and health because money affects living standards and lifestyle.There are many ways in which our finances can affect our health. Some people have to work more, including taking on more hours at work, having a second job, and so on when their income is not enough to pay the bills. Working long hours can increase stress and indirectly affect health.

Many people have money worries (e.g. stress over saving for retirement, paying off a credit card bill or finding the money to just put food on the table).Worrying about money can affect our health as stress has been linked to a variety of ailments, including anxiety, depression, diabetes, hair loss, heart disease, obesity and ulcers. Money worries can also lead to poor sleep and insomnia. Some people might find themselves lying awake at night thinking about their finances and what to do next. This will then affect how they eat, work and function.

Recent research shows that there is a link between a lack of wealth and obesity. A study in the USA shows that those with lower wealth have poorer health outcomes due to poor physical and social environments. The lack of economic resources associated with having little wealth may limit an individual's access to healthcare, quality housing and nutritious foods. Less wealthy individuals are also likely to live in deprived areas with unsafe streets, insufficient infrastructure (such as lack of parks) and higher prevalence of liquor and convenience stores. These can lead to increased isolation, a more sedentary lifestyle and poor diets, resulting in a higher incidence of obesity and smoking among the less wealthy (Hajat et al., 2010). A study on the connection between health and obesity in the UK also supports the above findings: higher wealth is associated with lower weight and better health because of a superior diet (Mazzocchi and Traill, 2008).

1.2.8 Pull: relationship between wealth and longevity

Wealth affords better health and so it is not surprising that those who have wealth live longer. Research shows that wealth and, more broadly, socioeconomic status, play a powerful role in determining how long we live. The connection is so widely accepted that researchers call it 'the wealth gradient in mortality'.

Table 1.1 shows that wealthier nations tend to have a longer life expectancy. Switzerland, one of the wealthiest countries in the world, has the highest life expectancy (83 years) at birth. People in South Africa, on the other hand, have a life expectancy of 57 years (26 years lower than the Swiss), due to the prevalence of

Table 1.1 Global wealth distribution and life expectancy

Country	Population (millions)	Mean wealth ($)	Median wealth ($)	Total wealth (trillions $)	Number of dollar millionaires (thousands)	Life expectancy at birth
USA	331	352,996	49,787	85.9	15,656	79
China	1,369	22,513	7,357	22.8	1,333	76
Japan	126	190,230	96,071	19.8	2,126	84
India	1,286	4,252	868	3.4	185	68
UK	63	320,368	126,472	15.6	2,364	81
Switzerland	8	567,122	107,583	3.5	667	83
Russia	138	11,726	1,388	1.3	92	70
Singapore	5	269,408	98,922	1.1	142	83
Australia	22	364,896	168,291	6.2	961	82
Indonesia	243	9,031	1,615	1.5	98	69
South Africa	52	21,402	3,379	0.7	50	57

Sources: data from Credit Suisse (2015) and World Bank (2016).

infectious diseases, injury and violence as well as non-communicable diseases (stroke, heart disease, cancer, diabetes) (Geach, 2014).

In the USA, research found that higher income was associated with greater longevity – the gap in life expectancy between the richest 1 per cent and poorest 1 per cent of individuals was 14.6 years for men and 10.1 years for women (Chetty et al., 2016). A recent study shows that the difference in life expectancy between the rich and poor in London can be as high as 25 years (Pickett and Wilkinson, 2014).

While many believe that income is the key determinant of life expectancy, others argue that education is the key. George Vaillant, professor of psychiatry at Harvard Medical School, in a longitudinal study of health, found education to be one of the biggest determinants of longevity, along with behavioural factors such as smoking and drinking. According to Professor Vaillant, there are several possible reasons for higher life expectancy among the educated. People who go to college tend to drink less, smoke less and are less likely to be obese. In addition, he argues that people who pursue higher education tend be more focused on the future, which probably also helps them make healthier choices (such as avoiding excessive drinking, smoking and drugs) (Palmer, 2012). Other researchers argue that another possibility is that people with higher levels of education are more likely to maintain their health, have better access to healthcare, and follow doctors' directions when it comes to taking pills or other instructions.

Wealth contributes to better health, but research also suggests that health contributes to wealth as well. A healthy individual is able to work and earn an income and build wealth. In the USA, an individual with poor health may face double trouble: loss of income as a result of inability to work and expensive medical treatments.

Besides better health and longer life, wealth can give individuals lifestyle choices such as stop work early, take regular holidays overseas, work for pleasure rather than for money to make ends meet, spend more time with the family or have the resources to leave a legacy.

Wealth is also powerful because it can affect the life chances of the next generation. Research on the relationship between parental wealth and children's economic well-being shows that there is a close link. In the USA, for example, research shows that wealth can have a significant effect on children's educational attainment, as parental wealth can meet the direct financial costs of schooling, and extra-curricular activities such as computer use or tutoring. In countries where income is low and employment intermittent, parental wealth can have a greater life–chances effect. In Mexico, for example, parental wealth has a substantial influence on children's educational attainment, consumption level and wealth holdings (Orr 2003; Torche and Spilerman, 2009).

The greatest power of wealth is that it can give us the ability to make a difference to the lives of others and allow us to give through philanthropy. The world's richest man is Carlos Slim Helú from Mexico who has a fortune of more than $70 billion, ahead of Bill Gates and Warren Buffett. However, the world's great donors are Bill and Melinda Gates who have given more than $28 billion for various causes and Warren Buffett $8.3 billion. Globally, leading philanthropists spend between 2 per cent and 5 per cent of their net worth on philanthropy annually. Indeed, Andrew Carnegie, industrialist and philanthropist (1835–1919) believed that a 'man who dies ... rich dies disgraced' and advocated giving surplus wealth away during the lifetime of the giver for the common good as this was more efficient and fulfilling.

Table 1.2 The world's great philanthropists

Givers	Donations ($ billion)	Net-worth ($ billion)	Causes	Source of wealth
Bill Gates	28	56	Education, health, Bill & Melinda Gates Foundation	Computers
Warren Buffett	8.30	50	Bill & Melinda Gates Foundation, education, health and economic development, nuclear threats, children and community services	Berkshire Hathaway
George Soros	8	14.5	Education, human rights causes	Investor (speculating on the market), author
Gordon Moore	6.8	4	Science, environmental conservation, nursing education	Intel co-founder
Carlos Slim Helú (Mexico)	4	74	Digital education, health	Banking, retail, mining, construction, restaurants, printing and insurance, telecommunications (Movil phone company)
Azim Premji (India)	2.1	16.8	Education	Head of tech titan Wipro
Li Ka Shing (Hong Kong)	1.6	>26	Children's centres, churches, health	Varied including banking, construction, real estate, plastics, cellular phones, satellite television, retail outlets (pharmacies and supermarkets), hotels, domestic transportation, airports, electric power, steel production, ports and shipping

Source: www.therichest.com/celebnetworth/celebrity-lifestyle/giveaway/the-worlds-biggest-givers/.

1.3 How much money do you need in retirement?

The period of time we need financial reserves the most to cover the difference in income and expenditure is retirement. Many people are worried about having enough money to live when they stop work but few know how much they might need in retirement. The amount an individual requires in retirement depends on their lifestyle. A survey by Scottish Widows (2015) shows that £23,000 per year is an average amount of income people think they will need to be comfortable in retirement. Using a 5 per cent annuity rate, the capital amount needed is £460,000. Worryingly, 20 per cent of the UK population have no savings for retirement.

There is a clear difference between retirement aspiration and reality. Research by True Potential (2015) shows that to have an income of £23,000 per year in retirement, individuals need to save £10,425 per year. However, individuals save only a fifth

Table 1.3 Income need in retirement

	Annual savings (£)	Total pension fund size after 45 years (£)	Desired annual income (£)	Number of years fund could support desired annual income
Amount needed for a comfortable retirement	10,425	469,140	23,457	20
Amount currently being saved	2,671	120,213	23,457	5

Source: Jefferies (2014).

of the required amount. David Harrison, managing director of True Potential, believes that these figures

> show the size of the problem we face as a nation. Britain is sleepwalking towards an impoverished retirement and the reality for many in society today is that they will simply be unable ever to retire. That is a scary prospect and we should be in no doubt about the radical overhaul of financial education, regulation and culture that will be required to address this. The seeds of the savings gap were sown in non-existent personal finance education, overly-complicated products and a buy-now-pay-later culture that has become part of society.

One of the UK's largest insurers, Aviva, estimates that a pensioner needs a basic annual income of £12,590 a year, or £242 a week, to get by. Even at this low estimate, it is clear that the state pension will not be enough. The annual state pension averages £6,556 (including entitlements to the state second pension), so that leaves individuals having to find an additional income of £6,034 a year (Papworth and Collinson, 2015). Assuming an annuity rate of 5 per cent, the capital amount needed is £120,680. However, many people in the UK have a lot less than this: the average pension pot in the UK is £30,000.

In countries where there is no free healthcare, the expected amount of money needed in retirement is much higher. A recent report from insurer AIA says mainland Chinese residents believe, on average, they require $1.79 million for a comfortable retirement. Those surveyed in larger tier-one cities believe they will require $1.94 million, while those living in smaller tier-two cities expect they will need $1.64 million. For comparison, in Australia, industry estimates say an Australian couple with no welfare entitlements will need around $750,000, or just over A$1 million, to fund a comfortable retirement (Scutt, 2015).

In the USA, a survey by Legg Mason (global investment management firm) shows that some expect to have a much higher amount. Those who surveyed said they require $2.5 million in retirement to enjoy the quality of life they have today. Yet, the average 401(k) balance invested with Fidelity (the largest retirement planner) was $91,300 at the end of 2014. On average, they told Legg Mason they spend an hour and 18 minutes worrying about money *each day*. That's 475 hours, or nearly 20 full days, of financial worrying a year (Anderson, 2015).

Most people do not need $2.5 million. Fidelity estimates most investors require about eight times their ending salary to increase the chances that their savings will last during a 25-year retirement. But every retirement is different. People also tend to spend lavishly in their first years of retirement before their spending declines in later years.

The amount of income required in retirement depends on lifestyle and so the amount varies. However, many people do not know how much income they may need in retirement. The first step in achieving the income required is to calculate the requirement and then plan for the future.

1.4 Examples of students who became millionaires

In the UK, there are many examples of students who went on to be financially successful and became multi-millionaires. Table 1.4 is a list of famous former-student millionaires with details of what and where they studied. J.K. Rowling tops the list with an estimated fortune of more than $1 billion.

Other examples show that we do not need to become best-selling authors to become extremely wealthy. The case of billionaire Zhang Xin illustrates this. Born in China during the time of the Cultural Revolution in 1965, Xin fled to Hong Kong with her mother in 1979 and lived in a room just big enough for two bunk beds. For five

Table 1.4 Students turned millionaires in the UK

Name	Where and what they studied	Fortune	What they are famous for
Rowan Atkinson	Newcastle University & Oxford University Degree – Electrical Engineering	£60 million	Actor, comedian, screenwriter
Sacha Baron Cohen	University of Cambridge Degree – History	£70 million	Actor and comedian
David Gill	Birmingham Business School Degree – Industrial, Economic and Business Studies	£20 million	Football
Sir Chris Hoy	University of Edinburgh Degree – Applied Sports Science	£52 million	Cyclist
E.L. James	University of Kent Degree – History	£37 million	Author (*Fifty Shades of Grey*)
Sir Terry Leahy	University of Manchester Institute of Science & Technology Degree – Management Science	£45 million	Retailing (Former Tesco chief executive)
Christopher Nolan	UCL Degree – English literature	£60 million	Film director
J.K. Rowling	University of Exeter Degree – French and Classics	>$1 billion	Author (*Harry Potter*)
Chris Tarrant	University of Birmingham Degree – English	£20 million	TV presenter

Source: www.savethestudent.org/make-money/uk-millionaires-where-and-what-they-studied.html.

years from the age of 14, she toiled in small factories making sleeves, collars, zippers and electrical parts. She saved enough money to buy a plane ticket to come to England and won a scholarship to study Economics at the University of Sussex before going to Cambridge to study a Masters degree in Development Economics. After completion, she went to work for Goldman Sachs before returning to China. In 1995, she founded the SOHO (Small Office, Home Office) company with her husband. She is now estimated to be worth more than $2.2 billion, ranking her alongside Oprah Winfrey (Bloomberg Markets, 2010). In 2013, she successfully out-bid Brad Pitt, Leonardo DiCaprio and a Saudi prince for a $26 million Manhattan mansion (Cole, 2014).

❖ **BOX 1.2 RIPPLE EFFECT OF WEALTH**

China's growing wealth is having a ripple effect around the world. House prices in cities such as Vancouver, London and New York are soaring as Chinese buyers snap up properties. A recent survey conducted with 3,000 high net worth Chinese shows that 30 per cent mentioned property as one of the top three investments they'll make overseas. One reason many wealthy Chinese are buying up properties outside of China is the desire for asset diversification. It is also a way to get money out of China. Many fear that the government will come after their riches.

Foreign businesses are also prospering as wealthy Chinese are seeking to buy vineyards and chateaux in Europe. Companies selling luxury items – Gucci, Burberry, Louis Vuitton – also experience a boom.

It is unclear what is the long-term impact but two things are clear – Chinese are getting richer and they are spreading their money globally.

Source: www.bbc.com/capital/story/20140203-
the-rise-of-chinas-wealth-dragon.

1.5 Ways to create wealth

How people create wealth is a topic that fascinates many and there are many books written on this topic. Napoleon Hill's *Think and Grow Rich* is a classic text. After studying America's 500 most successful people, Hill distilled 13 steps to riches. The starting point of all achievement is having a desire to be and to do something. A burning desire will stir the imagination and creativity. Following this, faith is important because it will strengthen convictions and ensure perseverance, while planning allows the translation of desires and beliefs into concrete actions. Wealth accumulation, then, starts with the mind and motivation.

For others, dream is a powerful motivator. In *The One Minute Millionaire*, Mark Victor Hansen offers a clear three-step approach to build wealth. First, there must be a dream, an end game. Money after all is a means to an end and so it is important to have a clear end in mind. Second, there must be a team to help us achieve our dreams. We need advisers and professionals who can help us make things happen, such as accountants, lawyers and financial planners. Third, we need to choose a theme to focus on – property, investments, business or internet. Many people seek diversification and so tend to have a range of assets in their portfolios. However, when starting out, it might be easier to focus on one asset in which we may have an interest, insight into or experience in.

1.5.1 Guiding principles

In *The Richest Man in Babylon*, George Clason offers seven useful guiding principles to build wealth:

1. **Start saving:** savings are necessary because they can give us an emergency fund as well as the capital to invest (recommended putting aside 10 per cent of income).
2. **Control expenditures**: a golden rule is that expenditure must be less than income to avoid debt and have surplus income for investment.
3. **Make the gold multiply**: to build wealth, it is important to increase the value of our savings and investments and to ensure that inflation does not erode the value of money.
4. **Guard your treasures from loss**: protect investments or wealth from losses, by avoiding taking unnecessary risks and making sure that assets are protected.
5. **Make your home a profitable investment**: for many people their home is an important source of wealth and so it is important to make a wise decision.
6. **Insure a future income**: ill-health can have a devastating impact and so it is important to insure a future income stream.
7. **Increase your ability to earn**: prices tend to rise over time, and so it is important to ensure that earnings are higher than prices. Continuous learning or professional development can help individual earnings rise over time.

After studying more than a thousand millionaires in the USA between 1995 and 1996, *The Millionaire Next Door* by Stanley and Danko reaches the same conclusions: the secrets of building wealth lie in planning, controlling consumption (budgeting), being frugal and actively investing (15 per cent of income). They found that the millionaires shared seven common traits:

1. They live well below their means.
2. They allocate their time, energy and money efficiently, in ways conducive to building wealth.
3. They believe that financial independence is more important than displaying wealth.
4. Their parents did not provide economic subsidies ('economic outpatient care').
5. Their adult children are financially independent.
6. They are proficient in targeting market opportunities.
7. They choose the right occupation.

However, self-control or the lack of willpower may pose a problem in wealth accumulation. An individual may be aware of the importance of saving and spending less, but may not have the discipline or self-control to set aside income regularly. To overcome

Figure 1.7 Steps to build wealth

this behavioural problem, the author of *The Automatic Millionaire*, David Bach, suggests that the process must be *automated*. This can be done through the direct debit system. To ensure this is effective, individuals must *pay themselves first*, requiring them to save *before* they start spending their income.

In short, wealth accumulation requires a desire to be wealthy, planning and taking action as shown in Figure 1.7.

1.5.2 Financial literacy

Extensive research shows that our financial behaviour and decision-making is influenced by financial literacy, defined as the ability to process economic information and make informed decisions about financial planning, wealth accumulation, debt and pensions. (Lusardi and Mitchell, 2014).

People with high financial literacy tend to be less likely to have problems with debt, more likely to participate in the stock market, more likely to choose funds with lower fees, more likely to accumulate wealth and manage wealth, and more likely to plan for retirement.

All the above factors contribute to wealth accumulation. One study shows that there are two possible channels through which financial literacy might facilitate wealth accumulation. First, a high level of financial knowledge lowers the costs of gathering and processing information and reduces barriers to investing in the stock market. Individuals with high financial literacy are thought to be more likely to invest in the stock market. This participation in the stock market is believed to be the key to wealth accumulation because it allows knowledgeable individuals to take advantage of the equity premium. Second, financial literacy is found to be positively associated with retirement planning because those who have more confidence in their financial knowledge have a higher propensity to plan. The study found that once such individuals calculate saving needs in retirement, they set up a retirement plan and are successful in sticking to their plan (Lusardi and Mitchell, 2009; van Rooij *et al.*, 2012).

Despite its importance, financial illiteracy is pervasive throughout the world with a large proportion of the adult population knowing very little about finance and basic concepts such as risk diversification, inflation, interest compounding, mortgage and other debt instruments (Lusardi, 2008). In a study of financial literacy among the young in the USA, it is found that financial literacy is low, with fewer than one-third of young adults possessing basic knowledge of interest rates, inflation and risks (Lusardi *et al.*, 2010).

Low levels of financial literacy are also evident elsewhere, as highlighted by an OECD report in 2005 of financial illiteracy in Europe, Australia and Japan, among others. In countries with generous social security benefits, people have fewer incentives to save and accumulate wealth, and a lower desire to invest in financial literacy (Lusardi and Mitchell, 2014).

However, increased financial literacy is found to have a positive impact on people's personal and business life. Financial knowledge helps reduce social and psychological pressures and increases welfare of the family by lowering stress, illness, financial disputes, abuse of children and conflict among family members. People who grow up in families with a higher level of financial knowledge and well-being are less likely to be depressed, less likely to display aggressive and anti-social behaviour, and are more likely to possess self-confidence (Taft et al., 2013). Acquiring financial literacy skills, then, is the first step in wealth acquisition.

1.5.3 Planning

In addition to financial literacy, planning too plays an important role in wealth accumulation (Ameriks et al., 2003). The example below is often quoted to illustrate this: the Yale University graduating class of 1953 was asked the following question, 'How many of you have clearly established goals for your life?' Three per cent of the class replied that they had clearly established goals. Twenty years later the group was surveyed again and it was found that the original 3 per cent with clearly established goals had greater financial net worth than the remaining 97 per cent combined. In *Wealth Secrets of the One Percent*, Sam Wilkin found that the uniting personality trait among billionaires is they tend to declare their financial objectives as young children. 'Bill Gates did it to his high school friends, [and] Andrew Carnegie, too. Having the objective just to have money is a major driver of people who become super rich' (The Telegraph, 2015).

Lusardi's study (1999) found a positive link between planning and wealth. Households that had given little thought to retirement had far lower wealth than those that had given the subject more thought. Yet, Lusardi and Mitchell (2011) found that most workers have not planned or thought much about retirement. They also found that retirement planning is a good indication of retirement wealth: those who have calculated how much they need to save for retirement reach retirement with as much as three times the wealth of those who did no such calculations (Lusardi and Mitchell, 2011). One reason why those with a high propensity to plan may be wealthier is because they may be better able to control their spending, and thus are more likely to have surplus income to invest.

1.6 Conclusion

With rapid demographic and social changes, and diminishing role of the government, employer and the family, it is more important than ever that individuals take steps to provide for themselves. Building wealth should be an important life goal, because its possession allows individuals to take care of themselves, derive significant well-being benefits, reduce burden on the state, as well as have the ability to help others through charity and philanthropy.

Answers to Activity 1.2

1. What factors do you think have contributed to the rising life expectancy in the UK and the rest of the world?
2. Suggest which countries are likely to have the highest rate of life expectancy. Suggest reasons why.

1. Some reasons for the global increase in life expectancy are advances in income, nutrition, education, sanitation and medicine (Oeppen and Vaupel, 2002). However, as the World Health Organization (2016) notes, there can also be dips in life expectancy in some countries due to specific causes such as AIDS (in Africa) and the break-up of Russia (in Eastern Europe). The ONS (2015) records UK life expectancy trends and gives the main reason for improving life expectancy as health improvements in young population (e.g. childhood immunisation) and older population (e.g. heart disease treatment)). There is an interesting distinction by time period with younger ages benefiting historically and older ages more recently.
2. It follows that the countries that are most likely to have high rates of life expectancy are those which are wealthier, have well developed healthcare and are more politically stable.

End of chapter test

1. How does attitude towards money affect wealth accumulation?
2. Explain the patterns of wealth distribution in the UK and globally.
3. What are the key demographic and social changes taking place that make it necessary for us to look after ourselves?
4. Discuss different ways to build wealth. What do you think is the most critical factor?
5. How important is financial literacy in wealth creation?

References

Age UK (2016), 'Later life in the UK', Age UK Factsheet, October, p.8, available at https://www.ageuk.org.uk/Documents/EN-GB/Factsheets/Later_Life_UK_factsheet.pdf?dtrk=true (Accessed 31 October 2016).

Ameriks, J., Caplin, A. and Leahy, J. (2003), 'Wealth accumulation and the propensity to plan', *Quarterly Journal of Economics*, 118(3), pp. 1007–48.

Anderson, T. (2015), 'Do you really need $2.5 million for a good retirement?', available at www.cnbc.com/2015/03/10/do-you-really-need-25-million-for-a-good-retirement.html (Accessed 30 March 2016).

Bach, D. (2004), *The Automatic Millionaire: A Powerful One-Step Plan to Live and Finish Rich*. New York: Broadway Books.

Bloom, D., Canning, D. and Fink, G. (n.d.), 'Population ageing and economic growth', available at http://siteresources.worldbank.org/EXTPREMNET/Resources/489960-1338997241035/Growth_Commission_Vol4_Globalization_Growth_Ch13_Population_Aging_Economic_Growth.pdf (Accessed 11 June 2016).

Bloomberg Markets (2010), 'Beijing billionaire who grew up with Mao sees no housing bubble', 3 August.

Chetty, R., Stepner, M., Abraham, S. *et al.* (2016), 'The association between income and life expectancy in the United States, 2001–2014', *The JAMA Network*, 315(16), available at http://jama.jamanetwork.com/article.aspx?articleid=2513561 (Accessed 11 June 2016).

ChinaFile (2012), 'A comparison of China's and America's richest people', available at www.chinafile.com/multimedia/infographics/comparison-chinas-and-americas-richest-people (Accessed 4 June 2016).

Clason, G. (2004), *The Richest Man in Babylon*. New York: Signet Books.

CNTV (2014), 'Single-person households in China double in ten years', available at http://english.cntv.cn/2014/05/16/VIDE1400197683694828.shtml (Accessed 11 June 2016).

Cole, M. (2014), 'Chinese now top foreign buyers in Manhattan property market', available at www.forbes.com/sites/michaelcole/2014/04/27/chinese-now-top-foreign-buyers-in-manhattan-property-market/#673b69a21953 (Accessed 4 June 2016).

Credit Suisse (2015), *Wealth Report 2015*, available at https://publications.credit-suisse.com/tasks/render/file/?fileID=F2425415-DCA7-80B8-EAD989AF9341D47E (Accessed 4 June 2016).

Economist (2014), 'Paying for the grey', available at www.economist.com/news/china/21600160-pensions-crisis-looms-china-looks-raising-retirement-age-paying-grey (Accessed 4 June 2016).

Euronews (2015), 'Europe's ageing population: how will healthcare systems cope?', available at www.euronews.com/2015/03/23/europes-ageing-population-how-will-healthcare-systems-cope (Accessed 11 June 2016).

Fidelity (2015), 'Health care costs for couples in retirement rise to an estimated $245,000', available at www.fidelity.com/about-fidelity/employer-services/health-care-costs-for-couples-retirement-rise (Accessed 6 June 2016).

Frank, R. (2016), 'China has more billionaires than US: Report', available at www.cnbc.com/2016/02/24/china-has-more-billionaires-than-us-report.html (Accessed 4 June 2016).

French, P. (2014), 'China's changing demographics – old age becomes a key factor for China', *Europe China Research & Advice Network* (ECRAN), p. 20.

Gasiorowska, A. (2014), 'The relationship between objective and subjective wealth is moderated by financial control and mediated by money anxiety', *Journal of Economic Psychology*, August, 43, p. 65.

Geach, C. (2014), 'Four reasons for SA's low life expectancy', available at www.iol.co.za/news/south-africa/western-cape/four-reasons-for-sas-low-life-expectancy-1798106 (Accessed 11 June 2016).

Geoba (2016), 'The world: fertility rate', available at www.geoba.se/population.php?pc=world&type=10 (Accessed 11 June 2016).

Hajat, A., Kaufman, J.S., Rose, K.M., Siddiqi, A. and Thomas, J.G. (2010), 'Do the wealthy have a health advantage? Cardiovascular disease risk factors and wealth', *Social Science & Medicine*, 71(11), p. 1941.

Ibtimes (2013), 'Living alone: more US residents forming single-person households than before', available at www.ibtimes.com/living-alone-more-us-residents-forming-single-person-households-charts-1401580 (Accessed 11 June 2016).

Japantimes (2015), 'Fertility rate dips again', available at www.japantimes.co.jp/opinion/2015/06/21/editorials/fertility-rate-dips/#.V1u6EOYrJE4 (Accessed 11 June 2016).

Jefferies, T. (2014), 'Savers think they need £23k a year for a comfortable retirement – which would empty the average pension pot in five years', available at www. thisismoney.co.uk/money/pensions/article-2797270/savers-want-23k-year-retirement-money-run-5-years.html (Accessed 30 March 2016).

Lafrance, A. and LaRochelle-Côté, S. (2012), 'The evolution of wealth over life cycle', *Perspectives on Labour and Income*, 24(3), pp. 1–16. Also available at www.statcan. gc.ca/pub/75-001-x/2012003/article/11690-eng.pdf (Accessed 11 June 2016).

Lusardi, A. (1999), 'Planning for retirement: the importance of financial literacy', available at www.dartmouth.edu/~alusardi/Papers/PPAR09.pdf (Accessed 31 October 2016).

Lusardi, A. (2008), 'Financial literacy: an essential tool for informed consumer choice?', available at www.dartmouth.edu/~alusardi/Papers/Lusardi_Informed_Consumer.pdf (Accessed 31 October 2016).

Lusardi, A. (2011), 'Americans' financial capability', NBER Working Paper Series, Working Paper 17103.

Lusardi, A. and Mitchell, O. (2009), 'How ordinary consumers make complex economic decisions: financial literacy and retirement readiness', NBER Working Paper Series, Working Paper 15350.

Lusardi, A. and Mitchell, O. (2011), 'Financial literacy around the world: an overview', *Journal of Pension Economics & Finance*, 10(4), pp. 497–508.

Lusardi, A. and Mitchell, O. (2014), 'The economic importance of financial literacy: theory and evidence', *Journal of Economic Literature*, 52(1), pp. 5–44.

Lusardi, A., Mitchell, O. and Curto, V. (2010), 'Financial literacy among the young', *Journal of Consumer Affairs*, 44(2), pp. 358–380.

McGrath, D. (2016), 'Are health-care costs really "just" $245K in retirement?', available at www.cnbc.com/2016/02/13/are-health-care-costs-really-just-245k-in-retirement.html (Accessed 4 June 2016).

Martin, S. (2014), 'ONS: UK healthcare spend tops £144bn in 2012', available at www. ibtimes.co.uk/ons-uk-healthcare-spend-tops-144bn-2012-1446713 (Accessed 4 June 2016).

Mazzocchi, M. and Traill, W. (2008), 'A structural model of wealth, obesity and health in the UK', IDEAS Working Paper Series from RePEc, pp. 6–7.

Noack, R., Gamio, L. and Cai, W. (2015), 'These charts show how much of your life you will spend being sick', *The Washington Post*, available at www.washingtonpost. com/news/worldviews/wp/2015/09/19/these-charts-show-how-much-of-your-life-you-will-spend-being-sick/ (Accessed 11 June 2016).

Oeppen, J. and Vaupel, J.W. (2002) 'Broken limits to life expectancy' in *Science*, 296, 10 May, pp. 1029–31, available at www.econ.ku.dk/okocg/VV/VV-economic%20 growth/articles/artikler-2006/broken-limits-to-life-expectancy.pdf (Accessed 4 June 2016).

Office for National Statistics (2014), 'Families and households, 2014', available at www. ons.gov.uk/ons/rel/family-demography/families-and-households/2014/families-and-households-in-the-uk--2014.html (Accessed 11 June 2016).

Office for National Statistics (ONS) (2015a), 'Article: main results from the Wealth and Assets survey, July 2012 to June 2014', available at http://webarchive. nationalarchives.gov.uk/20160105160709/www.ons.gov.uk/ons/dcp171776_428683.pdf (Accessed 4 June 2016).

Office for National Statistics (2015b), 'Past and projected cohort expectations of life (ex) from the 2014-based life tables for the UK (1981 to 2074, 0 to 105+yrs)', available at https://www.ons.gov.uk/peoplepopulationandcommunity/birthsdeathsandmarriages/lifeexpectancies/adhocs/005114pastandprojectedcohortexpectationsoflifeexfromthe2014basedlifetablesfortheuk1981to20740to105yrs (Accessed 4 June 2016).

Office for National Statistics (ONS) (2015c) *How Has Life Expectancy Changed Over Time* available at http://visual.ons.gov.uk/how-has-life-expectancy-changed-over-time/ (Accessed 6 January 2017).

Orr, A. (2003), 'Black-white differences in achievement: the importance of wealth', *Sociology of Education*, 76(4), pp. 281–304.

Palmer, K. (2012), 'Do rich people live longer', available at http://money.usnews.com/money/personal-finance/articles/2012/02/14/do-rich-people-live-longer (Accessed 11 June 2016).

Papworth, J. and Collinson, P. (2015), 'Want a comfortable retirement? You only need to save £86 a month', available at www.theguardian.com/money/2015/jul/18/comfortable-retirement-save-86-month (Accessed 30 March 2016).

Pickett, K. and Wilkinson, R. (2014), 'A 25 year gap between the life expectancy of rich and poor Londoners is a further indictment of our unequal society: one of the greatest determinants of a person's health is their income', available at www.independent.co.uk/voices/comment/a-25-year-gap-between-the-life-expectancy-of-rich-and-poor-londoners-is-a-further-indictment-of-our-9061888.html (Accessed 11 June 2016).

van Rooij, M.C.J., Lusardi, A. and Alessie, R.J.M. (2012), 'Financial literacy, retirement planning and household wealth', *The Economic Journal*, 122, p. 450.

Rui, S., Heqian, X., Boling, Z. and Jiayi, Y. (2015), 'Slowly, China prepares to raise retirement age', available at http://english.caixin.com/2015-04-01/100796734.html?hvocvqxlnydqesiq (Accessed 4 June 2016).

Sabri, I.F., Hayhoe, C.R. and Ai, G.L. (2006), 'Attitudes, values and belief towards money: gender and working sector comparison', *Pertanika J. Soc. Sci. & Hum.*, 14(2), pp. 121–130, p. 122. Also available at https://core.ac.uk/download/files/452/12222836.pdf (Accessed 11 June 2016).

Scottish Widows (2015), *Retirement Report*, available at http://reference.scottishwidows.co.uk/docs/46273-2015.pdf (Accessed 11 June 2016).

Scutt, D. (2015), 'China's middle class expects to be vastly rich in retirement, and it might tell us something about the crazy stock market', *Business Insider Australia*, available at www.businessinsider.com.au/chinas-middle-class-expects-to-be-vastly-rich-in-retirement-and-it-might-tell-us-something-about-the-crazy-stock-market-2015-7 (Accessed 30 March 2016).

Shi Rui and Xu Heqian (2015), 'Slowly, China prepares to raise retirement age', available at http://english.caixin.com/2015-04-01/100796734.html (Accessed 11 June 2016).

Stanley, T.J. and Danko, W.D. (1998), *The Millionaire Next Door*. New York: Pocket Books.

Taft, M.K., Hosein, Z.Z. and Mehrizi, S.M.T. (2013), 'The relation between financial literacy, financial wellbeing and financial concerns', *International Journal of Business and Management*, 8(11), pp. 63–75.

The Telegraph (2015), 'Wealth secrets of the one percent: how the super-rich became super rich', available at www.telegraph.co.uk/money/fame-fortune/wealth-secrets-of-the-one-percent-how-the-super-rich-became-supe/ (Accessed 11 June 2016).

This is Money (2016), 'New state pension age: as we're all told to work longer, when will you be able to retire?', available at www.thisismoney.co.uk/money/pensions/article-1679780/New-state-pension-age-retire.html (Accessed 4 June 2016).

Torche, F. and Spilerman, S. (2009), 'Intergenerational influences of wealth in Mexico', *Latin American Research Review*, 44(3), p. 97.

True Potential (2015), 'Tackling the savings gap', available at www.tpllp.com/wp-content/uploads/2015/05/Tackling-the-Savings-Gap-Q1-2015.pdf (Accessed 11 June 2016).

Tycehurst, R. and Roberts, H. (2015), 'The responsibility of wealth – should rich people give away their money?', *Legal Week*, 26 October. Also available at www.legalweek.com/legal-week/analysis/2431969/the-responsiblity-of-wealth-should-rich-people-give-away-their-money (Accessed 11 June 2016).

UN (2015), 'World population ageing, 1950–2050', Population Division, DESA, UN, p.12, available at www.un.org/esa/population/publications/worldageing19502050/pdf/80chapterii.pdf (Accessed 11 June 2016).

World Bank (2015a), 'Fertility rate', available at http://data.worldbank.org/indicator/SP.DYN.TFRT.IN/ (Accessed 11 June 2016).

World Bank (2015b), 'World population prospects: the 2015 revision', available at https://esa.un.org/unpd/wpp/Publications/Files/Key_Findings_WPP_2015.pdf (Accessed 11 June 2016).

World Bank (2016), 'Life expectancy at birth, total (years)', available at http://data.worldbank.org/indicator/SP.DYN.LE00.IN (Accessed 4 June 2016).

World Health Organisation (WHO) (2016) *World Health Statistics 2016*, available at www.who.int/gho/publications/world_health_statistics/2016/en_whs2016_chapter3.pdf?ua=1 (Accessed 4 June 2016).

Chapter 2

Defining and achieving your desired lifestyle and legacy

Jason Butler

Financial planning is the process by which individuals are directed towards achieving their goals or objectives in the simplest, most efficient manner possible. It follows, therefore, that you need to have a clear understanding of your goals and objectives in order to develop a planning strategy and tactics to achieve them. Life goals and other preferences will influence your decisions on everything from education and skills; work and career; lifestyle and experiences; relationships and family; and opportunities and risk taking.

Money is likely to be a key component in enabling you to achieve many of your life goals, but money itself is only a means to an end, not the end itself. Throughout your life you will need to make key financial decisions on the basis of what is important to you and what action you need to take to realise your ambition.

Learning outcomes

By the end of this chapter you will:

- have an awareness of the role and impact of human motivations and beliefs in relation to money;
- understand the importance of setting clear life goals and developing and maintaining a personal expenditure budget;
- be aware of the impact of self-efficacy in achieving goals and developing resilience;
- understand the main financial behavioural biases and how they can influence financial decisions.

2.1 Human motivations and needs

In this section we examine how human motivations, beliefs and needs can affect how we relate to money and make financial decisions.

2.1.1 Classical and behavioural finance

The foundation of standard or traditional finance is called *classical economic theory*, and it provides a framework for understanding human motivation. At its foundation is the theory of consumer choice, which is that individuals are motivated by the goal of seeking the highest level of satisfaction possible. They do this by buying as many goods and services as they can afford, based on their personal preferences, and they gain more satisfaction from higher spending. Consumers' spending is only limited by their income, known as the **budget constraint**.

Where an individual chooses not to spend all their money when they receive it, but to do so over a longer period of time, this is known as **intertemporal choice**. In simple terms this means they can save and invest some of their income for use at a later date. Other individuals may choose to spend more than their current income, in which case they borrow money temporarily or run down previous savings.

The model also assumes that individuals act rationally (**rational behaviour**), but, as we will discuss later, people do not always act in a logical way, consistent with achieving their goals and objectives.

Franco Modigliani (1980) developed the **Life Cycle Hypothesis** as a way of explaining people's spending and savings habits over a lifetime. Modigliani asserts that humans are motivated to plan and seek to maximise their resources over their lifetime by spending a consistent amount throughout, saving for retirement while earning, and then eventually dying with no savings.

The concept concludes that the **propensity to consume** is greatest among young and ageing people, with the young borrowing against future income, and ageing and retired people living off savings. Middle-aged people, however, have the greatest propensity to save rather than consume.

The concept's weakness is that it does not take into account the various risks associated with longevity, earnings security, living costs or investment returns. In addition, many people are uncomfortable planning to die penniless, while others wish to leave a financial legacy to their family. Despite these weaknesses, Modigliani's approach, with the emphasis on forward thinking, is considered to be the foundation for modern personal financial planning.

The Life Cycle Hypothesis has been further refined by incorporating behavioural aspects into the model. Thaler and Shefin (1981) find that people are seen to have two motivation preferences: short-term and long-term, which often conflict. The planner side is motivated by lifetime satisfaction and is farsighted. The doer side is selfish and myopic and purely concerned with immediate satisfaction. The authors conclude that people welcome help to control their short-term temptations, to achieve their long-term goals.

2.1.2 Hierarchy of needs and humanism

Abraham Maslow (1943; Maslow and Frager, 1987) was a psychologist who developed the theory of the **hierarchy of needs**, which provides a basic framework for all human motivation and associated actions. At the bottom of the pyramid (see Figure 2.1 overleaf) are basic needs like food, shelter, etc. Once these basic needs have been met the individual will seek to fulfil higher level needs that serve to meet their wider personal desires like friendship, love, material possessions and status.

Once these intermediate needs have been met, an individual will seek much higher level needs, referred to as 'self-actualisation'. These needs generally relate to wider society and the desire of the individual to find their real meaning or place in the world. The self-actualisation stage is where real meaning and contentment can be found. Maslow also identified two other needs not included in the hierarchy of needs. One is the need to know, understand and be curious. The other is the aesthetic need people have to seek out beauty.

Maslow's hierarchy of needs has its critics, with the main objections being that values vary by country, interests and income level. For example, in the United States people value materialism, personal success and achieving goals. In Japan, individual opinions are usually subjugated to the goal of the group, risk aversion is

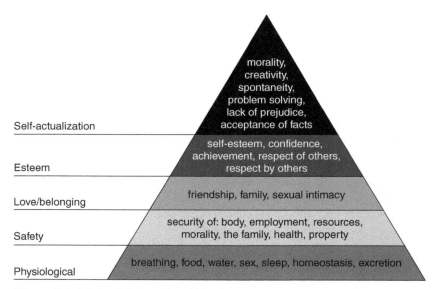

Self-actualization

Esteem

Love/belonging

Safety

Physiological

Figure 2.1 Maslow's Hierarchy of Needs

higher and creative lifestyles are not celebrated. Some countries have strict religious doctrines or less expressive cultures. In some countries work is considered a perfunctory activity, compared to the United States where many people seek fulfilment through their work.

Even within countries, people can have different interests. For example, someone can have a low income but engage in altruistic acts, which is a higher level need. Another person might have a very successful career, have attained significant recognition and be able to afford a lavish lifestyle but not have satisfied their need for sex and love, which is a lower level need.

Gratton (1980) found that people's values produce different priorities depending on their social class. Lower class people valued physiological and belonging; working-class people valued esteem and belonging; and middle-class people valued esteem and self-actualisation.

Despite its weaknesses, Maslow's theory provides a simple, powerful and popular framework for understanding human motivation, which is widely understood. Meeting lower level (basic) human needs, before moving on towards higher level needs, is easy to define and quantify. Defining higher level needs and their importance to motivation, however, is more difficult.

ACTIVITY 2.1

1. Think of examples for each of the levels of motivation as established by Maslow's hierarchy of needs in Figure 2.1.

Satisfaction is closely linked to motivation and relates to fulfilment of and pleasure derived from a person's needs, expectations and wishes. Life satisfaction is considered to be mainly a mental rather than emotional process. As such it provides people with a more effective means of assessing their progress and life status. Life satisfaction is also more closely linked to self-esteem than happiness, which is more associated with fleeting emotions and moods.

Lutz's (1999) additional research into Maslow's theory contends that humans have competing motivations. Some desires are basic whereas others relate to personal development such as love, integrity and truth; and that for people it 'is not so much the optimal satisfaction of our desires to consume but the development of a meaningful life embedded in human community and the natural environment'.

Material desires and needs have an obvious financial implication, whereas higher level altruistic desires may not.

2.1.3 Money beliefs and life planning

We develop our attitudes and beliefs about money from childhood, whether from parents, peers, culture or other life experiences. Sometimes these beliefs are positive and empowering and sometimes they can be negative and regressive.

Because your relationship with money will have a big impact on your overall life satisfaction, it makes sense to develop greater self-awareness of what is important to you about money, how it fits into your life and how to make better financial decisions.

Life planning is an approach that emerged in the 1990s and which combines financial insights with an individual's desire to go beyond basic needs and materialism. Some describe life planning as essentially about living life on purpose, whatever that means to you, by uncovering what motivates you and how you can derive satisfaction from your efforts. By taking into account both human behaviour and money factors in the financial planning process, life planning seeks to go beyond building wealth so that people live happier, fulfilling and more satisfying lives.

For life planning to be appropriate and effective, Anthes and Lee (2001) suggest that the following conditions need to be met:

- motivation – an intense desire for the change;
- all the required information necessary for the decision;
- the ability to focus on the changes necessary (today);
- preparation for problems and upside that can come;
- an ability to make changes as circumstances change;
- a keen understanding of your own policy;
- preparation of some people for unselfish behaviour.

George Kinder is considered by many to be the father of life planning, and his book, *The Seven Stages of Money Maturity*, sets out a radically different way of approaching managing wealth. A key element of the Kinder approach is to ask yourself the three difficult questions in Box 2.1.

╭───╮
❖ BOX 2.1 KINDER'S LIFE-PLANNING QUESTIONS

- **Question one.** I want you to imagine that you are financially secure – you have enough money to take care of your needs, now and in the future. The question is, how would you live your life? What would you do with the money? Would you change anything? Let yourself go. Don't hold back your dreams. *Describe a life that is complete, richly yours.*
- **Question two.** This time, you visit your doctor who tells you that you have five to ten years to live. The good part is that you won't ever feel sick. The bad news is that you will have no notice of the moment of your death. What will you do in the time you have remaining to live? *Will you change your life and how will you do it?*
- **Question three.** This time, your doctor shocks you with the news that you have only one day left to live. Notice what feelings arise as you confront your very real mortality. Ask yourself: 'What dreams will be left unfulfilled? What do I wish I had finished or had been? What do I wish I had done? What did I miss?'

Source: © Copyright 1999/2015 George Kinder and the Kinder Institute of Life Planning. All Rights Reserved. This material was developed by George Kinder and the Kinder Institute of Life Planning. It is part of a programme of trainings that lead to the Registered Life Planner® designation. Used by permission of George Kinder and the Kinder Institute of Life Planning.
╰───╯

The purpose of these questions is to help uncover your deepest and most important values. Equally important is uncovering what is standing in the way of leading the life that is truly the one you want to live. In this context another home or expensive car might not be the answer.

Kinder sets out a framework for helping us to identify what is really important in life. The values grid, as it is known, determines between 'heart's core' – what really matters; 'ought to' – things that you feel obliged to do; and 'fun to' – irreverent things that aren't really important but nevertheless are possible goals.

Maria Nemeth is a clinical psychologist and a Master Certified Coach (a professional recognition for trained coaches) who has been involved in life planning for many years. Maria has developed a useful tool called the 'Life's Intentions Inventory' and this is reproduced in Table 2.1. The tool is designed to help elicit goals, aspirations and lifestyle experiences which may be important, but as yet not articulated.

╭───╮
ACTIVITY 2.2
1. Answer the three Kinder questions.
2. Go through the Life's Intentions Inventory and score the relative importance of each of the intentions.
╰───╯

Table 2.1 Life's Intentions Inventory

The Life's Intentions Inventory

Life's intentions represent underlying purposes that give meaning to our goals and dreams. Please rate the intentions that are currently important to you. Use 1 for Relatively Unimportant and 5 for Very Important. This is only a snapshot in time, reflecting where you are today. How you rate your intentions could change at a later date.

My intentions are to be:
Financially successful
Physically fit and healthy
A successful painter or sculptor
A successful author, playwright or poet
A contributor to my community
A visionary leader
Spiritually developing
A loving family member
A trusted friend
A well-respected professional
An effective manager
An effective teacher
Well-educated
An effective coach
A successful business owner
An effective mediator
Well travelled
An effective mentor
A successful entrepreneur
An adventurer
Politically active
A successful communicator

Reproduced by kind permission of Maria Nemeth, Founder and Executive Director of the Academy for Coaching Excellence.

2.2 Desired lifestyle and the role of money

Beyond basic subsistence needs we all have different ideas of what represents a good lifestyle, with some lifestyles more expensive than others. This can have significant implications for how you manage your personal finances and the choices you make throughout life.

2.2.1 Defining and prioritising goals

People don't have financial goals, but rather they have life goals that may have financial implications. For example, taking a one-year sabbatical to volunteer in a developing country may have implications for retirement funding – an obvious financial factor. However, not taking the sabbatical could lead to less fulfilment and life satisfaction – a non-financial, well-being factor.

Extrinsic motivation relates to our desire to pursue a goal or action because someone else encourages us to do so, whether that be for financial or emotional reward. **Intrinsic motivation,** on the other hand, relates to our desire to pursue a goal or action because we want to do so, i.e. it comes from within. It is widely thought that intrinsic motivation is more effective at enabling people to achieve goals. From a financial planning perspective, it therefore makes sense to spend time and thought defining, quantifying and prioritising life goals, so these can be taken into account in analysing the financial implications (which are discussed in Chapter 3).

Life goals that will be common to everyone are maintaining **financial independence** and staying fit and well. This means being able to fund your desired lifestyle until you die, regardless of your desire or ability to work, and that your money lasts a lifetime, including a time when paid work is optional because you have enough financial resources available to fund your desired lifestyle.

In an ideal world you would work for money because you want to, not because you have to. The term 'financial independence' can be more empowering to people than the concept of 'retirement' and is something worthwhile to aim for. This is because, unlike retirement, which for some people means being too old to be productive or engaged in meaningful activities, financial independence means you have the choice of doing whatever you wish, including continuing to work.

An emerging trend is that people are likely to have many different jobs over their working lives; potentially two or more careers; and a series of 'mini-retirements' involving part-time work combined with travel and leisure in later life as described by Timothy Ferris (2011) in his recent best-selling book, *The 4-Hour Work Week: Escape the 9-5, Live Anywhere and Join the New Rich.*

❖ BOX 2.2 THE CHANGING FACE OF RETIREMENT

For many, a conventional retirement may not be welcome. More than ever before, we are enjoying good health to an older age and many of us are not only capable of working well beyond retirement age, we also often have the desire to do so. Today's older generation can often be found using their retirement years to start a new career, set up a business or to consult in their specialist field. As a result, the notion that an individual should cease working at a pre-defined age is more of an illusion than a reality.

Source: Barclays Wealth Insights (2010, p.4).

The five main factors that will affect your ability to achieve financial independence include: how long you will live; how much you earn and spend; whether you receive any financial legacy or help from your family; the return you achieve on your capital; and the rate at which the cost of living rises. These issues, which are covered in more depth in later chapters of this book, determine what financial resources you might have throughout your lifetime.

ACTIVITY 2.3

1. Think about the following questions to explore your own thoughts about retirement in the context of goals and financial planning:
   - What does retirement mean to you?
   - How will you live your life differently when you are retired?
   - Do you have a role model of someone who is retired and, if so, what is it about their lifestyle that you admire?
   - Do you have concerns about retirement and, if so, what are they?
   - How would you feel about working less but for longer?

There may be a number of other life goals that are important to you. The following are examples that have a financial implication:

- **Education goals.** For example: funding part or all of the education costs of a child, grandchild or other family member or friend; taking up further study or further education at a university or college; learning a foreign language and staying in the home country for some time; learning a new skill such as dancing, martial arts or rock climbing.
- **Family and altruistic goals.** For example: leaving a specific legacy to an individual or charity; funding the cost of a child's or children's wedding; helping children or other family members to buy their first home.
- **Lifestyle goals.** For example: taking up a hobby, such as sailing, shooting, scuba-diving or flying, which has a cost implication; indulging an interest in culture such as opera, ballet, musicals or performance art at home and abroad; buying a second home; moving abroad to live permanently; travelling around the world to indulge an interest in historical buildings and/or interesting places; buying a boat, classic car or plane; collecting art, fine wine or other items; buying an expensive musical instrument; visiting relatives more often, particularly those living overseas.
- **Career and business goals.** For example: mentoring young businesses and possibly providing development funds; setting up a small 'lifestyle' business such as a café, wine bar, restaurant or shop; writing a book or making a documentary film.

Different goals will require different approaches based on whether they are short-, medium- or long-term goals. Funding a wedding or house in a couple of years means that it will be important to avoid capital loss and inflation is less of a concern. Building capital to become financially independent in the long term, however, means that inflation will be more of an issue and, given the much longer time horizon, you could accept some risk to capital, in the form of stockmarket volatility, in return for the potential of generating meaningful real (post inflation) investment returns over the long term.

2.2.2 Converting human capital to financial capital

As described in Chapter 1, total wealth comprises human capital and financial capital. When we are young the human capital is at its highest, representing the **present**

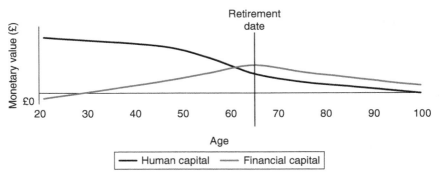

Figure 2.2 Human and financial capital

value of all future potential earnings from work. Assuming no financial legacies have been received, financial capital is either non-existent or very low in the early adult years.

As we progress through our working life our human capital gradually reduces and, to the extent that there is a surplus of income over expenditure, financial capital gradually increases. As shown in Figure 2.2, once human capital has been exhausted, we need to have sufficient financial assets to fund lifestyle expenditure until death.

While it is true that the earlier one starts saving and accumulating financial capital the better, sometimes a higher total wealth return can be achieved by younger people investing in improving their skills and knowledge to increase future earnings. Respected financial planning expert Michael Kitces has looked at this issue in some detail and he made the observations in Box 2.3, which are particularly relevant for young people.

❖ BOX 2.3 DO YOU SHOW HUMAN CAPITAL ON THE BALANCE SHEET?

... making investments that alter the trajectory of an individual's future earnings can have a dramatic impact on the value of human capital and therefore on lifetime wealth. Whether it's a slight increase in earnings (that becomes the new base for future raises and income growth) or merely an increase in the growth rate of future earnings in the years to come, small changes have a big effect.

For instance, imagine a 25-year-old client who is looking ahead at a 40-year working life. Current earnings a few years out of college are $40,000. Assuming earnings increase at 3 per cent/year for inflation, the client is anticipated to earn just over $3 million of cumulative earnings over the working years; at a discount rate of 8 per cent, the client's human capital is effectively an $808,424 'asset' on the balance sheet.

So what happens if the client gets a $1,000 raise, pushing up base salary to $41,000 (upon which all future inflation adjustments are applied). Over the 40-year working career, a $1,000 raise isn't just a $1,000 increase in income, but a $20,210 increase in the total (net present) value of the human capital asset.

On the other hand, improving the client's career trajectory has an even greater impact – if the client can generate a 1 per cent real growth rate in income (i.e., grow income at 4 per cent/year where inflation is only 3 per cent), the human capital asset jumps in value (on a present value basis) by a whopping $112,374! Small changes have a significant impact over extended periods of time.

Source: kitces.com (2011).

At Berkshire Hathaway's annual meeting in 2008, Warren Buffett made the point, 'Invest in as much of yourself as you can. You are your own biggest asset by far.' He echoed those sentiments in a CNBC interview in July 2009 when he said, 'Anything you do to improve your own talents and make yourself more valuable will get paid off in terms of appropriate real purchasing power.' Returns from investing in your ability to earn can be significant. 'Anything you invest in yourself, you get back tenfold.' And unlike other assets and investments, 'nobody can tax it away; they can't steal it from you'.

Social capital

The extent to which you need to convert human capital to financial capital may be affected by your level of *social capital*. Definitions of social capital vary, but the main aspects include citizenship, 'neighbourliness', social networks and civic participation. The definition used by ONS, taken from the Office for Economic Co-operation and Development (OECD), is 'networks together with shared norms, values and understandings that facilitate co-operation within or among groups'. Research has shown that higher levels of social capital are associated with better health, higher educational achievement, better employment outcomes and lower crime rates. In other words, those with extensive networks are more likely to be 'housed, healthy, hired and happy' (ONS, n.d.).

Those who have high social capital may have less need of financial capital if, for example, their family or community will provide support that leads to a lower need for savings or insurance. By contrast, those who are more isolated must rely more on their own financial resources, for example needing to pay for later life care. Additionally, there seems to be some evidence that social capital promotes human capital and vice versa (Keeley, 2007).

ACTIVITY 2.4

Think about your education and work experiences so far and those you expect to acquire in future. How do you expect them to affect your future income* (in other words, the value today of your human capital)?

* Bear in mind that your future income may include elements other than wages and salary, for example contributions employers make to pension schemes on your behalf (see Chapter 10).

2.2.3 Personal expenditure budgeting

The clearer you can be about what your current and future lifestyle costs are, and where you are spending your money now, the better your overall plan and associated financial decisions will be. How much you earn will clearly be a key factor in your financial planning, but what really matters is how much you spend relative to what you earn throughout your working life.

If you spend all that you earn, and don't accumulate any financial capital by regular saving, you'll have nothing to support you when you can't or don't wish to work. In his 2009 biography *The Snowball: Warren Buffett and the Business of Life*, Warren Buffett advises, 'Do not save what is left after spending; instead spend what is left after saving.'

My experience is that many people rarely have a clear idea of the cost of their current or future desired lifestyle and they typically consistently underestimate how much they are spending. It is good practice to set out a clear annual expenditure **budget** each year, broken down by fixed and discretionary items. Most online banking services allow you to download your bank statement into a financial management programme or app. There are also a number of budgeting apps now available for monitoring personal spending.

The more you can control your non-core, discretionary spending, the more likely you are to have sufficient money to save for the longer term.

2.2.4 Self-efficacy – the key to achieving life goals

Whether you believe you can do a thing or not, you are right.

Henry Ford (1947)

Believing that you are capable of doing something, such as achieving life goals, has been shown to be a major determinant of success. Albert Bandura (1977, 1995) is a psychologist who introduced the term 'self-efficacy' to describe the psychological phenomenon that enhances goal achievement. According to Bandura, a self-efficacy belief is, 'The belief in one's capabilities to organize and execute the courses of action required to manage prospective situations' (Bandura, 1995, p.2). In other words, if you believe you can do something you are much more likely to achieve it and if you don't believe you can achieve it you are more likely to fail. From a financial planning perspective, this means that as well as setting life goals that are important and meaningful to you, you also need to believe that they are achievable.

People who have high self-efficacy also develop higher emotional resilience – the ability to bounce back from failure, mistakes or setbacks. They also see failures as a learning opportunity and use their past experiences to achieve success. Thomas Jefferson, Walt Disney and J.K. Rowling are well-known high achievers with high self-efficacy because they experienced significant failure on their route to achieving significant success.

To increase the chance of your financial plan becoming a reality you can use the following techniques:

1.   Break your goal down into a series of smaller, more achievable milestones and celebrate the success of reaching them.

2. Find a mentor, role model or adviser to show you how to create and maintain a plan and give you encouragement and support.
3. Picture how your life will be when you have achieved your various goals, and what they will mean to you. The more you can paint a picture in your mind of your future self, the more you'll be motivated to stick with the plan.
4. Cultivate happiness and a positive outlook by integrating as many things into your life which lift your mood and help you to remain positive, such as music, exercise, comedy, hobbies or social interactions.
5. Be pragmatic when you start to doubt yourself. Accept you are only human and not perfect but don't let it dominate your thinking.

2.3 Emotions and behavioural biases – impact on financial decision making

Behavioural finance is the study of human psychology as it relates to money. There have been numerous books and research papers written on this subject over the years. What follows is an overview of the key theories and hypotheses.

2.3.1 The role of emotions

We all have individual idiosyncrasies, traits, experiences and preferences and make decisions, including those involving money, at an emotional level. In his book on investor psychology, *Your Money and Your Brain* (2008), Jason Zweig makes two important points: 'emotions overwhelm reason' (p.221) and 'financial losses are processed in the same areas of the brain that responds to mortal danger' (p.6).

The 2008–9 global stockmarket downturn offers an example of how the cycle of fear and greed can drive an investor's decisions. Some investors fled the market in early 2009, just before the rebound began. They locked in their losses and then experienced the stress of watching the markets climb. Figure 2.3 depicts the main emotions experienced at different stages of the stockmarket cycle.

Figure 2.3 Emotions and investing

Table 2.2 Morningstar behaviour gap results

Investor returns Group	Asset-weighted 10-year investor return, % p.a.	Average 10-year total return, % p.a.	10-year return gap, % p.a.
2014			
US Equity	6.49	7.47	−0.98
Sector Equity	7.18	6.16	0.02
Allocation	5.40	5.42	−0.02
International Equity	4.55	5.74	−1.19
Taxable Bond	3.75	4.44	−0.69
Municipal Bond	2.36	3.66	−1.30
All Funds	5.21	5.75	−0.54
2013			
US Equity	6.52	8.18	−1.66
Sector Equity	6.32	9.46	−3.14
Allocation	4.81	6.93	−2.12
International Equity	5.76	8.77	−3.01
Taxable Bond	3.15	5.39	−2.24
Municipal Bond	1.65	3.53	−1.88
All Funds	4.81	7.30	−2.49
2012			
US Equity	6.88	7.89	−1.01
Sector Equity	9.07	9.44	−0.37
Allocation	5.53	6.37	−0.84
International Equity	6.84	9.95	−3.11
Taxable Bond	4.76	5.63	−0.87
Municipal Bond	2.71	4.06	−1.35
All Funds	6.10	7.05	−0.95

Source: Morningstar, asset-weighted and average total investor returns – trailing through 31 December 2014.

Return gap – asset-weighted investor return less average total return.

Source: Kinnel (2015).

The phenomenon of investors receiving lower investment returns than would otherwise have been available is known as the behaviour or performance gap. Recent research by Barclays (2013) has estimated that the true cost to the average investor in forgone long-term returns, due to their inability to make rational decisions in the short term, is in the region of 2 per cent per year, with the cost for many being even higher.

Morningstar, the **investment fund** information provider, publishes an annual review of US investors' performance compared to the funds they are invested in. They found that the behaviour gap for all funds to the end of 2014 was 0.54 per cent p.a., down from 2.49 per cent the previous year (Kinnel, 2015). Table 2.2 shows the performance gap for major fund sectors, which shows the gap for the main **equities** and **bonds** sectors to be around 1 per cent p.a. (You may be unfamiliar with some of the terms in the table, but they will be explained in Chapter 9.)

Research into the behaviour gap by Clare and Motson (2010, p.4) found that:

On average the investment timing decisions of retail investors with regard to equity mutual funds has cost them performance of just under 1.2 per cent a year over the eighteen year period of our study. Although 1.2 per cent may not sound very high, compounded over 18 years it represents a cumulated under performance of 20 per cent, compared with a simple buy and hold strategy.

An annualised return gap of 'just' 1.2 per cent p.a. on a £1m portfolio invested over 20 years would have translated into £940,000 in lost returns (see Figure 2.4) for the average investor, purely as a result of bad decision making. Staying disciplined through rising and falling markets can pose a challenge, but it is crucial for long-term success.

The brain makes decisions in one of two ways. One is **automatic** and intuitive and the other is **reflective** and rational. For example, learning to speak a foreign language requires reflective thinking. The learner has to think slowly and deliberately about each word and sentence until they become so familiar with the language that the automatic thinking process takes over. Learning to drive is another example of using reflective thinking to become proficient at the activity before it becomes instinctive and less mental thought is required.

ACTIVITY 2.5

1. Have a look at the following three questions (Frederick, 2005, p.27) and answer them as quickly as you can.
   (1) A bat and a ball together cost $1.10 in total. The bat costs a dollar more than the ball. How much does the ball cost?
   (2) If it takes 5 minutes for 5 machines to make 5 widgets, how long would it take 100 machines to make 100 widgets?
   (3) In a lake there is a patch of lily pads. Every day the patch doubles in size. If it takes 48 days for the patch to cover the entire lake, how long will it take to cover half the lake?

Your intuitive (System 1) answers to these questions were probably $0.10, 100 minutes and 24 days (see the end of the chapter for the actual answers). Don't

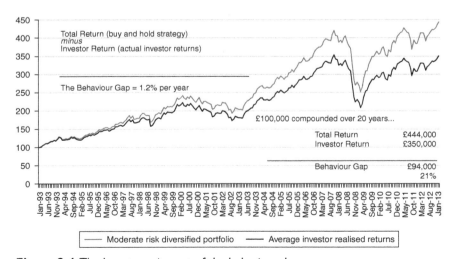

Figure 2.4 The long-term impact of the behavioural gap

worry if you got them wrong, it's just your intuitive rather than rational thinking system kicking in.

2.3.2 Heuristics and biases

Psychologist Daniel Kahneman (2011), who was awarded the Nobel Prize for Economic Science in 2002, describes the brain's thinking as System 1 and System 2. System 2 is slow, deliberate, analytical and involves conscious effort to make rational decisions. To minimise the brain's work, it also has System 1 thinking. This is fast, automatic, intuitive and largely unconscious. System 1 thinking enables us to use trial and error to develop rules of thumb and mental shortcuts for making decisions, otherwise known as heuristics. Academics have identified a number of common biases and heuristics which influence how we make financial decisions, some of which are described below.

Over-confidence

People think that they make better financial and investing decisions than they really do. It's similar to how most people think that they are above-average drivers. A mistaken belief in your financial capabilities can lead you to take too much risk by putting too much money in one investment (over concentration) or switching investments too frequently in the belief that you can generate higher returns.

Extrapolation

People often base their financial decisions too heavily on recent events, or they give more weight to facts which support their beliefs and opinions, assuming that recent returns (good or bad) will continue in the future.

❖ BOX 2.4 EXAMPLE OF BEHAVIOURAL BIASES AT WORK

A good example of over-confidence and extrapolation was shown in a survey of about a thousand individual investors, on three separate occasions between 1998 and 2001 (see Figure 2.5). Participants were asked to give their prediction for how much they thought the stockmarket and their own investment portfolio would rise over the next 12 months. On two of the occasions, when the stockmarket had experienced a strong rise, investors' predications for the rise in the stockmarket were bullish and of own portfolios even higher. On the occasion when the stockmarket had experienced a significant fall, investors' expectations for the stockmarket performance in the next year and their own portfolios was about half of what it had been on the two previous occasions.

Anchoring and adjustment

This relates to using a known amount to estimate an unknown amount. For example, if you are asked to estimate how much time people spend watching television your starting point (anchor) might be how much time you spend watching television.

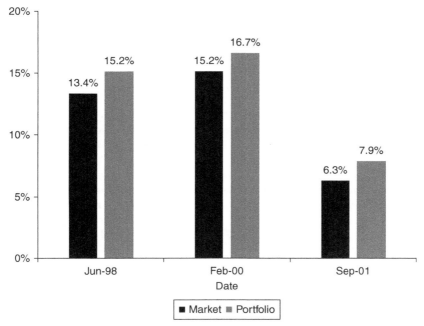

Figure 2.5 Over-optimism, extrapolation and investor predictions
Source: Data from Fisher and Statman (2002).

Where the anchor is higher than the true answer there is a tendency to over-estimate, and where the anchor is lower, there is a tendency to underestimate.

For example, if you browse the internet for 45 minutes, you might estimate that the average person browses more than you, say two hours. If, however, you browse for six hours a day then you might estimate the average to be a bit less, perhaps four hours.

Availability

The availability heuristic relates to how people use freely available information to answer a question or make a decision. Ricciardi (2008, p.96) describes the availability heuristic as, 'in various experiments in psychology ... individuals tend to be biased by information that is easier to recall, influenced by information that is vivid, well-publicized, or recent'.

You might think dying in a car accident a remote possibility, but if you learned that someone local to you had died from a car crash you might think that the probability of it happening to you to be higher. Environmental disasters are another good example of the effect of the availability heuristic. Floods may occur in an area where they have never been experienced in living memory. Many householders won't have flood insurance, even those in areas considered at risk.

The purchase of flood insurance usually increases significantly after a flood, even in areas that never suffered flooding, as householders perceive the risk to be much higher. If flooding doesn't occur in the subsequent few years policy purchases and renewals decline.

From a financial planning perspective, someone who has several relatives who are/were long or short lived, might have more or less inclination to save for retirement as a result.

Hindsight bias
As the saying goes, hindsight is a wonderful thing. After the event, things seem obvious and we wonder why we didn't see them coming: 'How could I have been so stupid?' Hindsight bias therefore lulls us into thinking that it is easy to predict the future.

Representativeness
When an individual assesses a new situation against their past experiences, they often rely on stereotypes as a guide to decision making. For instance, making an assumption about someone by the type of car they drive or how they speak. In personal finance this bias is often related to manipulation of statistics to support a particular outcome.

Thaler and Sunstein (2009) give a good example of how, during the Second World War, London newspapers plotted VI rocket strikes on an area of Central London measuring 3 miles by 2.5 miles. This implied that the Germans could accurately aim the rockets, and were targeting two quadrants – the South East and North West – with the majority of the strikes.

The reality was that the VI could not accurately target strikes and, as such, bombings were entirely random. Redrawing the quadrants with diagonal lines, rather than vertical or horizontal lines, made the strikes look more random and thus not targeted as initially thought.

Gambler's fallacy
Gambler's fallacy is the heuristic that describes the common misunderstanding individuals have about random sequences.

Say you tossed a coin five times and each time you came up with tails. What probability do you think you'll come up with heads on the sixth toss? You might think that a head is most probable, based on the previous five outcomes, when in fact the probability remains just under 50 per cent (it might land on the edge).

In the UK the government-owned National Savings & Investments agency offers savings accounts called Premium Bonds, which give savers a potential return in the form of random monthly cash prize draws of various amounts. In mid-2016, the odds of winning any prize in return for each £1 invested were 30,000 to 1. Thus someone holding the maximum holding of £50,000 would expect to win, on average, 1.6666 prizes per month. If an investor goes several months without winning any prizes he or she may feel that they are more likely to win as they are 'overdue' a prize. The reality is the odds of them winning remain 30,000 to 1 for each pound invested, regardless of how long they have been invested or what has happened previously.

Self-attribution bias
We like to take the credit for when things go right and blame other influences or factors when they go wrong. There is always a pundit who was so clever and smart that

they made the right call on the direction of investment markets, interest rates, the price of oil or gold, etc., because they could see what others didn't see or chose to ignore. Investors in Apple or even Facebook now say, 'Look how smart I am', whereas when Enron went bust investors said, 'No one could see that coming!'

Prospect theory and loss aversion

This heuristic suggests that we are more sensitive to investment losses than gains, perhaps twice as much. Say you are given the chance to flip a coin, i.e. a 50/50 chance, and heads means you lose £1,000. How much would you need to win by landing tails to make the deal attractive? Logic suggests that a gain of £1,000 should be sufficient, but most people would require a gain of £2,500.

This heuristic also suggests that investors will avoid crystallising a loss on an investment and would prefer to retain the holding in the hope that it will recover, at least to break even. The history of a holding should have no bearing on whether to retain it from an investment perspective.

The disposition effect

Consider this situation: you are holding two different investments, with £10,000 invested in each. One has grown to be worth £13,000, the other has fallen in value to £7,000. You are now faced with the situation where you need to realise £5,000 from these investments. Which one should you sell down to realise £5,000?

The disposition effect is an extension to loss aversion which relates to the fact that investors would rather sell an investment showing a gain, and retain an investment standing at a loss. Odean (1998) and Barber and Odean (2000) found that investors were 50 per cent more likely to sell down the investment showing the gain and retain the investment with the loss, leading to an adverse effect on portfolio returns. In Chapter 9 we'll discuss the role of portfolio 'rebalancing' to provide a disciplined structure for selling off investments which show gains.

Regret avoidance

This trait relates to the concept of 'once bitten, twice shy', in that when we have experienced the pain of losing money we try to avoid the behaviour which caused it. We kid ourselves that we have learned from our mistakes, which leads us to avoid, for example, technology after the crash in technology related equities in 2001, or the stockmarket as a whole after the heavy falls during the global financial crisis of 2008, even though we know that big market falls are usually followed by rapid market recoveries. Having a structured plan and a disciplined approach to decision making helps minimise such wealth-destroying behaviour.

Framing

The way that financial information and statistics are presented can have a significant effect on how investors process the information. Investors can make completely different decisions, even with identical information, purely on the basis of how it is presented or framed.

Tversky and Kahneman (1981) set out an interesting example of framing in action. Imagine that the United States is preparing for the outbreak of an unusual Asian disease, which is expected to kill 600 people. Two alternative programs to combat the disease have been proposed. Assume that the exact scientific estimate of the consequences of the programs is as follows:

- If Program A is adopted, 200 people will be saved.
- If Program B is adopted, a one-third probability exists that 600 people will be saved, and a two-thirds probability that no people will be saved.

Which of the two programs would you favour?

A second group of people is given the same problem but asked to choose between two different programs, as follows:

- If Program C is adopted, 400 people will die.
- If Program D is adopted, a one-third probability exists that nobody will die, and a two-thirds probability that 600 people will die.

Which of the two programs would you favour?

When given the choice between programs A and B, the majority of Kahneman and Tversky's respondents choose A (72 per cent), whereas when choosing between C and D, the majority choose D (78 per cent).

In terms of outcomes A and C are equivalent, as are B and D. If decisions were being made on a purely rational basis a risk taker would consistently choose B and D and a risk-adverse person would choose A and C. The conclusion Kahneman and Tversky drew from this experiment is that when the problem is presented in terms of net gains, the majority of people are risk averse, but when presented in terms of losses, the majority of people are risk taking.

Mental accounting

An extension of framing is the tendency for investors to compartmentalise or identify different pots of their wealth with specific goals, time horizons or objectives. The process, known as *mental accounting*, involves people using certain rules to keep track of their financial situation. Thaler (1999) explains how mental accounting enables us to understand a wide range of financial behaviours. Mental accounting explains why some investors, where taxation is similar, prefer cash dividends over capital gains. The investor's mental accounting sees them keep the dividend payments in a 'current income' account and capital gains in a separate 'long-term savings' account.

Mental accounting can cause investors to make differing and often sub-optimal decisions for each financial pot compared to if they had viewed their wealth as a whole. For example, some people retain cash in a low-interest savings account while also having borrowing at a much higher interest rate. On the other hand, mental accounting can also help people with day-to-day money management (budgeting), which is discussed in Chapter 5.

2.4 Conclusion

Financial planning encompasses identifying and reconciling an individual's competing needs, higher level motivations, latent aspiration, specific goals and money values, with their current and future human and financial resources. In addition, better financial decisions arise from an awareness and acceptance of the role that emotions can have on behaviour and financial decision making.

Answers to Activity 2.5

1. *Bat = $1.05 and Ball = $0.05*
2. *5 minutes (one widget per machine for 5 minutes)*
3. *47 days (if it's half covered and then doubles that means it's fully covered the next day)*

End of chapter test

1. Explain self-actualisation and how life planning might be used in this regard.
2. Explain what is meant by financial independence and how this differs from the traditional concept of retirement.
3. Describe the differences between human capital and financial capital and the implications and considerations for financial planning.
4. Explain the term behavioural biases and give three examples of different heuristics.

References

Anthes, W. and Lee, S. (2001) 'Experts Examine Emerging Concept of Life Planning', *Journal of Financial Planning* 14:6, 90–101.

Bandura, A. (1977) 'Self-efficacy: Toward a Unifying Theory of Behavioural Change', *Psychological Review* 84, 191–215.

Bandura, A. (Ed.) (1995) *Self-efficacy in Changing Societies*. New York: Cambridge University Press.

Barber, B. and Odean, T. (2000) 'Trading is Hazardous to Your Wealth: The Common Stock Investment Performance of Individual Investors', *Journal of Finance* 55:2, 773–806.

Barclays (2013) 'Overcoming the Cost of Being Human (or, the Pursuit of Anxiety-adjusted Returns)', March.

Barclays Wealth Insights (2010) 'How the Wealthy Are Redefining Their Retirement', Vol. 12, p. 4.

Clare, A. and Motson, N. (2010) 'Do UK Retail Investors Buy at the Top and Sell at the Bottom?' (p. 4). Working Paper, available at https://www.cass.city.ac.uk/__data/assets/pdf_file/0003/69933/Do-UK-retail-investors-buy-at-the-top-and-sell-at-the-bottom.pdf (Accessed 17 October 2016).

Ferris, T. (2011) *The 4-Hour Work Week: Escape the 9-5, Live Anywhere and Join the New Rich*. London: Vermilion.

Fisher, K.L. and Statman, M. (2002) 'Bubble Expectations', *Journal of Wealth Management* 5:2, 17–22.

Ford, H. (1947) Quotation attributed to Henry Ford in *The Reader's Digest* at http://quoteinvestigator.com/2015/02/03/you-can/ (Accessed 17 October 2016).

Frederick, S. (2005) 'Cognitive Reflection and Decision Making', *The Journal of Economic Perspectives* 19:4, 25–42.

Gratton, Lynda C. (1980) 'Analysis of Maslow's Hierarchy of Needs with Three Social Class Groups', *Social Indicators Research* 7:1–4, 463–476.

Kahneman, D. (2011) *Thinking Fast and Slow*. London: Penguin Books.

Keeley, B. (2007) *Human Capital: How what you know shapes your life*. Paris: OECD.

Kinder, G. (2000) *The Seven Stages of Money Maturity: Understanding the spirit and value of money in your life*. New York: Dell Publishing Company.

Kinnel, R. (2015) *Mind the Gap 2015*. Morningstar. http://news.morningstar.com.

Lutz, M. (1999) 'Humanistic Perspective', in Peter E. Earl and Simon Kemp, eds, *The Elgar Companion to Consumer Research and Economic Psychology*, 314–319. Cheltenham, UK: Edward Elgar.

Maslow, Abraham H. (1943) 'A Theory of Human Motivation', *Psychological Review* 50:4, 370–396.

Maslow, Abraham H. and Frager, R. (1987) *Motivation and Personality*, 3rd ed. New York: Addison Wesley Longman.

Modigliani, F. (1980) 'The Life Cycle Hypothesis of Saving', *The Collected Papers of Franco Modigliani*, Vol. 2. Cambridge, MA: MIT Press.

Odean, T. (1998) 'Are Investors Reluctant to Realise Their Losses?', *Journal of Finance* 53:5, 1775–1798.

Office for National Statistics (ONS) (n.d.) 'Guide to Social Capital', available at http://webarchive.nationalarchives.gov.uk/20160105160709/www.ons.gov.uk/ons/guide-method/user-guidance/social-capital-guide/the-social-capital-project/guide-to-social-capital.html (Accessed 17 October 2016).

Ricciardi, Victor (2008) 'The Psychology of Risk: The Behavioral Finance Perspective', in Frank J. Fabozzi, ed., *The Handbook of Finance, Volume 2: Investment Management and Financial Management*, 85–111. Hoboken, NJ: John Wiley & Sons.

Thaler, Richard H. (1999) 'Mental Accounting Matters', *Journal of Behavioural Decision Making* 12:3, 183–206.

Thaler, Richard H. and Shefin, Hersh M. (1981) 'An Economic Theory of Self-Control', *Journal of Political Economy* 89:2, 392–406.

Thaler, R. and Sunstein, C. (2009) *Nudge: Improving decisions about health, wealth and happiness*. London: Penguin.

Tversky, A. and Kahneman, D. (1981) 'The Framing of Decisions and the Psychology of Choice', *Science* 211:4481, 453–458.

www.kitces.com (2011) Michael Kitces at Nerd's Eye View. www.kitces.com/blog/do-you-show-human-capital-on-the-balance-sheet/ (Accessed 17 October 2016). Extract and chart reproduced by kind permission.

Zweig, J. (2008) *Your Money and Your Brain: Become a smarter, more successful investor, the neuroscience way*. New York: Simon & Schuster.

Chapter 3

Money and happiness

Jason Butler

We all want to live happy, fulfilling and healthy lives, but what role does money play in achieving those outcomes? Can money really buy you happiness and a long life or is there more to it than just being wealthy? In this chapter you'll gain insights into how to get the biggest happiness return from your money and how to avoid the money blues.

Learning outcomes

By the end of this chapter you will:

- be aware of the role that money plays in achieving and sustaining happiness;
- have an understanding of the main financial factors which influence life happiness;
- be able to describe the main personality traits and the impact on happiness from a financial perspective;
- have an awareness of how money influences health and life expectancy.

3.1 The role of money in achieving and maintaining happiness

We all have different perspectives, views and values about money, based on our culture, parents, education, peers, life experiences and personality traits. Our deep-seated feelings about money can have a significant influence on our behaviours, habits and decisions about money. The theory of planned behaviour is a theory originally created by Icek Ajzen (1991) that links *beliefs* and *behaviour*. The implications are that:

- the more positive your beliefs and attitudes about money;
- the more you believe that good money behaviour is what others expect of you (the social norm); and
- the more you have belief in your ability to adopt positive money behaviours, the better you'll be with money and as a result you'll be happier.

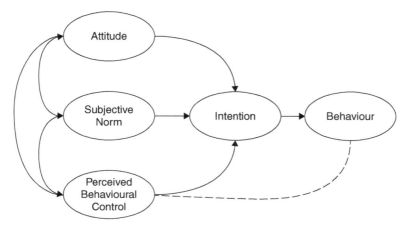

Figure 3.1 Theory of planned behaviour
Source: Orzanna (2015).

Table 3.1 Well-known English money proverbs

'Money doesn't grow on trees'	Money is hard to get or is scarce
'Money is the root of all evil'	Religiously based view that money is evil/corrupting
'Money is a necessary evil'	Money is a bad thing and doesn't enable one to live an honest life
'Money talks'	People who are rich have a lot of power and influence
'Fortune favours the bold'	People who bravely go after what they want are more successful than people who try to live safely
'Easy come, easy go'	When you get money quickly, like by winning it, it's easy to spend it or lose it quickly as well

The messages we hear as we grow up can sometimes embed a strong negative association about money. Every culture has a collection of wise sayings that offer advice about how to live your life – known as 'proverbs'. Have a look at the common English sayings in Table 3.1 above and what they mean.

ACTIVITY 3.1

List as many common money proverbs as you can from your own culture, together with the meaning. Have a think about how these might re-enforce a negative money value in someone.

Some people are obsessed with accumulating as much money as possible, they flaunt it and are big spenders. At the other end of the spectrum some people are totally uninterested in money, live a frugal, low-cost lifestyle and have no material aspirations or motivations. Some people find it hard to save for later life, living purely for the moment, even though they know this is not in their best interests. Sometimes, people with reasonable wealth find it difficult to spend their money, due to insecurities or worries. For others money is seen as a source of power, control, status and meaning, which often leads to unhappiness.

A significant number of people find money is a source of anxiety, worry and frustration. A survey (Mann 2015) for the *Guardian* newspaper of a thousand people in the UK (demographically weighted) found that money was by far the biggest source of anxiety for all age groups with 30 per cent of respondents citing it as their main worry, ahead of family (16 per cent) and health (16 per cent).

Before we go further it is appropriate to clarify what we mean by money and happiness. The consensus seems to be that money means income, work, spending and money attitudes, while happiness means daily mood, life satisfaction and living a meaningful life. Happiness should not be confused with pleasure, which can only be sustained by the activity that produces it. Happiness, on the other hand, is a state of mind that comes from a series of actions, thoughts, feelings and attitudes.

ACTIVITY 3.2

1. Explain why money might be the biggest source of anxiety for many people.
2. Explain why the level of money anxiety might vary (higher or lower) in different countries.

A review of research into money and happiness finds that:

- money purchases financial security and satisfaction of financial needs (Howell et al. 2012);
- money has a material impact and influence on how people view themselves, including feelings of self-esteem, control, security and indebtedness (Belk 1999);
- while most research has explored the role of money in levels of happiness, there is also evidence that happier people also make more money (De Neve and Oswald 2012).

Recent analysis by the UK's Office for National Statistics (ONS) in 2015 showed that for Britons aged 16 and over there is a clear link between household wealth and happiness, life satisfaction and personal sense of self-worth. The report concluded (p.1):

> An individual's level of personal well-being is strongly related to the level of wealth of the household in which they live. Life satisfaction, sense of worth and happiness are higher, and anxiety less, as the level of household wealth increases. The levels of household income are less strongly related, with relationships found only with life satisfaction and sense of worth. The net financial wealth of the household appears to be the type of wealth most strongly associated with personal well-being. In particular, life satisfaction will be higher in households with greater net financial wealth.

Other research (Lyubomirsky et al. 2005), however, argues that money has much less impact on overall happiness because 50 per cent of individual happiness is based on our innate genetic predisposition to happiness, with some people being naturally happier than others. Life circumstances, by contrast – including income – account for only 10 per cent of individual happiness. The remaining 40 per cent relates to 'intentional activities', that is activities and behaviours we can pursue to make ourselves happier.

We discussed the concept of social capital in Chapter 2 and how it can influence the degree to which you need to develop financial capital. Social capital has also been found to influence our level of happiness and, other things being equal, people with higher levels of social capital are generally happier (Leung et al. 2010).

3.2 The main factors affecting happiness

The main financial factors that appear to have the biggest impact on happiness are income, work, spending and the degree of materialism.

3.2.1 Income

There is ample evidence of a strong link between an individual's level of income and their overall happiness. One study (Diener and Biswas-Diener 2002) found happiness increased as personal income rose from low to middle levels. Other research (Kahneman and Deaton 2010) found that happiness didn't increase significantly from middle to high levels of income, with $75,000 per annum being the level at which happiness plateaued.

However, more recent research (Stevenson and Wolfers 2013) refutes the idea that there is an income plateau in relation to happiness. The researchers looked at the happiness levels and general life satisfaction in rich and poor people in a number of rich and poor countries. Rich was defined as an annual income of more than $15,000 (£10,000, €13,000, ¥ 97,500). The researchers concluded, 'The relationship between wellbeing and income … does not diminish as income rises. If there is a satiation point, we are yet to reach it' (p.1).

While money and happiness are highly correlated, and perhaps having too much is a safer bet for ensuring happiness than not having enough, it seems that people also care about their relative income i.e. how much they earn compared to their peers and colleagues (Blanchflower and Oswald 2004). So even if you have a middle to high income, if this isn't the same as or higher than your compatriots, you might feel aggrieved and less happy. It is for this reason that many private sector employers do not permit their staff to discuss their wages with colleagues. This is unlikely to be because they are particularly worried about staff happiness, but more that unhappy staff are more likely to request a salary raise.

People are also happy when they receive a rise in income, but the effects of this eventually wear off, known as the *adaptation effect*. Analysis (Di Tella and MacCulloch 2010) of affluent Germans found that happiness arising from a rise in income lasted about three years, whereas for wealthy Europeans happiness lasted about five years. But regardless of exactly how long happiness lasts from a rise in income it seems that the most happiness results from continual and meaningful rises in salary throughout one's working life.

Most research has been on whether income affects happiness, but there has been much less research into whether happier people make more money. One study (Graham et al. 2004) of young Russians found that people who had a happier disposition in 1995 made more money and had better health five years later. Another study (De Neve and Oswald 2012) of young adults in the USA found that, after adjusting for IQ, education, health and mental state, those with higher life satisfaction earned significantly more income in later life.

There is also another interesting phenomenon relating to how we view and value time as income and wealth rises. As income and wealth rise, people place a premium on their time and feel that it is a scarce commodity (DeVoe and Pfeffer 2011). People also feel more 'time pressured' the more that they think about their wealth, particularly if they believe they are 'rich' (DeVoe and House 2012). So the message is clear, stop thinking you are rich and don't look at your net worth too often.

ACTIVITY 3.3

Explain why someone might be unhappy despite having amassed significant wealth.

Markus Persson is the founder of gaming software company Minecraft, which he sold to Microsoft for £2.5bn in 2014. In August 2015 Persson tweeted, 'Hanging out in Ibiza with a bunch of friends and partying with famous people, able to do whatever I want, and I've never felt more isolated.' So just because you become seriously rich doesn't guarantee that you will be happy, particularly if your main drive and motivation is working to create new products and services and interacting with like-minded colleagues you enjoy working with.

3.2.2 Career and work

While we have seen that the absolute and relative level of income make a significant contribution to an individual's happiness, the type of job they do also seems to be an important happiness influencer. Job fit, total number of hours worked and whether the individual is employed or self-employed have been found to be key factors.

Research (Harter and Arora 2010), based on data from the Gallup World Poll, to assess life satisfaction on a scale of 1 (low) to 10 (high), found that the highest score was among those who had a very high job fit and who worked between 35 and 44 hours a week. Another study (Clark 1996) found the lowest life satisfaction among well-educated men aged between 30 and 39, who worked long hours for a large employer. Analysis of OECD data found a large gap in life satisfaction between those who were employed and self-employed, with self-employed having the highest life satisfaction (Clark 2010).

Careers research in the UK found that florists and gardeners had the highest life satisfaction and bankers and IT workers had the lowest. In addition to the job fit, self-employment and reasonable working hours, it seems that the highest satisfaction

Table 3.2 Career Happiness Index 2012

Profession	Percentage agreeing they are happy
Florists and gardeners	87
Hairdressers and beauticians	79
Plumbers and water workers	76
Marketers and PR	75
Scientists and researchers	69
Leisure and tourism workers	67
Construction workers	66
Doctors and dentists	65
Lawyers	64
Nurses	62
Architects	62
Child care and youth workers	60
Teachers	59
Accountants	58
Car workers and mechanics	57
Electricians	55
Caterers	55
HR and personnel staff	54
IT and telecoms workers	48
Bankers	44

Source: City & Guilds (2012).

is associated with those jobs where the individual has a high degree of control and autonomy and sees the end results from their efforts.

ACTIVITY 3.4

How happy does your work make you and why is that so? If you are a student, ask a family member this question.

While for some people work will be a means to an end, rather than the end in itself, for many people work is an important part of their identity and sense of purpose. If, however, you are mainly motivated to earn a high income you'd better be successful because research (Nickerson *et al.* 2003) suggests that if you don't become rich you are highly likely to be very unhappy.

The desire for material and financial success from work in the anticipation of greater rewards later on can lead people to make life choices which lead them to be unhappy through much of their career, as the classic Brazilian story of the fisherman and the businessman described in Box 3.1 illustrates.

❖ BOX 3.1 HAPPINESS AND LIFE CHOICE

There was once a businessman who was sitting by the beach in a small Brazilian village. As he sat, he saw a Brazilian fisherman rowing a small boat toward the shore having caught quite a few big fish. The businessman was impressed and asked the fisherman, "How long does it take you to catch so many fish?" The fisherman replied, "Oh, just a short while." "Then why don't you stay longer at sea and catch even more?" The businessman was astonished. "This is enough to feed my whole family", the fisherman said. The businessman then asked, "So, what do you do for the rest of the day?" The fisherman replied, "Well, I usually wake up early in the morning, go out to sea and catch a few fish, then go back and play with my kids. In the afternoon, I take a nap with my wife, and [when] evening comes, I join my buddies in the village for a drink – we play guitar, sing and dance throughout the night."

The businessman offered a suggestion to the fisherman. "I am a PhD in business management. I could help you to become a more successful person. From now on, you should spend more time at sea and try to catch as many fish as possible. When you have saved enough money, you could buy a bigger boat and catch even more fish. Soon you will be able to afford to buy more boats, set up your own company, your own production plant for canned food and distribution network. By then, you will have moved out of this village and to Sao Paulo, where you can set up an HQ to manage your other branches."

The fisherman continues, "And after that?" The businessman laughs heartily. "After that, you can live like a king in your own house, and when the time is right you can go public and float your shares in the Stock Exchange, and you will be rich." The fisherman asks, "And after that?" The businessman says, "After that, you can finally retire, you can move to a house by the fishing village, wake up early in the morning, catch a few fish, then return home to play with [your] kids, have a nice afternoon nap with your wife, and when evening comes, you can join your buddies for a drink, play the guitar, sing and dance throughout the night!" The fisherman was puzzled. "Isn't that what I am doing now?"

Source: Translated from *The Fisherman and the Businessman* by Paulo Coelho (2010).

As we discussed in Chapter 2, one of the most important attributes of those who enjoy a long and fulfilling life is having a strong sense of purpose. Viktor Frankl was a psychiatrist who, with his entire family, was held in a Nazi concentration camp. Only he and his sister survived. He wrote about his observations of human motivation in the face of terrible suffering, degradation and humiliation.

In the preface to the 1992 edition of his seminal book – *Man's Search for Meaning* – Frankl gave this advice:

Don't aim at success – the more you aim at it and make it a target, the more you are going to miss it. For success, like happiness, cannot be pursued; it must ensue, and it only does so as the unintended side-effect of one's dedication to a cause greater than oneself or as the by-product of one's surrender to a person other than oneself. Happiness must happen, and the same holds for success: you have to let it happen by not caring about it. I want you to listen to what your conscience commands you to do and go on to carry it out to the best of your knowledge. Then you will live to see that in the long run – in the long run, I say! – success will follow you precisely because you had forgotten to think of it.

(pp.12–13)

3.2.3 Spending habits and behaviour

As stated earlier it has been found (Lyubomirsky *et al.* 2005) that '*intentional activities*', of which spending is one, accounted for 40 per cent of an individual's happiness. An analysis (Xiao *et al.* 2009) of college students found that life satisfaction was positively correlated with positive financial behaviours – with spending being a major financial behaviour. Analysis (Headey *et al.* 2008) of data from Hungary and the United Kingdom found that spending had as much impact on life satisfaction as income.

As well as having a direct impact on your ability to save and accumulate wealth for use at a later date, *how* we spend our money, rather than how much money we have, appears to determine our overall level of happiness. So let's look at the positive types of spending which most contribute to happiness.

Buy experiences, not things

The excitement and satisfaction we derive from buying material things – a new car, clothes, jewellery, gadgets, etc. – soon wears off. On the other hand, we remember things we've done, people we've met and places we've visited long after we forget the price we paid. This is because it takes longer for the brain to adapt to the happiness arising from an experience, compared to a material possession (Van Boven and Gilovich 2003). For example, attending a music concert or festival would deliver more happiness than buying a new music system.

Your happiness is also affected by the extent to which you compare yourself to your peers – known as 'social comparison'. In one experiment (Frank 2004) individuals were given a choice between buying an experience or a possession. The people who chose the experience, experienced much less social comparison, which in turn improved their happiness. This makes sense because it is much harder to compare the emotional and pleasurable benefits arising from, say, a music concert than a new sports car. If you recount an experience this will also make people like you more than if you talk about your possessions (Van Boven et al. 2010).

So the message is clear. Buy less stuff and do more stuff!

ACTIVITY 3.5

1. Think about a past experience and possession that you bought and how happy each made you feel at the time.
2. Write down how you feel about each purchase now and why that is so. Did the experience make you happier for longer than the possession?

Invest in others

Psychologists Elizabeth Dunn and Michael Norton contend that spending on others and being generous, known as 'pro-social spending' also seems to have a link to well-being and increased happiness (Dunn et al. 2008). They conducted an experiment involving 46 people, whose existing happiness levels were recorded. Each participant was then given either $5 or $20, with some instructed to spend it on themselves and others to give it away. Those who had given their windfall away showed a greater increase in well-being than those who had spent the money on themselves.

If we spend on others in a way which helps build and strengthen personal relationships, this also improves happiness. In another experiment people were given $10 Starbucks gift cards. One group was asked to spend the card on themselves, another group was asked to give the card to someone else. A third group was asked to use the card to take someone out for a coffee. The happiest group was the one that had used the card to take someone out for a coffee. So spending on others while also spending time with them – altruism and connection – increased their happiness.

In another study, for the National Institute of Health in the United States (Moll et al. 2006), researchers found a strong link between charitable giving and activation in the part of the brain associated with pleasure, triggering the release of endorphins – the hormones which promote happiness.

Whether it's sponsoring someone for a charitable event, making a small loan to help them achieve something, paying for them to have a meaningful life experience or buying them something special, it improves how we feel and makes us happy.

ACTIVITY 3.6

In the next week or so, make a point of taking someone for a coffee, lunch, cinema or other low cost social treat and note how happy you feel afterwards compared to spending on yourself.

Match your spending to your personality

Research from Cambridge University (Matz *et al.* 2016) shows a link between different types of spending and personality types. The study, which was conducted in conjunction with a major UK bank, was based on the spending habits of 625 bank customers. Each participant was asked to complete a standard personality and happiness questionnaire, and to consent to their responses being matched anonymously for research purposes with their bank transaction data. A total of 76,863 spending transactions were then grouped by the bank into 59 categories that had at least 500 transactions over a six-month period. The researchers matched spending categories on the 'Big Five' personality traits – openness to experience (artistic versus traditional), conscientiousness (self-controlled vs easy-going), extraversion (outgoing vs reserved), agreeableness (compassionate vs competitive) and neuroticism (prone to stress vs stable) – see Table 3.3.

'Historically, studies had found a weak relationship between money and overall wellbeing', says Joe Gladstone, one of the report's authors. 'Our study breaks new ground by mining actual bank-transaction data and demonstrating that spending can increase our happiness when it is spent on goods and services that fit our personalities and so meet our psychological needs.'

The researchers also backed up their findings by running a second experiment, where they gave people a voucher to spend in either a bookshop or at a bar. Extroverts who were forced to spend at a bar were happier than introverts forced to spend at a bar, while introverts forced to spend at a bookshop were happier than extroverts forced to spend at a bookshop. This follow-up experiment overcomes the limitations of correlational data by demonstrating that spending money on things that match a person's personality can cause an increase in happiness.

'Our findings suggest that spending money on products that help us express who we are as individuals could turn out to be as important to our well-being as finding the right job, the right neighbourhood or even the right friends and partners', said Sandra Matz, one of the report's authors. 'By developing a more nuanced understanding of the links between spending and happiness, we hope to be able to provide more personalised advice on how to find happiness through the little consumption choices we make every day.'

Table 3.3 Categories with the lowest and highest scores on each of the big five personality traits

The big five	Low	High
Openness to experience	Traffic fines, residential mortgages	Entertainment, hair and beauty
Conscientiousness	Gambling, toys and hobbies	Home insurance, health and fitness
Extraversion	Home insurance, accountant fees	Entertainment, travel
Agreeableness	Traffic fines, gambling	Charities, pets
Neuroticism	Stationery, hotels	Traffic fines, gambling

ACTIVITY 3.7
1. Which personality trait do you think best fits you?
2. What products and services do you buy which you think best express who you are and why?

3.3 Health and longevity outcomes related to money

So far we have looked at how money contributes to making people happy. However, money can affect people's health, quality of life and lifespan, which in turn can influence their happiness. A recent review by the Joseph Rowntree Foundation (2014) of 272 research papers on how money affects health identified four key theories:

1. **Material:** money buys goods and services that improve health; the more money families have, the more/better goods they can buy; and the greater ability people have to engage in a social life in ways that enable them to be healthy.
2. **Psychosocial:** managing on a low income is stressful; comparing oneself to others and feeling at the bottom of the social ladder can be distressing. Such stress can lead to biochemical changes in the body, damaging its systems and eventually causing ill health.
3. **Behavioural:** for various reasons, people on low incomes and living in disadvantaged circumstances are more likely to adopt unhealthy behaviours (smoking and drinking, for example) while those on higher incomes are more able to afford healthier lifestyles.
4. **Reverse causation** (poor health leads to low income): health may affect income by preventing people from taking paid employment. More indirectly, childhood health may affect educational outcomes, in turn affecting employment opportunities and earnings potential.

The report's authors concluded

> Our review has found a strong theoretical consensus that money does matter for health and the relationship is a positive one. However, we found less clarity regarding the particular role of income as a health determinant or the mechanisms by which income modification interventions might affect health.

While the research evidence supports the idea that higher levels of income and wealth all contribute to good health and longevity through the four theories – material, psychosocial, behavioural and reverse causation – the review researchers were unable to quantify the contribution played by each factor.

A recent study by the CASS Business School in London (Mayhew and Smith 2016) found that for men aged 30 in the UK the gap in lifespan between the highest 5 per cent and lowest 10 per cent is now 33.3 years. According to the UK's Office for National Statistics (2012), deaths from potentially avoidable causes account for approximately 23 per cent of all deaths in England and Wales, with the leading causes being chronic heart disease in males and lung cancer in females. This suggests that lifestyle choices and behaviours are now much more important factors that influence life expectancy and good health.

The CASS study (Mayhew and Smith 2016) found that

> Men in lower socio-economic groups are the most likely to make damaging life-style choices. They put themselves in harm's way on average more than women do ... they smoke more, drink more and there are periods in their lives when they partake in riskier activities.
>
> (p.4)

> Although long run data connecting wealth and longevity is almost non-existent, the link between poverty and mortality is consistent with other research from the more recent period. Work by Smith et al. using millions of UK personal medical records in the period 2005 to 2010 identifies a mortality gradient between the poorest and richest quintiles in middle age in which mortality rates in the poorest poverty quintile are up to 2.5 times higher than in the richest quintile.
>
> This finding does not mean that lack of wealth or income is directly responsible for the difference ... The most likely explanation is that the wealthier used to be just as vulnerable as the poor to lifestyle related diseases ... the wealthier are more likely to adopt healthy behaviours and hence are better placed to avoid or defer them to later in life ... healthy behaviour spreads much faster through wealthier educated networks: for example, the educated better off were the first to quit smoking. In other words, more educated people can process information relevant to their health better than less educated people.
>
> (pp.4–5)

So it appears that wealthier people on average adopt healthier lifestyles, have more choice, can buy healthier goods and services and can afford to buy more experiences, all of which improve their quality of life and overall life expectancy.

3.4 Putting money in context

Paul Dolan is a Professor of Behavioural Science at the London School of Economics and an internationally renowned expert on happiness, behaviour and public policy. In his recent book *Happiness by Design* (2014), Professor Dolan had this to say about money and happiness:

> [I]t's better if you don't pay too much attention to money at all. Given my upbringing, I appreciate that money matters when circumstances dictate that every penny counts but it might generally be worth chilling out a bit about it if you are not in that position. Sure, money matters and you should respect it, but not so much that it overruns your life. It's certainly not worth making yourself miserable over. Rob Metcalfe and I have shown that, while poorer people have more intrusive thoughts about money than do wealthier people, the latter's happiness is more negatively influenced by those thoughts.
>
> (p.160)

3.5 Conclusion

So can money buy happiness? Yes, but only to a point. The research suggests that we need to have enough income to fund the basics in life, plus some modest extra pleasures. We need our income to rise by a meaningful amount periodically and not compare this to what our friends and colleagues earn. We need to ensure that the job we do is the right fit for our personality, even if we don't yet have the necessary skills.

We need to spend less money on things and more on experiences. We also need to spend money on other people and charities and make social investments, as well as focus on nurturing and strengthening personal relationships. We need to use money to make healthier lifestyle choices, buy better healthcare and help minimise stress. And we should avoid over-fixating on our personal finances, but review them once or twice a year.

But perhaps the most powerful thing we can do to be happier is to cultivate a healthy and constructive relationship with money by ensuring we have a positive money 'story' by examining our core money beliefs. We can then choose flexible strategies to meet our continual and evolving needs and remain focused on cultivating our own human capital resource so we can build sufficient financial capital and property to meet post-work needs.

Your value as a human being is not defined by your net worth, but by the quality of your personal relationships, your life experiences and the meaning you derive from your existence. So in a nutshell it's not really how much money you have, but how you choose to think about and use it.

End of chapter test

1. Discuss how childhood experiences, parental messages and cultural factors might affect a person's money values and beliefs.
2. Explain how money beliefs, behaviours, habits and actions combine to influence financial decisions.
3. Explain how income and work interact to influence happiness and give an example.
4. Describe three main spending factors which have a significant influence on happiness.
5. Discuss the health implications related to money and the key risks affecting life expectancy.

References

Ajzen, Icek. 1991. "The Theory of Planned Behavior." *Organizational Behavior and Human Decision Processes* 50:2: 179–211.

Belk, Russell W. 1999. "Money." In Peter E. Earl and Simon Kemp, eds, *The Elgar Companion to Consumer Research and Economic Psychology*, 383–388. Cheltenham, UK: Edward Elgar.

Blanchflower, David G., and Andrew J. Oswald. 2004. "Well-Being over Time in Britain and USA." *Journal of Public Economics* 88:7, 1359–1386.

City & Guilds. 2012. 13 November. www.cityandguilds.com/news/November-2012/careers-happiness-index-2012#.VysOffkrLic (Accessed 30 April 2016).

Clark, Andrew E. 1996. "Job Satisfaction in Britain." *British Journal of Industrial Relations* 34:2, 189–217.

Clark, Andrew E. 2010. "Work, Jobs, and Well-Being across the Millennium." In Ed Diener, John F. Helliwell and Daniel Kahneman, eds, *International Differences in Well-Being*, 436–468. Oxford: Oxford University Press.

Coelho, P. 2010. "The Fisherman and the Businessman", available at http://paulocoelhoblog.com/2015/09/04/the-fisherman-and-the-businessman/ (Accessed 4 June 2016).

De Neve, Jan-Emmanuel and Andrew J. Oswald. 2012. "Estimating the Influence of Life Satisfaction and Positive Affect on Later Income Using Sibling Fixed Effects." *Proceedings of the National Academy of Sciences* 109:49, 19953–19958.

DeVoe, S.E., and J. House. 2012. "Time, Money, and Happiness: How Does Putting a Price on Time Affect our Ability to Smell the Roses?" *Journal of Experimental Social Psychology* 48: 466.

DeVoe, S.E., and J. Pfeffer. 2011. "Time is Tight: How Higher Economic Value of Time Increases Feelings of Time Pressure." *Journal of Applied Psychology* 96: 665.

Di Tella, Rafael, and Robert J. MacCulloch. 2010. "Happiness Adaptation to Income beyond 'Basic Needs'." In Ed Diener, John F. Helliwell and Daniel Kahneman, eds, *International Differences in Well-Being*, 139–165. Oxford: Oxford University Press.

Diener, Ed, and Robert Biswas-Diener. 2002. "Will Money Increase Subjective Well-Being?" *Social Indicators Research* 57:2, 119–169.

Dolan, P. 2014. *Happiness by Design: Finding pleasure and purpose in everyday life*. London: Penguin.

Dunn, Elizabeth W., Lara B. Aknin and Michael I. Norton. 2008. "Spending Money on Others Promotes Happiness." *Science* 319:5870, 1687–1688.

Frank, R.H. 2004. "How Not to Buy Happiness." *Daedalus* 133, 69–79.

Frankl, Viktor E. 1992. *Man's Search for Meaning: The classic tribute to hope from the Holocaust*. London: Rider (new edition 6 May 2004).

Graham, Carol, Andrew Eggars and Sundip Sukhtanker. 2004. "Does Happiness Pay? An Exploration Based on Panel Data from Russia." *Journal of Economic Behavior & Organisation* 55:3, 319–342.

Harter, James K., and Raksha Arora. 2010. "The Impact of Time Spent Working and Job Fit on Well-Being around the World." In Ed Diener, John F. Helliwell and Daniel Kahneman, eds, *International Differences in Well-Being*, 398–435. Oxford: Oxford University Press.

Headey, Bruce, Ruud Muffels and Mark Wooden. 2008. "Money Does Not Buy Happiness: Or Does It? A Reassessment Based on the Combined Effects of Wealth, Income and Consumption." *Social Indicators Research* 87:1, 65–82.

Howell, Ryan T., Mark Kurai and Wing Yin Leona Tam. 2012. "Money Buys Financial Security and Psychological Need Satisfaction: Testing Need Theory in Affluence." *Social Indicators Research* 110:1, 17–29.

Joseph Rowntree Foundation. 2014. "How Does Money Influence Health?", available at https://www.jrf.org.uk/sites/default/files/jrf/migrated/files/income-health-poverty-full.pdf (Accessed 1 May 2016).

Kahneman, Daniel, and Angus Deaton. 2010. "High Income Improves Evaluation of Life But Not Emotional Well-Being." *Proceedings of the National Academy of Sciences* 107:38, 16489–16493.

Leung, A., C. Kier, T. Fung, L. Fung and R. Sproule. 2010. "Searching for Happiness: The Importance of Social Capital." *Journal of Happiness Studies* 12:443–462, also available at http://link.springer.com/article/10.1007/s10902-010-9208-8#page-2 (Accessed 17 October 2016).

Lyubomirsky, Sonia, Kennon M. Sheldon and David Schkade. 2005. "Pursuing Happiness: The Architecture of Sustainable Change." *Review of General Psychology* 9:2, 111–131.

Mann, J. 2015. "Britain Uncovered Survey Results: The Attitudes and Beliefs of Britons in 2015", available at www.theguardian.com/society/2015/apr/19/britain-uncovered-survey-attitudes-beliefs-britons-2015 (Accessed 29 April 2016).

Matz, S., J. Gladstone and D. Stillwell. 2016. "Money Buys Happiness When Spending Fits Our Personality." Published online (April 2016) by *Psychological Science* http://pss.sagepub.com/content/early/2016/04/05/0956797616635200.abstract (Accessed 17 October 2016).

Mayhew, L., and D. Smith. 2016. "An Investigation into Growing Inequalities in Adult Lifespan", available at www.ilcuk.org.uk/index.php/publications/publication_details/an_investigation_into_inequalities_in_adult_lifespan (Accessed 17 October 2016).

Moll, Jorge, Frank Krueger, Roland Zahn, Matteo Pardini, Ricardo de Oliveria-Soza and Jordan Grafman. 2006. "Human Fronto–mesolimbic Networks Guide Decisions about Charitable Donation", available at www.pnas.org/content/103/42/15623.abstract (Accessed 17 October 2016).

Nickerson, C., N. Schwarz, E. Diener and D. Kahneman. 2003. "Zeroing in on the Dark Side of the American Dream: A Closer Look at the Negative Consequences of the Goal for Financial Success." *Psychological Science* 14:6, 531–516.

Office for National Statistics (ONS). 2012. "Avoidable Mortality in England and Wales, 2012", available at http://webarchive.nationalarchives.gov.uk/20160105160709/www.ons.gov.uk/ons/dcp171778_362295.pdf (Accessed 17 October 2016).

Office for National Statistics (ONS). 2015. "Relationship between Wealth, Income and Personal Well-being, July 2011 to June 2012", available at http://webarchive.nationalarchives.gov.uk/20160105160709/www.ons.gov.uk/ons/dcp171776_415633.pdf (Accessed 2 May 2016).

Orzanna, R. 2015. "The Theory of Planned Behavior." Downloadable from https://en.wikipedia.org/wiki/Theory_of_planned_behavior#/media/File:Theory_of_planned_behavior.png (Accessed 5 May 2016).

Stevenson, Betsey, and Justin Wolfers. 2013. *Well-Being and Income: Is There Any Evidence of Satiation?* University of Michigan, available at http://users.nber.org/~jwolfers/Papers/Satiation(AER).pdf (accessed 25 October 2016).

Van Boven L., and T. Gilovich. 2003. "To Do or to Have? That is the Question." *Journal of Personality and Social Psychology* 85: 1193–1202.

Van Boven, L., M.C. Campbell and T. Gilovich. 2010. "Stigmatizing Materialism: On Stereotypes and Impressions of Materialistic and Experiential Pursuits." *Personality and Social Psychology Bulletin* 36: 551–563.

Xiao, Jing Jian, Chuuanyi Tang and Soyeon Shim. 2009. "Acting for Happiness: Financial Behaviour and Life Satisfaction of College Students." *Social Indicators Research* 92:1, 53–68.

Chapter 4

Plan your future

Jason Butler

❖ CONTENTS

Financial planning is officially defined as 'the process of determining whether and how an individual can meet life goals through the proper management of financial resources' (cfp.net). In reality financial planning is an iterative, ongoing process that is a mixture of art and science, which involves both qualitative and quantitative factors, and a need to accept trade-offs and compromises in the face of many variables. In this chapter we'll explore the theory and practice of creating and maintaining a personal financial plan.

As we have seen from the previous chapters, having a good idea of what you are trying to achieve and why is a vital first step to making good financial decisions. But before you can make any decisions about your finances you'll need to take stock of where you are now financially and determine what, if any, action is necessary to ensure that you are on track to achieve those life goals which have financial implications.

Learning objectives

By the end of this chapter you will:

- have an understanding of the importance of having a structured written financial plan;
- be able to explain the main components of a simple personal financial plan;
- have an awareness of key financial planning principles and practices;
- be able to carry out simplified financial calculations as the basis of the financial planning strategy.

4.1 Why a plan is essential to success

A goal without a plan is just a wish.

Antoine de Saint-Exupéry (French writer, 1900–1944)

People who have a personal financial plan are invariably more confident about their financial situation and more likely to achieve better financial outcomes than those who don't. There are several reasons why this is the case. A recent study (Matthews 2010) into successful goal setting identified that there are three key elements to achieving goals: accountability, commitment and writing down the goals. The researchers randomly assigned participants to five groups:

- Group 1 – carefully thought about their goals and the resources they had available to accomplish them.
- Group 2 – wrote down their goals after the careful thought.
- Group 3 – set action commitments after writing down their goals.
- Group 4 – did all of the above and shared them with a friend.
- Group 5 – did all of the above and sent a weekly progress report to their friend.

Follow-up interviews found that Group 5 did the best. An average of 76 per cent of participants in Group 5 completed their stated goals versus 43 per cent in Group 1. Therefore, writing down your financial goals, sharing them with someone, making a commitment to achieving them and regularly reviewing your progress increase the likelihood of success.

A survey by the CFP (Certified Financial Planner) Board of Standards conducted in the USA found that people who do more financial planning feel more confident in managing their finances. About 50 per cent of people who had a comprehensive plan said they feel very confident, compared with less than 25 per cent of people who did little or no planning.

Having a plan also provides the context and foundation for all financial planning decisions, so that you know what you are doing and why. This is particularly important when your emotions and personality traits might otherwise lead to wealth destroying actions and behaviours. Reminding yourself of your 'big picture' and key life goals will help keep you on track and have the discipline and patience to stay the course.

A financial plan essentially represents your best current guess or estimate of your financial related life goals and associated long-term assumptions such as life expectancy, investment returns and inflation. In this sense it will almost certainly turn out to be wrong because there are so many variables involved and the time horizon for most people is very long.

A written plan will, however, enable you to measure your progress from year to year. Even if in some years you are slightly off course, progress is still progress and celebrating and acknowledging this will help you to protect your confidence. It will also document any financial planning policy statements which set out how you make decisions and what you will do if certain events or scenarios happen, so as to avoid making emotionally charged decisions.

I recall that my first written financial plan was created when I was 30. Looking back on it 17 years later, while everything hasn't turned out exactly how it was planned, I have achieved many of my goals and am on course to meet my long-term financial goals. I also have a sense of optimism and confidence about my long-term future, because I can see the progress that I have made over those 17 years of formal planning. We learn by doing and experiencing and eventually financial planning becomes a habit.

He who is fixed to a star does not change his mind.

Leonardo Da Vinci (artist, mathematician, inventor, writer)

ACTIVITY 4.1

Think about two similar personal experiences that involved achieving a defined outcome; one where you had written down some form of plan and the other where you didn't. Were you more organised, happier, effective and efficient working with a written plan? If so, think why this was the case.

4.2 Life stages, planning principles and practices

We all go through various life stages, and each of these presents different financial challenges, needs, choices and resources. In addition, life stages can be influenced by cultural norms, religion, gender, family circumstances and personal preferences. For example, if you do not wish to raise a family you will have fewer demands on your money than someone who does, and this has implications for housing, lifestyle and education costs, as well as your ability to work and earn. If you envisage working beyond your country's statutory retirement age, perhaps continuing to run a business or work part-time, then your financial goals might be more achievable than someone who wishes to achieve financial independence at, say, age 55.

Each life stage and transition represents a key trigger point when it is essential to review and possibly change your financial plan, by updating goals, changing planning assumptions, and revising key financial calculations and projections (known as 'gap analysis'). This will enable you to determine what, if any, changes are required to your planning strategy. It may be the case that your own life stages might not necessarily follow the stages shown in Figure 4.1.

For example, there is a global trend for more young people to remain living with parents well into their 30s, or to rent, rather than buy, their own home, whether through a desire to maintain lifestyle flexibility or due to lack of affordability. In addition, more people are working for longer but more flexibly compared to the old model, particularly in western societies, of working full-time for 40 years, followed by retirement at an arbitrary age of, say, 65. Second marriages and families can have significant financial implications for retirement funding, as they create additional expenses in mid-life, which means less money available to save for older age.

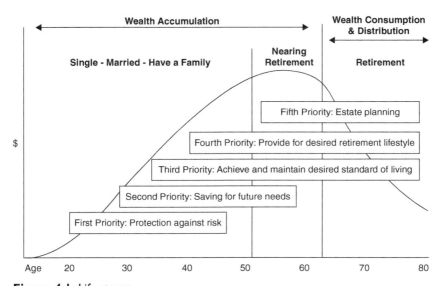

Figure 4.1 Life stages

4.3 Planning principles

Before we look at the components of a typical financial plan, we need to explore some general planning principles.

4.3.1 How you see money

One of the most important principles is to understand where money comes from. There are three sources of money: labour, land/property and capital. If you think of money in terms of income to fund spending, you are unlikely to build meaningful wealth, because you are consuming (in the form of lifestyle spending) whatever money flows in. If, however, you think of money as assets which produce future cashflow, your mindset will be entirely different, and you will see the importance of using earned income to buy property/land and financial assets. As we discussed in Chapter 2, financial independence is achieved by converting human capital to financial capital over time.

Learning to spend less than you earn, possibly by deferring certain spending, using cheaper alternatives, or earning higher income through increased work, involves more effort than having what you want, whenever you want it. Budgeting is one of the key skills to learn and is the foundation upon which financial freedom, choice and security are based. If you spend more than you earn, you will incur debt which will act as a drag on your ability to save and accumulate wealth.

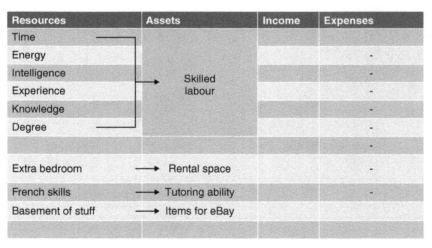

Figure 4.2 How income maps to resources
Source: Sarah Newcomb (2016), *Loaded: Money, Psychology, and How to Get Ahead Without Leaving Your Values Behind* (Wiley: Hoboken)

4.3.2 Compound interest

> Compound interest is the eighth wonder of the world ... he who understands it, earns it ... he who doesn't ... pays it.
>
> Albert Einstein (theoretical physicist)

When we earn interest or other investment income and retain this with the principal capital, it is available to earn further income. Earning returns on returns is a fundamental financial planning concept, with the higher the rate of return achieved and the longer the time horizon, the greater the effect **compounding** will have. For example, to build up £1 million (in today's money), a 3 per cent a year post-inflation investment return over a 10-year time horizon requires monthly savings of £7,300, compared to over a 30-year time horizon which requires £1,800pm at the same rate of return. This is the classic trade-off that we all have to make each day between consumption now and deferring gratification to the future. This is why it is so important to start saving as soon as you can, so that you have the longest possible holding period and thus maximise the effect of compounding. Compounding is described in more detail in Chapter 5, Section 5.4.

The 'Rule of 72'
A really simple, but highly useful and quick, rule of thumb for working out compound investment returns, without having to do complicated calculations, is called the 'Rule of 72'. If you take the compound rate of return and divide it into 72, you can estimate the number of years it will take for you to double your money, as illustrated in Table 4.1. For example, 72/7 is about 10, so with 7 per cent a year investment return it would take roughly ten years for capital to double. The higher the return, the less time it takes. The rule can also be used to estimate the annualised return required to double the value of money over a given time period, by dividing the time period into 72 as illustrated in Table 4.2.

4.3.3 Inflation
The price of goods and services can stay the same, fall or rise from year to year. The most common position is that the price of the majority of goods and services will tend to rise over the long term. This gradual rise, known as mild positive **inflation**, is measured by ongoing monitoring of the prices of a broad range of goods and services. Thus the annual inflation rate refers to the average rise in that basket of prices over the previous 12 months. Price rises do not always conform to a mild, positive rate. Historically, in the UK, inflation has peaked at nearly 30 per cent a year in 1975 and occasionally been negative (falling prices) (ONS 2016).

Table 4.1 Years to double your money at different rates of return

Return	1%	2%	3%	4%	5%	6%	7%
Years	72	36	24	18	14	12	10

Table 4.2 Rate of return to double your money over a specified time horizon

Time	5 years	10 years	15 years	20 years	25 years
Return required	14%	7%	5%	4%	3%

Positive inflation means that the same amount of money in future buys less than it does today. At its simplest, suppose you spend £100 a week on groceries; if prices doubled but you still only had £100 cash to spend, you would only be able to buy half as many items. It would be as if someone had halved your money, so you only had £50. The amount of cash you have (in this example, £100) is called the **nominal value** of your money. The amount that your cash will buy (in this example, £50) is called its **real value**.

Because the impact of inflation is felt most acutely over the long term, it is a particular threat to savings that are accumulated or earmarked to fund lifestyle in older age, when one can't, or no longer wishes to, work. Even low rates of inflation can have a devastating effect on the purchasing power of money as Table 4.3 shows. For example, even if inflation averaged a modest 2 per cent a year (the third column), the table shows that after ten years (find the row labelled '10') the buying power of £1,000 would have fallen to £820 (in other words, lost nearly a fifth of its buying power) and after 35 years would be worth only £500 (half as much) in terms of what it can buy.

Just as with the 'Rule of 72' above, there is a similar simple rule for working out how many years it takes for the value of your money to halve. It's called the 'Rule of

Table 4.3 The effect of inflation on the buying power of your money

Number of years	Real value of £1,000 nominal if annual inflation averages									
	1%	2%	3%	4%	5%	6%	7%	8%	9%	10%
1	£990	£980	£971	£962	£952	£943	£935	£926	£917	£909
2	£980	£961	£943	£925	£907	£890	£873	£857	£842	£826
3	£971	£942	£915	£889	£864	£840	£816	£794	£772	£751
4	£961	£924	£888	£855	£823	£792	£763	£735	£708	£683
5	£951	£906	£863	£822	£784	£747	£713	£681	£650	£621
6	£942	£888	£837	£790	£746	£705	£666	£630	£596	£564
7	£933	£871	£813	£760	£711	£665	£623	£583	£547	£513
8	£923	£853	£789	£731	£677	£627	£582	£540	£502	£467
9	£914	£837	£766	£703	£645	£592	£544	£500	£460	£424
10	£905	£820	£744	£676	£614	£558	£508	£463	£422	£386
11	£896	£804	£722	£650	£585	£527	£475	£429	£388	£350
12	£887	£788	£701	£625	£557	£497	£444	£397	£356	£319
13	£879	£773	£681	£601	£530	£469	£415	£368	£326	£290
14	£870	£758	£661	£577	£505	£442	£388	£340	£299	£263
15	£861	£743	£642	£555	£481	£417	£362	£315	£275	£239
16	£853	£728	£623	£534	£458	£394	£339	£292	£252	£218
17	£844	£714	£605	£513	£436	£371	£317	£270	£231	£198
18	£836	£700	£587	£494	£416	£350	£296	£250	£212	£180
19	£828	£686	£570	£475	£396	£331	£277	£232	£194	£164
20	£820	£673	£554	£456	£377	£312	£258	£215	£178	£149
25	£780	£610	£478	£375	£295	£233	£184	£146	£116	£92
30	£742	£552	£412	£308	£231	£174	£131	£99	£75	£57
35	£706	£500	£355	£253	£181	£130	£94	£68	£49	£36
40	£672	£453	£307	£208	£142	£97	£67	£46	£32	£22
45	£639	£410	£264	£171	£111	£73	£48	£31	£21	£14
50	£608	£372	£228	£141	£87	£54	£34	£21	£13	£9

Table 4.4 How long it takes the buying power of your money to halve

Inflation	1%	2%	3%	4%	5%
Years to halve capital	70	35	23	18	14

70'. Simply divide 70 by the rate of inflation. For example, if inflation is 2 per cent a year, the buying power of your money is halved after 35 years. Table 4.4 shows some further examples.

To beat inflation, you need savings or investments with a higher rate of return than the inflation rate. Although strictly the maths is a bit more complicated, to check whether you are getting a **real return** (above-inflation return) that is positive, subtract the inflation rate from your **nominal return**. For example, if the nominal return on your savings is 1.5 per cent a year and inflation is 2 per cent a year, you are making a real return of minus 0.5 (1.5 − 2.0). This means your savings are failing to keep pace with inflation and the buying power of your money is falling.

If we take a look at the longer-term historical returns that different investment asset classes have delivered, such as equities (owning a part share in a company), bonds (lending to governments and companies) and cash, the mantra that comes to mind is 'get (or stay) rich slowly'. Attempting to 'get rich (or richer) quick' is no different to gambling. Over the past 115 years cash has delivered a return of around 0.80 per cent a year above inflation, government bonds around 1.3 per cent a year and global equities 5 per cent a year.

ACTIVITY 4.2

1. Using Table 4.3, what is the real value of £1,000 in 15 years' time if inflation averages 3 per cent a year?
2. If you invested £1,000 today intending to leave it invested for 15 years, what nominal rate of return would you need to make sure your money had just kept its buying power if inflation averaged 3 per cent a year?
3. If you invested £1,000 for 15 years and your nominal return averaged 8 per cent a year, what real rate of return would you have got if inflation averaged 3 per cent a year?

[Answers to this Activity are at the end of the chapter.]

4.4 Planning practices

The following are a range of practical actions which can help you to achieve your lifestyle and financial goals.

Watch your spending

It doesn't matter how much you earn. If you spend all, or more than, you earn, you'll always be poor. While it is easy to be seduced into buying what you want (or think you want), deferring gratification and living within your means is the cornerstone of financial success. It's a good idea to track your spending for a week or a month to get an idea where your money goes. Most online banking allows transaction data to be downloaded into a spreadsheet or money management app. Small but regular changes in expenditure can free up cash that you can use to build financial security. As the old saying goes, 'Fools work for money and money works for the rich.'

Pay yourself first

Your financial security is the most important priority when it comes to devising a personal expenditure budget, before rent, travel, socialising, etc. This means adopting a mindset which prioritises regular saving as the *first* expense that needs to be meet. Or as Warren Buffett advises, 'Don't save what is left after spending; spend what is left after saving.' Regular saving is a bit like running a marathon, where you start out doing small regular runs and gradually increase your distance. Just begin by saving a small amount each week or month and then gradually increase the amount over time. It's also a good idea to increase the amount you save every time you receive a pay rise, because you don't miss what you haven't had.

Good debt not bad debt

Debt can be used responsibly to enable you to invest in yourself (like education or skills) or acquire assets like property (as long as it brings in more than it costs). Whatever the reasons for which you borrow money, remember two things: interest is a definite and regular cost that will reduce your ability to save and the capital must eventually be repaid.

While global interest rates after the global financial crisis have been low, they may not stay like that forever and you need to think very carefully about the impact on your expenditure if interest rates were, say, three times higher than at present (as they have been in the past). For this reason, even though buying a home with a mortgage can be a good long-term use of funds, make sure that you don't overstretch yourself.

Borrowing on credit/store card or payday loans to finance consumption is to be avoided at all costs. This type of borrowing will be a continual drain on your cashflow and will hold back your ability to accumulate assets that generate cashflow. Borrowing is discussed in more detail in Chapter 5, Section 5.1.

Keep it simple stupid (KISS)

Keep your personal financial planning as simple as possible.

If it looks too good

If anyone tells you that an investment is virtually risk-free and will generate a 20 per cent a year return, give them a wide berth. If it looks too good to be true, then it probably is.

Tax isn't everything

You need to avoid becoming obsessed about avoiding tax. By all means minimise your tax bill by using all the legitimate and tried and tested products and solutions available, but not to such an extent that you don't have enough money to live on today or fall foul of the tax authorities and end up paying penalties and fines.

The media is not your friend

The media, in the form of newspapers, 24-hour news, websites or magazines, is not designed to help you to make good decisions. It focuses on what personal finance professionals call 'noise' or 'financial pornography' in the form of negative stories or sensationalist 'get rich quick' ideas because they are newsworthy. People who participate in such media comment are chosen because they make the media outlet more marketable, not because of their insight. In general, the news is not the truth but a form of entertainment, so remember that when forming your opinions about money.

Keep costs low and diversify

As a general rule with long-term investing you get everything that you don't pay for. There is no evidence to support the commonly voiced (usually by those with an interest in the outcome) assertion that it is better to buy an expensive invest-ment fund than a similar lower cost one. Costs are certain whereas investment returns aren't.

Build a cash reserve

Having a cash reserve available is essential to enable you to cope with the inevita-ble ups and downs that arise in life. Your cash reserve should represent between three and twelve months' expenditure, or however many months it would take you to find new employment or earn an income from self-employment. In addi-tion, your cash reserve needs to include any funds that you will need to spend on non-living costs within the next few years, such as a house deposit or education/training expenses.

Protect your income

At the beginning of your working life your greatest asset is your human capital, i.e. your ability to earn an income. If you were unable to work due to disability or ill-ness for the medium to long term, it could consign you to poverty for life. Income protection insurance will keep paying you a proportion of your income until you can return to work or reach a certain age (usually when you expect to retire). Healthy young people can usually get this type of cover easily and at relatively low cost, so if your employer doesn't offer cover (as most don't) buy your own per-sonal policy – see Chapter 6.

Invest in yourself

In addition to a positive mental attitude, increasing your relevant skills and knowledge is the best way to increase your earning power. It therefore makes sense to look for ways to invest in your capability, whether attending business school, evening classes, distance learning or day release by your employer.

Join a pension plan

If you are offered the chance to join an employer-sponsored pension plan, then do so. Some countries require workers to be automatically enrolled in a pension plan through their employer, unless they actively opt out. If this applies to you DO NOT opt out if the employer is required to make contributions in addition to your own. If you are self-employed then contribute to a low cost tax-favoured retirement savings account with a choice of index funds (discussed in Chapter 9) and limit your risk by spreading your contributions across global markets, whether via one fund or several. As we discussed earlier, the earliest contributions make the most growth and can make the difference between a decent retirement income or not.

Don't rush to buy property

Although buying your own home generally makes more sense than renting over the long term, avoid rushing to buy a house until you have established your earning power, know where you want to live (which may be dictated by your work) and have a clearer idea of who, if anyone, will be your life partner. Buying and selling property can be expensive, and if you have to sell at a time when the value of the property has fallen and your equity is reduced, it can set you back years.

Repay debt

An interest-free loan from your family is the cheapest form of borrowing and payday loans are among the most expensive. As a general rule you should avoid debt, but otherwise repay it as fast as possible, starting with the most expensive debt.

Invest most of your long-term money in equities and property

Assuming you have followed all the previous suggested actions above, you should invest the bulk of any surplus income, plus your pension fund, into worldwide equities. Don't worry about volatility (the value moving up and down) because, with an asset class which is expected to rise over the long term (20 years+), regular savings benefit from pound cost averaging (explained in Chapter 9). This means that the average price you pay for the investments should be less than their average price over time.

Table 4.5 illustrates this principle by comparing investing £100 a month to investing the full £1,200 in one go during 2002, when the stockmarket was falling. The investment is a large UK equity index fund. As the fund's unit price falls the regular investor ends up buying more equities and at a cheaper price, with the average purchase cost for the monthly investor being 100p, compared to the lump sum investor paying 111p.

Table 4.5 Pound-cost averaging

Legal & General UK Index: the benefits of pound cost averaging			
Month	Price of units	No. of units purchased (monthly)	No. of units purchased (lump sum)
January	1.11	90.1	1,081
February	1.11	90.1	0
March	1.10	90.1	0
April	1.14	87.7	0
May	1.12	89.3	0
June	1.10	90.1	0
July	1.02	98.04	0
August	0.91	109.9	0
September	0.92	108.7	0
October	0.82	122.0	0
November	0.86	116.3	0
December	0.91	109.9	0
Total units		1,202.24	1,081
End value		1,094.04	983.71

As you get older you may need to reduce your exposure to equities, but by then pound cost averaging and the compounding of returns over time will have worked its magic and reduced the relative risk of price fluctuations because your capital should be worth many times what you invested.

ACTIVITY 4.3

Write down ten of your own financial planning principles and practices based on your own knowledge, experience and understanding and explain why each is relevant to your financial success.

4.5 Key components of a financial plan

A financial plan can be very simple, typically focused around a single goal, such as achieving financial independence. Alternatively, the plan can be comprehensive, taking into account multiple goals, scenarios and greater resource complexity.

Whether simple or complex, the plan needs to include a number of things as shown in Figure 4.3. A key element will be an analysis of your current and future financial position. This analysis, otherwise known as a *gap analysis*, will be based on a number of assumptions including inflation, investment returns, income, life expectancy and taxes, to forecast possible future income, asset value and sustainable regular portfolio withdrawal rates, to determine if your financial goals can be met in the future, or what steps need to be taken to ensure that they are.

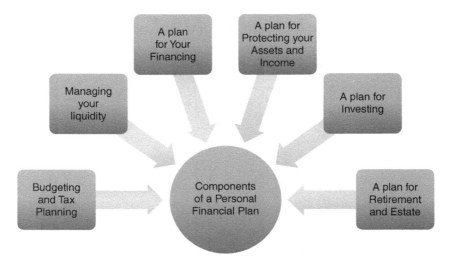

Figure 4.3 Key components of a financial plan

4.5.1 Values and goals

It's a good idea to state your overarching money values/beliefs in terms of how money fits into your life, because this serves as a very useful reminder of what's really important to you when formulating your goals and priorities and making associated financial decisions. The following are some examples of money values and beliefs:

- Maintaining relationships with family and friends, doing meaningful work and having interesting hobbies are more important to me than material possessions and status.
- I would rather take big financial risks while I am young and can recover from any failures or mistakes, as long as these risks are carefully considered and relate mainly to my human capital.
- Variety, flexibility and making a difference are more important to me in a job than a high salary, even if this means I have to potentially work for longer.
- Owning my own home is really important to me because it gives me a sense of security and I don't feel that the monthly cost of a mortgage is wasted money.
- Too much inheritance blunts ambition, reduces motivation and creates inertia among certain heirs.

ACTIVITY 4.4

Have a think about your own money values and write them down.

As we discussed in Chapter 2, it is important to define, quantify and prioritise your financial planning goals. More precisely, they need to be **SMART goals**: Specific,

Measurable, Attainable, Relevant and Timely. You need to prioritise your goals based on how important they are to you and whether they are short-, medium- or long-term goals.

If you are below age 35 then most of your goals will probably be short- to medium-term ones and as such that is where most of your financial resources will be directed. Don't worry if you don't have any SMART goals at present. It's perfectly OK to not know where you want to go in life when you are just starting out. If this is the case for you just make sure that you have an emergency fund to meet 3–6 months' expenses; you mitigate (with insurance) the risk of losing your income if you become ill or disabled for longer than your emergency fund can support; and bear in mind the need to convert your human capital into financial capital.

The term retirement is increasingly being replaced by the term *financial independence*, being that time when paid work is optional; you only work for money if you want to, not because you have to. You can aim to become financially independent at a specific age or over a period of years as you transition gradually from full-time to part-time work and then eventually to no work. The longer your working life and later the age you aim to become financially independent, the shorter your post-work period will be and the easier it will be to build up sufficient financial resources.

Behavioural science tells us that we find shorter-term goals like buying a house, getting married or travelling the world much more emotionally evocative than more abstract and distant goals like saving for retirement. This makes sense because when you are in your 20s and 30s, 60 seems so far away that you can't really comprehend its relevance and importance financially. For very long-term goals like financial independence it makes sense to start saving as soon as possible but initially at a very low level, while you focus on your shorter-term goals and build your earned income.

Your base plan will include all those goals, regardless of time frame, which are most important to you. The time frame is when the goal is intended to be achieved, not when you intend to start working towards it. In the case study of Amur (see Box 4.1 overleaf), his goals seem to meet the SMART test, but we won't know for sure if they are attainable until we complete a gap analysis. If these goals are SMART, then Amur could add other goals until he reaches the point where current and future financial resources are unlikely to be sufficient to fund a further goal.

4.5.2 Current position

Your financial statement sets out your current financial reality, which you will use as the basis to carry out the gap analysis to determine whether your goals are SMART and what actions are required to achieve them. The financial statement is split into the income statement and the balance sheet as illustrated in Figure 4.4. Another way of looking at your current financial position is the four quadrants of cash reserve, growth assets, debt and risk management. This is shown graphically in Figure 4.5.

❖ BOX 4.1 CORE GOALS CASE STUDY

Amur is 25 and earns €40,000 as a website coder in Berlin. He is currently renting an apartment with his girlfriend who is from the UK. Amur's parents live in India and his brother lives in Spain. Amur's main goals are as follows:

18 months
- To maintain existing cash reserve of €25,000
- To gain additional coding skills at cost of €6,000 to increase annual salary by €10,000

2–5 years
- To move to UK with girlfriend and get married at cost (to me) of £10,000
- To buy a house with deposit (in today's terms) of £80,000 and balance with a mortgage of c.£320,000

10 years+
- To continue to repay student loan at minimum rate permitted
- To start modest saving towards retirement with aim of providing income of about 50 per cent of current salary (in today's terms)

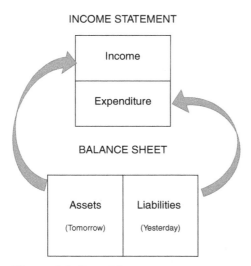

Figure 4.4 Financial statement

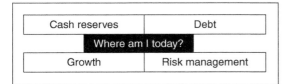

Figure 4.5 Four planning quadrants

ACTIVITY 4.5

1. Have a think about your own life goals which need money to achieve and write them down in as much detail as you can, including: target date to achieve, amount and how important they are to you.
2. Complete your own financial statement.

For people who have accumulated some assets and pension benefits, the *Back of the Envelope Retirement Tool* (BERT) is a really simple way of estimating how much income you might have in retirement and whether there is a gap. It is a signature exercise in Kinder Institute's lifeplanningforyou.com website for consumers. In the example shown in Figure 4.6 we can see that the pre-tax income is in the region of £47,500 per annum. However, income tax will need to be deducted from this amount, so if we assume an average rate of 20 per cent the net income expected to be received would be in the region of £38,000 per annum.

A. Sum total amount of your invested assets (e.g. shares and bonds)	250,000
B. Percent of invested assets you might reasonably expect to withdraw each year (A x 3%)	7,500
C. Number of remaining years you expect to live	40
D. Total home equity - the value of your real estate (property)	300,000
E. Total amount you expect from any inheritance	250,000
F. The amount of state pension you expect	10,000
G. Expected annual pension or annuity benefits	5,000
H. Any remaining yearly income you expect, such as from part-time work, rental etc.	10,000
AVAILABLE PRE-TAX INCOME*	47,500

* (B + (D/C) + (E × 3%) + F + G + H) Estimate of potential income using highly simplified assumptions

Figure 4.6 Back of the Envelope Retirement Planning Tool
Source: www.lifeplanningforyou.com © Copyright 2015 George Kinder and the Kinder Institute of Life Planning. All Rights Reserved. Used by permission of George Kinder and the Kinder Institute of Life Planning.

4.5.3 Gap analysis and 'what if?' scenarios

Once you have ascertained your current financial position, you'll need to analyse whether you are on track to achieve your financial goals. Initially you should create a base plan scenario based on your most important goals, to see how viable these are, before creating further scenarios including other, but less important, goals. There are many personal finance software applications that can be used to do the financial projections and calculations. If you want to use a spreadsheet the following formulae will enable you to calculate your own basic analysis.

$$\text{Annual contributions} = \frac{(\text{final value} \times \text{rate of return})}{[(1 + \text{rate of return})\,^\wedge\, \text{number of years} - 1]}$$

$$\text{Future value} = \frac{\text{annual contributions} \times [(1 + \text{rate of return})^\wedge \text{number of years} - 1]}{\text{rate of return}}$$

$$\text{Capital required} = \frac{\text{required income}}{\text{withdrawal rate}}$$

You can use simplified calculations to work out whether or not there are any shortfalls between what you want/need and what you are likely to have. These will give you a rough idea of whether you are on track and whether it is necessary (and worthwhile) doing more detailed analysis. Tables 4.4, 4.5 and 4.6 provide a range of calculation factors that you can use as shortcuts for doing your initial approximate gap analysis.

Three key variables which can have a significant impact on these calculations is the assumption used for investment returns, inflation and the percentage withdrawn from investments during wealth decumulation. In order to look at future values in today's money terms, you must use real, i.e. post-inflation, returns in financial calculation. This applies to both sides of the balance sheet, so inflation reduces the real value of assets (such as savings and investments) but it also reduces the real value of liabilities (debts).

Research from Morningstar in 2016 across a number of countries suggests that a 3 per cent a year real return (i.e. after inflation) and an annual portfolio withdrawal rate of 3 per cent (inflation adjusted) are reasonable planning assumptions and have a high probability of success for the majority of countries studied, including the USA and UK. Figure 4.7 shows the probability of portfolio viability at different levels of annual withdrawal.

Calculating savings required to provide an income

In our example in Figure 4.6 we ascertained that the net annual retirement income was likely to be in the region of £38,000. Let's assume that the target retirement lifestyle annual expenditure goal is £45,000 and this is required in ten years' time. The net shortfall in income is therefore £7,000 per annum. After grossing up the £7,000 to account for taxation at the assumed rate of 20 per cent, we arrive at a gross annual shortfall of £8,750.

Initial Withdrawal
Rate %

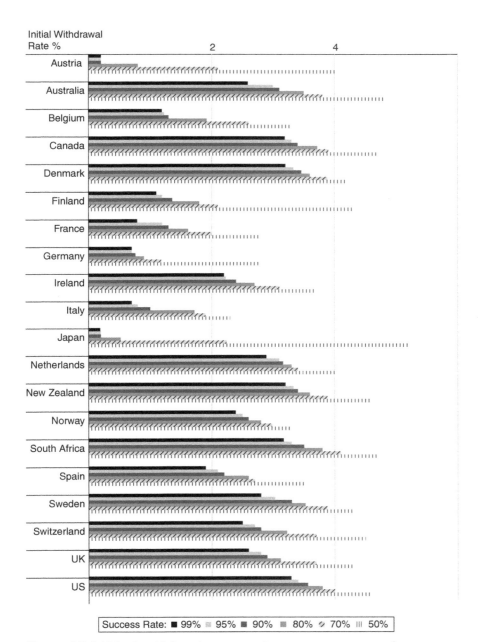

Figure 4.7 Initial safe withdrawal rates at various target success rates by country
Source: © 2016 Morningstar, Inc. All Rights Reserved. Reproduced with permission.

If we assume a 3 per cent a year withdrawal rate and real investment returns of 3 per cent a year, which are reasonably cautious, the calculation looks like this:

- income shortfall of £8,750/0.03 = £292,000 (rounded up);
- monthly contribution to build £1m @ 3 per cent a year real = £7,300;
- £7,300 x (£292,000/£1,000,000) = £2,130;
- monthly contribution required to meet goal is therefore £2,130 (to be increased each year in line with inflation).

ACTIVITY 4.6

Using the factors in Tables 4.6 (on page 77) and 4.7 (below) work out how much (using a 3 per cent a year real return and withdrawal rate) you would need to save each month (in today's terms) to be able to generate an income of 50 per cent of your current salary (or the starting salary that you expect to earn after education).

Calculating regular savings to produce a future lump

Let's assume that another goal is to accumulate £150,000 in today's terms to buy a second home in nine years' time and current savings amount to £75,000. If we assume a net annualised real return of, say, 3 per cent the calculation would look like this, using Table 4.8:

- £75,000 x 1.3 = £97,500;
- capital shortfall is £150,000 − £97,500 = £52,500;
- monthly contribution to build £52,500 @ 3 per cent a year real: (£52,500/£1,000,000 x £7,300) = £400 per month, to be increased each year in line with inflation.

Table 4.6 Capital required to meet different annual withdrawal amounts

| Withdrawal rate a year | Annual income required | | | | |
	10,000	20,000	30,000	40,000	50,000
2%	500,000	1,000,000	1,500,000	2,000,000	2,500,000
3%	333,333	666,667	1,000,000	1,333,333	1,666,667
4%	250,000	500,000	750,000	1,000,000	1,250,000

Table 4.7 Monthly savings required to accumulate £1,000,000

| Years | Expected real return | | | |
	1%	2%	3%	4%
10	£8,000	£7,600	£7,300	£6,900
20	£3,800	£3,400	£3,100	£2,800
30	£2,400	£2,100	£1,800	£1,500

Table 4.8 Growth of £1 over different periods and returns

Years	Expected real return				
	1%	2%	3%	4%	5%
10	£1.10	£1.20	£1.30	£1.50	£1.60
20	£1.20	£1.50	£1.80	£2.20	£2.70
30	£1.30	£1.80	£2.40	£3.20	£4.30

Don't worry that we've rounded up the contribution from £383 to £400 or that the return factors are for ten years compared to the actual time horizon of nine years. The objective is to get a rough estimate of funding levels, not spurious accuracy.

4.5.4 Financial planning policies

A financial planning policy is not a belief, goal or action point but 'a decision rule that embodies client goals and values, with financial planning best practices in a form that allows for rapid decision-making in the face of changing external circumstances' (Yeske and Buie 2014, p.192). A belief leads to a goal, which leads to a policy and that in turn leads to an action.

Belief – Goal – Policy – Action

Financial planners David Yeske CFP and Elissa Buie CFP have pioneered the practical application of financial planning policies and they make the point that such policies are particularly helpful to young people at the beginning of their careers – see Box 4.2.

❖ BOX 4.2 YESKE AND BUIE'S FINANCIAL PLANNING POLICY, EXAMPLE 1

These individuals generally have little income and few assets, and their family situation is likely to change dramatically because their most important decisions are in the future. They may also find themselves struggling to manage their cashflow as they begin to develop an independent life. For these individuals, simple, easy-to-follow policies that help them prioritize important needs in the face of limited cash flow can be very important.

The following is an example of just such a series of cashflow and investment policies:

I will save 10 per cent of every paycheck.

My savings will go first to my emergency fund until such time as this fund is equal to three months' living expenses.

Thereafter, my savings will go into a retirement savings vehicle up to the applicable contribution limit and according to the following principles:

A) If my employer offers a retirement plan, I will direct savings into this account, at least up to the amount of the employer match, if applicable.
    i)   If my marginal tax rate is 25 per cent or less then I will direct retirement savings above the employer match into a [non-pension savings vehicle].
    ii) If my marginal tax rate is greater than 25 per cent I will direct retirement savings above the employer match into the employer-sponsored pension plan.

B) If my employer does not offer a retirement savings plan I will direct retirement savings as follows:
    i)   If my marginal tax rate is 25 per cent or less then I will direct retirement savings into a [name of vehicle].
    ii) If my marginal tax rate is greater than 25 per cent I will direct retirement savings into [name of vehicle].

Any remaining savings will be directed to an after-tax 'opportunity fund' or supplemental retirement account.

With respect to investments:

A) The emergency fund will always be maintained in a money market account or similarly liquid account.
B) All retirement savings will be invested in a diversified mix of index mutual funds or, if unavailable, low-cost actively managed mutual funds, including in equal proportion as many as possible of the following categories:
    i)   Domestic large company stocks
    ii)   Domestic small company stocks
    iii) Foreign large company stocks
    iv)   Foreign small company stocks
    v)   High-quality, short-to-intermediate duration bonds.

Source: Yeske and Buie (2014, p.200).

The example (see Box 4.3) from Yeske and Buie shows financial planning policies for a retired couple who have, in addition to funding their own lifestyle, a desire to help their (free-spending) daughter and son-in-law, but not if this leads to reckless spending.

❖ **BOX 4.3 YESKE AND BUIE'S FINANCIAL PLANNING POLICY, EXAMPLE 2**

- We will spend each year from our portfolio a sum not to exceed the spending targets specified by our safe withdrawal rate (SWR) policy.
- We will not facilitate the purchase of assets by our children that they cannot afford to maintain with their own earnings.
- We will provide financial education and counselling to our children and other family members, but we will not provide direct financial support.

Source: Yeske and Buie (2014, p.204).

4.5.5 Strategy and action plan

Once you have determined the financial gaps under the base plan and any 'what-if?' scenarios, and devised appropriate financial planning policies, you will be in a position to decide on an appropriate strategy and associated actions.

Your strategy needs to include all of the following:

- amount of liquid cash reserve (minimum three months' expenditure);
- annual budget for lifestyle spending;
- monthly savings amount to be directed to growth assets (property and/or financial) or the amount of regular withdrawals to be taken from financial assets to fund lifestyle expenses;
- investment strategy for each goal or a combined single investment strategy;
- debt repayment strategy, i.e. term, repayment amounts, interest rate and frequency;
- use of insurance to mitigate risks such as disability, health and travel;
- tax management strategy, including utilisation of tax incentivised savings or borrowing;
- estate planning in the form of a valid will and life insurance nomination (if applicable).

The above items should suffice if your needs are reasonably simple. If, however, your needs are more complex (perhaps in the form of other, but less important, goals) or you have more significant assets and/or income, then your strategy will need to take these factors into account. Table 4.9 shows an example of a reasonably simple strategy and action plan.

The strategy and action plan should act as a reference document when you next review your finances. Your confidence and sense of progress should be strengthened by ticking off the items from your action list. Don't beat yourself up if you don't get everything on your action list done, just make sure that you include it on the next strategy and action plan if still relevant and make sure you deal with it first.

Table 4.9 Example strategy and action plan summary

Description	Target date	Current	Target	Action
STRATEGY & ACTION PLAN				
Cash reserve	12 months	£12,000	£15,000	Direct £250 of income surplus to cash reserve for 12 months
Annual expenditure (ex savings)	Now	£18,000	£20,000	Met from salary
Training course	6 months	£2,000	£3,000	Direct £170 per month to cash reserve
Investment strategy	Now	Default managed fund	Global lifestyle fund of index fund	Complete investment switch instruction online
Student debt repayment	Ongoing	£22,000	Maintain current repayments	No action required as payments taken from salary
Disability risk	Now	No cover	To have income replacement insurance which pays 70 per cent of gross salary after 3 months' incapacity from 'own' occupation	Apply to ABC Life for income protection policy to be funded within revised annual expenditure budget
Tax management	Now	N/A	To hold maximum amount of cash reserve in a tax-free savings account	Open tax-free savings account online with XYZ Bank
Estate planning	6 months	None	Create and sign simple will and nominate pension death benefits to mum and dad	1. Create will online using www.willsrus.com and have witnessed by two friends 2. Obtain death benefit nomination form from pension provider, complete, sign and return

---

ACTIVITY 4.7

Create your own strategy and action plan based on your own values, goals and basic gap analysis. Remember to be as specific and detailed as possible, including dates and amounts.

4.6 Conclusion

Son, if you really want something in this life, you have to work for it. Now quiet! They're about to announce the lottery numbers.

Homer Simpson

There are now many apps and money management packages and easy to use spreadsheet packages that you can use to plan your finances. However you choose to do it you need to end up with a written summary of your plan, but it is the planning process and the intentionality which it involves that will provide you the most value.

Whether you are embarking on your first job or well established in your career, have few assets or a significant amount, hate or love maths, or have simple or complex circumstances, you'll increase your chances of success and worry less about money if you follow the key principles set out in this chapter.

If you have very complex needs and the cost of financial mistakes could have a material impact on your well-being, it might make sense to take personalised advice from a professional financial planner. However, whether or not you take professional advice, having a proper understanding and appreciation of financial planning principles and practices will help you to be clear about what is important to you and the life goals which require money, and how you should go about planning to achieve them.

Answers to Activity 4.2

1. An inflation rate of 3% pa over 15 years would reduce the buying power of £1,000 to £642.
2. The nominal rate of return required to preserve the purchasing power of £1,000 over 15 years is the same as the inflation rate over that period. Thus 3% pa inflation requires 3% pa nominal return.
3. If £1,000 grew by 8% pa nominal over 15 years and the inflation rate of that period was 3% pa the real return will be about 5% pa (it is actually 4.854% pa).

End of chapter test

1. Give three reasons why it is a good idea to have a written financial plan.
2. Explain the main difference between a belief and a goal.
3. Outline the main reason for using real investment returns in a financial analysis.
4. Explain why it is not necessary, particularly for goals that have a long time frame, to be spuriously accurate with financial planning calculations.
5. Give an example of a financial planning policy and why this might be a useful thing to have in a financial plan.
6. Briefly outline the main components of a simple financial plan and the role that each plays.

References

Barclays (2016). *Barclays Equity Gilts Study 2016* [online] http://hungrydummy.com/media/pdf/EquityGiltStudy2016.pdf (Accessed 30 May 2016).

cfp.net (2013). 'Financial Planning Profiles of American Families'. Certified Financial Planner Board of Standards, Inc., available online at www.cfp.net/docs/public-policy/2013-fin-planning-profiles-of-amer-households.pdf?sfvrsn=2 (Accessed 5 May 2016).

Matthews, G. (2010). Goals-based research by Dr Gail Matthews of Dominican University, available online at www.dominican.edu/academics/ahss/undergraduate-programs/psych/faculty/assets/gail-matthews/researchsummary2.pdf (Accessed 5 May 2016).

Morningstar (2016). 'Safe Withdrawal Rates for Retirees in the United Kingdom – Where did the 4% rule come from and what is the impact of today's low bond yields?', available online at http://media.morningstar.com/uk%5CMEDIA%5CResearch_paper%5CUK_Safe_Withdrawal_Rates_ForRetirees.pdf?mc_cid=849258137e&mc_eid=91cb7ea5be (Accessed 15 May 2016). © 2016 Morningstar, Inc. All Rights Reserved. The information contained herein: (1) is proprietary to Morningstar and/or its content providers; (2) may not be copied or distributed; (3) does not constitute investment advice offered by Morningstar; and (4) is not warranted to be accurate, complete or timely. Neither Morningstar nor its content providers are responsible for any damages or losses arising from any use of this information. Past performance is no guarantee of future results. Use of information from Morningstar does not necessarily constitute agreement by Morningstar, Inc. of any investment philosophy or strategy presented in this publication.

Newcomb, Sarah (2016) *Loaded: Money, Psychology, and How to Get Ahead Without Leaving Your Values Behind*. Hoboken, NJ: Wiley.

Office for National Statistics (ONS) (2016). *Consumer Price Inflation Time Series Dataset*, available online at https://www.ons.gov.uk/economy/inflationandpriceindices/datasets/consumerpriceindices (Accessed 5 June 2016).

Yeske, D. and Buie, E. (2014). 'Policy-Based Financial Planning: Decision Rules for a Changing World'. *Investor Behavior – The Psychology of Financial Planning and Investing* Eds. H. Kent Baker and Victor Ricciardi. Hoboken, NJ: Wiley.

Part II

Build a secure foundation

Chapter 5

The pillars of wealth

Budgeting and saving

Tony Byrne and Lien Luu

Research on financial success shows that wealth accumulation is built on three pillars: ability to live below your means, commitment to regular saving to avoid debts and create a buffer, and growth of wealth through investing. Yet, the UK population is struggling to deal with these, and in many countries consumer debt is at historically high levels even years after the global financial crisis. This chapter examines the importance of budgeting, saving and investing as the essential building blocks for attaining your goals.

Learning outcomes

By the end of this chapter you will:

● be aware of the differences between different types of debt and its negative effects;
● understand how to compare the cost of credit including Annual Percentage Rate (APR);
● understand why living within your means is important and how this can be done through budgeting and delayed gratification;
● appreciate the importance of saving and how this can be made automatic;
● explore ways to increase income.

5.1 Living within your means

Living within your means is seen as the key to wealth and financial independence because it allows you to avoid debts and have the surplus income to save and invest.

5.1.1 Debt and saving in the UK

> It's not your salary that makes you rich, it's your spending habits.
>
> Charles A. Jaffe

Evidence suggests that people are not living within their means and rising consumer debt is an issue of national concern. Debt in the UK was estimated to total more than £1.46 trillion in January 2016, including mortgage debt (estimated at £1.294 trillion in November 2014), and this is predicted to increase by 55 per cent to £2.639 trillion by 2020. The average household debt will thus rise from approximately £54,000 to £94,000 (including mortgages).

Of particular concern is the rise of consumer debt – that is, money borrowed on loans and credit cards. This accounts for nearly 17 per cent of the total debt in the UK. Consumer credit lending was calculated at £168.8 billion in November 2014 and credit card debt at £61.0 billion, totalling £229.8 billion unsecured debt. By the end of March 2016, consumer credit lending had increased to £182.4 billion and credit card debt to £64.3 billion, giving a total of £246.7 billion (The Money Charity, 2015; Walker et al., 2012). In less than 18 months, consumer debt has risen by 7.3 per cent.

This figure excludes payday lending. The rise in payday lending has caused much concern in the UK. In 2013, payday lenders issued more than 10 million loans, to

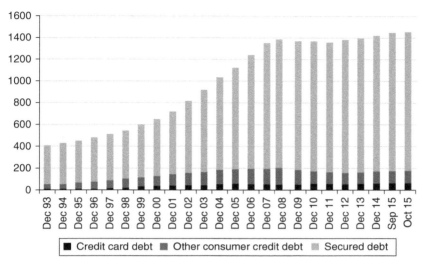

Figure 5.1 Total debt in the UK (£bn)
Source: The Money Charity (2015).

1.6 million payday customers, with a total value of £2.5 billion. The Archbishop of Canterbury told the House of Lords in 2013 that more than 5 million people in the UK used payday loans. Those with poor (or no) credit and unable to access mainstream credit are those most likely to turn to payday lending (Financial Ombudsman, 2014) and interest rates could be as high as a few thousand percentage. A high proportion (42 per cent) of young people use payday loans or pawn shops (Sheffield, 2016). Indeed, the report by the Financial Ombudsman (2014) showed that many young people used payday lending and the highest number of complaints came from those aged between 25 and 34. Those with poor credit history are being squeezed out of the mainstream market, but tackling the problem of high-cost short-term credit (e.g. through price caps) creates the risk of borrowers going to illegal lenders (loan sharks) instead.

Debt is continuing to soar in the UK. The household debt to income ratio was 145 per cent in 2016 and is expected to increase to 172 per cent by 2020 (see Figure 5.2). This is much higher than the 110 per cent in the USA and 85 per cent in Germany. Worryingly, the rise of debt to income is accompanied by a steep fall in the saving ratio. This will be discussed later in Section 5.3. With UK households spending on average 26.5 per cent of their annual income on servicing loans and credit cards, the situation is currently only affordable because of low mortgage interest rates (BBC, 2016a). Since the cut in interest rates in 2009, mortgage payments fell to 16 per cent of household income (see Figure 5.3).

Research by Aviva (2016) gives an insight into household finances in the UK – see Table 5.1. Average household debt in winter 2015 was £13,250. Couples with two children or more had on average £18,830 of debt, in comparison to £6,370 for lone parents. However, these average levels disguise the fact that some will have a much higher level of debt, while others have less. In 2008, a young man in his 30s had accumulated more than £120,000 of debt on numerous credit cards.

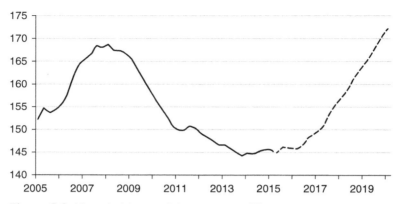

Figure 5.2 Household gross debt to income (%)
Source: The Institute of Economic Affairs (2015).

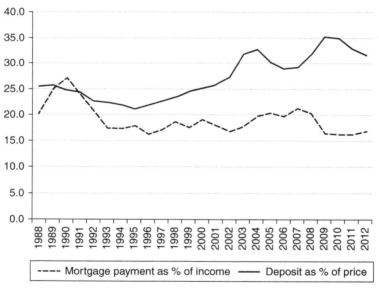

----- Mortgage payment as % of income —— Deposit as % of price

Figure 5.3 Mortgage payments and deposit as per cent of income
Source: Pettinger (2015).

The average saving was £105 per month in winter 2015 (down from £113), with a typical saving pot of £3,150, meaning that households have enough savings to cover just over one month of expenditure. This falls short of the recommended 3–6 months emergency fund. If the average monthly expenditure is £2,301, then UK households need to put aside between £6,903 and £13,806 to cover emergencies. In the UK, 9.61 million households are reported to have no savings at all (The Money Charity, 2016a).

The average net income was £2,024 per month in winter 2015,[1] but the Office for National Statistics found that the average UK spending was £531 per week or £2,301 per month in 2014. Aviva (2015), however, reported in August 2015 that the monthly

Table 5.1 UK household finances, 2011–15

	Winter 2011	Winter 2013	Winter 2014	Summer 2015	Winter 2015
Average household debt (exclude mortgages)	£10,870	£7,840	£9,050	£9,520	£13,520
Credit card debt				£1,960	£2,370
Overdrafts				£870	£1,190
Personal loans					£2,080
Savings per month	£77	£80	£99	£113	£105
Typical family saving pot	£696	£2,016	£3,303	£3,116	£3,150
Typical net income per month	£2,076	£1,917	£2,043	£2,126	£2,024
Average household monthly spending			£2,301 (1)	£2,259 (2)	
Monthly income shortfall			£258	£133	

Source: Aviva (2016); Notes: 1) Office for National Statistics (2015); 2) Aviva (2015).

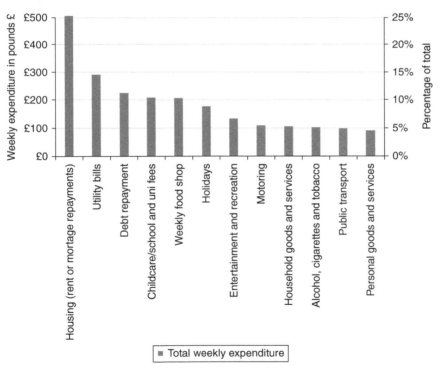

Total weekly expenditure

Figure 5.4 Breakdown of monthly expenditure in the UK, 2015
Source: Aviva (2015).

expenditure had reduced to £2,259. The shortfall between income and expenditure fell from £258 per month to £133, due to rising incomes and lower rates of inflation.

Figure 5.4 provides a breakdown of monthly expenditure in the UK in 2015. This shows that the biggest three expenditures are housing, utility bills and debt repayment.

Table 5.2 Breakdown of household expenditure in the UK, USA and China

Types of expenditure	UK	USA	China
Food	9.12	12.9	26.91
Housing	22.36	33.6	16.65
Household goods and services	4.69		
Utility bills	12.97		
Transport	10.36	17.6	19.74
Entertainment	4.87	4.9	
Holidays	7.79		
Childcare/school fees	9.25		
Debt repayment	9.96		
Alcohol, tobacco/cigarettes	4.56		
Personal goods and services	4.07		
Clothing		3.1	6.29
Healthcare		7.1	8.06
Pensions and social security		10.2	
Other		10.6	1.9
Daily necessities			5.85
Education and entertainment			14.6
Total %	**100**	**100**	**100**
Total amount	**£22,108**	**$51,100**	**¥53,485**

Source: UK (Aviva, 2015), USA (Foster, 2015 (US Bureau of Labour Statistics)), China (China Household Finance Survey, n.d.).

ACTIVITY 5.1

Using the information in Table 5.1, Table 5.2 and Figure 5.4 answer the following questions:

1. Identify which figures in Table 5.2 are stocks (assets or liabilities) and which are flows (income and spending). (See Chapter 1, Section 1.1 to review this distinction.)
2. Does the data suggest UK households were managing their debts in Winter 2014 and Summer 2015?
3. What does the breakdown of expenditure tell you about UK lifestyles?

Growth in car purchase is believed to be responsible for much of the increase in consumer debt in the UK. The number of new car purchases surged in 2015, and £28 billion was borrowed to finance these (Strauss, 2016). In fact, some 2.63 million new vehicles were registered in 2015, a 6 per cent increase from 2.48 million in 2014. The previous record for sales in the UK was in 2003 when 2.58 million new cars were sold (BBC, 2016b). The AA estimates that the average new car will have a residual value of around 40 per cent of its new price after three years (assuming 10,000 miles/year). In other words, it will have lost 60 per cent of its value, with an average depreciation rate of 20 per cent per year (The AA, 2016).

Debt is not unique to the UK, but a global problem, as can be seen in Figure 5.5. Countries with the highest level of household debt, expressed as per cent of

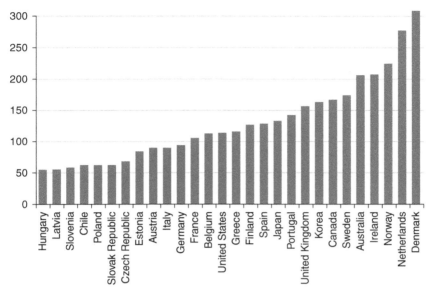

Figure 5.5 Total household debt as per cent of disposable income, 2014
Source: https://data.oecd.org/hha/household-debt.htm.

disposable income, are Denmark (over 300 per cent), Netherlands (275 per cent), Norway (220 per cent), Ireland (205 per cent), while the UK's household debt is 150 per cent of disposable income. The USA has a slightly lower level of debt (120 per cent), and the countries with the lowest level of debt are Hungary (55 per cent) and Slovenia (60 per cent). The financial crisis caused house prices to fall in many countries, and with less income and more precarious employment, many find it hard to meet their mortgage payments. By the end of 2011, real house prices had fallen from their peak by about 41 per cent in Ireland, 29 per cent in Iceland, 23 per cent in Spain and the USA, and 21 per cent in Denmark. Household defaults began to rise and, in the USA, debt fell largely due to defaults on loans (IMF, 2012).

5.1.2 Good debt – bad debt

Debt is generally divided into two types – *good debt* and *bad debt*. Good debt is when you borrow money to buy an asset that appreciates in value and allows you to increase your wealth over the life of the loan. Mortgages are often seen as good debts because in many countries homes have historically tended to appreciate in value over time. Home-improvement loans are also regarded as good debts because the costs of improvements to your home might be recovered when you sell as these (new kitchen or bathroom) make your home more desirable. The desirability of a property, however, does depend on its location and other factors (a change in the neighbourhood, subsidence). Investing in property is a risk because wealth is concentrated in one property (in other words, having all your eggs in one basket) – a change in the neighbourhood, subsidence, etc. could cause the value of your particular property to fall even if the market generally is rising. As the financial crisis of 2008 has shown, the property market can collapse when households cannot afford to meet mortgage payments. Some also regard student loans as good debts, because these loans can create opportunities for you to expand your career, and increase your earning potential.

Bad debt, on the other hand, refers to money borrowed to fund everyday spending or acquire disposable items or durable goods that lose value or do not maintain value from the day purchased. These include loans for holidays, money to buy clothing, furnishings, appliances, entertainment, weddings, Christmas presents and so on (*The Clergy Journal*, 2004; Shipman, 2007). In December 2012, a survey by Which? revealed that around 13 million in the UK (25 per cent) paid for their Christmas by borrowing. Overall, more than four in ten (42 per cent) used credit cards, loans or overdrafts to fund their spending over the festive period (Which, 2012).

Bad debt not only has financial but also emotional, psychological and mental consequences. Research shows that more than eight out of ten people with debt problems say that their financial difficulties are affecting their personal relationships, health and their ability to do their jobs. Debt is believed to affect health, with some suffering a nervous breakdown, loss of hair, palpitations and cessation of menstruation. Those in debt, for example, are also twice as likely to think about suicide, and often feel humiliated, disconnected and entrapped (Insley, 2010). These, combined with the process of debt collection (persistent phone calls and threatening letters), make them feel depressed and suicidal. The total number of suicides in the UK rose to 6,045 in 2011, a 7.8 per cent increase from 2010 (Pitas, 2013).

There are two possible factors which can help us understand why UK consumer debt has increased. First is the issue of over-confidence bias. It is argued that people take out more debt because they feel more confident about the future and therefore are more willing to spend. There are reasons for this consumer confidence: improving employment rates, low interest rates, prices at the petrol pumps and supermarket checkouts have been low, and the cost of debt (personal loans) is low (Strauss, 2016). However, psychologists believe that over-confidence makes people under-estimate their risks. By taking out more debt, consumers are making themselves vulnerable to any downturn in the economy.

The second factor, a lack of self-control, also helps us understand consumers' behaviour. In his book *Behavioural Finance and Wealth Management*, Michael Pompian explores how self-control bias, a human behavioural tendency, causes people to fail to act in pursuit of their long-term goals because of a lack of self-discipline. Many people are lacking self-control when it comes to money and self-control bias can cause investors to spend more today at the expense of saving for tomorrow (Pompian, 2012). However, we live in a 'buy now and pay later' culture and people want instant gratification. This culture is incompatible with wealth accumulation, as suggested by the Marshmallow Experiment by Professor Mischel (see Box 5.1). In an interview with the *Financial Times*, he concludes that individuals with good self-control who can regulate their emotions will have more experience of success, because they feel more confident and self-assured and have a sense that they are able to overcome negative outcomes (*Financial Times*, 2014). To help people break their bad money habits, a British firm, Intelligent Environments, has developed the world's first Internet of Things bank account (IoT) to detect over-spending and then give users an electric shock or turn their heating down to save money on heating bills. It does so by integrating two smart devices: *Nest Thermostat* and *Pavlok* (a wearable device that gives people an electronic shock to help them break bad habits) (Intelligent Environments, 2016).

❖ BOX 5.1 THE MARSHMALLOW EXPERIMENT

A Stanford professor named Walter Mischel conducted a series of important psychological studies in the 1960s. He and his team tested hundreds of children, mostly aged 4–5, and demonstrated what is now believed to be one of the most important characteristics for success in health, work and life.

The experiment consisted of bringing each child into a private room, putting a marshmallow on a table in front of each of them. The researcher told the children that he was going to leave the room and that if they did not eat the marshmallows while he was away he would reward them with a second one each. If, instead, they ate the marshmallows they would not get a second one. He then left the room for 15 minutes. Only a few of the children were able to resist the temptation to eat the marshmallow.

As the years passed the researchers conducted follow-up studies and they discovered that the children who were able to delay gratification ended up doing better in virtually all areas of life including education, health, stress, obesity, drugs, social skills, etc. The research carried on for more than 40 years and the experiments proved that the ability to delay gratification was critical for success in life.

Source: Shoda *et al.* (1990).

5.1.3 Types of borrowing

Debt should generally be avoided to pay for current spending or disposable items but at some point in your life you will need to borrow money (e.g. to buy a house). It is therefore important to understand different types of debt and the costs associated.

There are two main types of debt: *unsecured* and *secured debt*. Unsecured debt includes overdrafts, credit cards and loans and is more expensive as this is not secured on any collateral such as your property and so lenders as a consequence face a higher risk. They therefore compensate for the higher risk by charging customers a higher rate of interest. In August 2016, the average interest rate on credit card lending was 18.29 per cent, that is 18.04 per cent above the Bank of England Base Rate (0.25 per cent). British Bankers Association figures show that 57.1 per cent of credit card balances were bearing interest in August 2016. The rate for loans depends in part on the amount borrowed. The average APR for a £5,000 personal loan was 9.13 per cent, according to the Bank of England. For a £10,000 loan it was 4.14 per cent. Overdrafts are among the most expensive and the average rate for an overdraft was 19.68 per cent as shown in Figure 5.6 (The Money Charity, 2016a).

The rates above assume that the borrower has a good credit history. Those with a poor credit history will pay a higher rate, and interest rates of 20–30 per cent or more are not uncommon. This is why debts can spiral out of control when payments start being missed. At an interest rate of 24 per cent a credit card balance will on average double every three years assuming you did not have to make any repayments!

Also bear in mind that this example is based on the best rates available from a comparison website. The disparities would be far wider if the borrower did not shop around.

In comparison to unsecured debt, secured debt such as a mortgage is a cheaper form of lending because the lender has more security. If you do not pay your mortgage, the lender can repossess the house and sell it to get back the money. However, a mortgage is long-term lending and borrowed over many years.

Besides understanding the interest rate, the borrower needs to know the annual percentage rate (APR). All lenders have to disclose the APR as well as the headline interest rate. The APR is the true rate of interest calculated on a yearly basis including all fees and costs. It is in effect the real cost of credit. It is vital to understand this because otherwise one could be fooled into thinking that a mortgage or a loan with a particularly tempting low initial interest rate is a real bargain, whereas over the borrowing term it may not be good at all if the APR is high (see Chapter 8, Box 8.2).

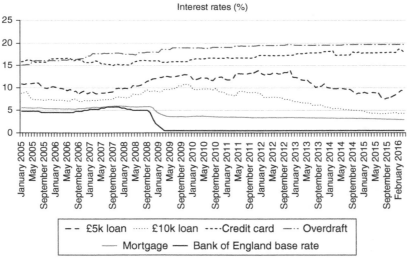

Figure 5.6 Costs of borrowings
Source: The Money Charity (2016b).

ACTIVITY 5.2

Read the following case study and answer the question that follows:

Case study: Martin is aged 24 and is employed as a landscape gardener. He lives at home with his parents. He earns £20,000 a year. He has a deposit of £1,000 but needs to borrow £5,000 to buy a second-hand Volkswagen Golf for £6,000. The maximum term he wants to borrow the money is over three years. He would like to pay by monthly instalments and would like the flexibility to be able to repay his borrowing early. He has asked his parents to lend him the money and they were unable to do so. He doesn't know any individual who could lend him the money he needs. He has a good credit record. He has two credit cards with combined limits of £7,000 and pays back in full what he borrows monthly. He has no debts.

What do you think might be the cheapest way he can borrow the money over three years with the most flexibility?

5.1.4 Credit referencing and scoring

Holding a good credit record is essential because it means you will be able to access prime lending rates and pay a lower interest rate. A credit record is a history of a borrower's past borrowing and repayments including information about late payments and bankruptcy. Your credit record is checked when you open a bank account, apply for a credit card, loan or a mortgage. Most lenders give information to the three main credit reference agencies in the UK: Experian, Equifax and Call Credit, who keep a record of the borrower's credit history. These credit reference agencies keep a record of information from four sources:

● Publicly available, e.g. electoral roll.
● Closed-user group. Lenders who choose to share information about what credit has been taken out and how good the borrower is at repaying that credit.
● Court data on County Court Judgments, bankruptcies and so on.
● Search information. Each time you apply for credit, your record is usually checked and this leaves a 'footprint' on your file. A lot of footprints in a short space of time may suggest you are borrowing too much or you are a victim of fraud.

When you apply for a credit card, loan or mortgage, many lenders use credit scoring and the score determines the outcome. Each lender uses its own credit scoring system, but credit reference agencies also make available 'indicative' scores to borrowers based on data the agency holds about them. These indicative scores – see examples in Table 5.3 – give an idea of whether or not you might be successful in applying for a loan or credit.

Table 5.3 Credit scoring: indicative scores

Excellent 961–999	You should get the best credit cards, loans and mortgages (but there are no guarantees).
Good 881–960	You should get most credit cards, loans and mortgages but the very best deals may reject you.
Fair 721–880	You might get OK interest rates but your credit limits may not be very high.
Poor 561–720	You might be accepted for credit cards, loans and mortgages but they may be at higher interest rates.
Very Poor 0–560	You are more likely to be rejected for most credit cards, loans and mortgages that are available.

Source: www.experian.co.uk/consumer/experian-credit-score.html.

Table 5.4 Factors affecting your credit score

Easy to do	Easy to avoid	Harder to fix
Electoral roll Make sure you are on it	**Late payments** Being even a few days late can decrease your score	**Defaulted accounts**
Credit accounts Not too many, not too few	**Applying for credit** Every application you make can decrease your score	**County Court Judgments (CCJs)**
Total credit balance Do not let it get too high	**Maxed-out cards** Spending up to your credit limits decreases your score	**Individual Voluntary Arrangements (IVAs)**
Highest card limit The higher the better		**Bankruptcies and insolvencies**

Source: Experian (2016).

If you have an 'excellent' rating, it should normally be easy to get credit (credit card, loan or mortgage) and you may be able to get the best rates as you are deemed to be low risk. If you have 'fair' or 'poor', you may still get credit but you will have to pay higher interest rates. For example, credit card companies such as Aqua and Luma offer credit cards to those with bad credit ratings but the APR is 34.9 per cent (almost twice the average rate for those with good credit) and the limit is low (£1,200 and £1,500, respectively). If your credit is 'very poor' it will be difficult to get credit. You might have to use expensive sources of lending such as payday lending. It is important therefore to maintain a good credit record.

There are several factors that affect a credit score and they fall into three categories as shown in Table 5.4.

A borrower can get a copy of his credit record by requesting one from each of the credit reference agencies and paying a small fee in the UK.

5.1.5 Why people borrow
People borrow money for many reasons:

1. **To be able to drive**: buying a car, especially a new car, is expensive and so people tend to borrow to pay for this.
2. **To pay for education**: e.g. by taking out a student loan.
3. **To buy a house**: buying a house is one of the biggest purchases and so people tend to borrow money over many years to pay for the cost.
4. **Home improvements**: home improvements (e.g. loft conversion, conservatory, extensions, renovations) can be expensive and so people tend to borrow to pay for these costs.
5. **For their children**: people might borrow money to pay for school fees, weddings and other expenses for their children.
6. **For Christmas**: Christmas can be an expensive time and so people tend to borrow to cover extra expenses. In 2015, the average family was calculated to spend more than £800 celebrating Christmas, with the majority of the money

being spent on food and drink, as well as cards and decorations. To meet extra expenses, 35 per cent of households borrowed money to buy Christmas gifts and 23 per cent to buy Christmas food (The Telegraph, 2015).

7. **Widen monthly budgets**: some people borrow to tide them over until the day they get paid.
8. **To save face from family and friends**: many people do not like to borrow money from family and friends in case it changes the relationship, and prefer to borrow on credit or take out a loan.

5.2 Budgeting

Living within your means is essential and forms the first pillar of wealth. This requires discipline, commitment and budgeting. This involves making a **cashflow statement**, which is the most important step in controlling your money because it allows you to see where your money is coming from and how you spend your money. The cashflow statement lists all your incomes and expenditures and will help you determine whether you are living within your means or over-spending. This awareness is essential, allowing you to tackle the problem before it arises.

5.2.1 Check your income

The first step is to calculate your **net income**, that is income you take home after all the taxes and deductions have been taken into account. All additional incomes such as rental income, self-employment income, interest/dividend income, child support and so on should be included. If you are unable to calculate your net income, you can estimate how much you get.

5.2.2 Control your expenses

The next step is to list all your **expenses**. Here it is important to understand the difference between what you need and what you want. Expenses can be divided into several categories: *fixed, variable, periodic* and *discretionary expenses*.

- **Fixed expenses** occur every month and the amount usually does not vary, and include rent/mortgage, car payments and childcare.
- **Variable expenses** also occur monthly but the amount may vary month to month. These include food expenses, utilities, petrol, household expenses and credit card payments, etc.
- **Periodic expenses** can be seen as those which occur on a regular, but not monthly basis. These include car insurance, medical expenses, home or car maintenance, and memberships.
- Unlike other categories, **discretionary expenses** are seen as luxuries that can be sacrificed. These include vacations, gifts, subscriptions, entertainment, eating out and treats (going to a cinema, buying coffees at Starbucks and Costa).

After doing these calculations the cashflow statement will enable you to see if you have a surplus or deficit. A **budget** is then your plan for cutting a deficit or increasing your capacity to save. Rental or mortgage costs, for example, are usually the largest monthly expense. There might be scope to reduce costs by changing to a better deal. Households have sought to reduce food expenses by shopping at discount stores such as Lidl and Aldi. These German-owned stores control 10 per cent of the grocery market in the UK in 2016 (Butler, 2015). The potential for increasing saving can easily be explored in discretionary expenses. In *The Automatic Millionaire*, David Bach illustrates how the Latte Factor can prevent us from achieving our financial goals. The Latte Factor refers to the long-term financial cost of expenditure on items such as coffee, bottled water, cigarettes, soft drinks and fast food. Bach tells the story of a lady who believes she cannot afford to save but spends $11.20 daily on various mid-morning drinks and snacks. He shows how, by investing $5 per day, 7 days a week and at 10 per cent return, she will accumulate $339,073 over 30 years or $948,611 over 40 years. Buying lunch can also cost a lot in the long term. Let's assume we buy a meal deal every day at the cost of £3 or £60 per month. Imagine if we invest £60 per month in shares with 10 per cent return over 40 years, we will receive nearly £158,000. Obviously, we need to balance between today's wants with tomorrow's needs. The compromise, perhaps, is to buy lunch once a week as a treat.

It is also possible to manage your budget using the 'jars system'. This involves putting money away for a designated purpose in each jar. The 'jars system' consists of six jars with the following labels: *Necessities* (living expenses), *Financial Freedom Account, Long-term Savings and Spending, Give* (for charity), *Education* (self-learning or self-development; as the saying goes, 'The more you learn the more you earn') and *Play* (spending money). The largest amount (50 per cent) is paid into Necessities, with the other jars receiving 10 per cent each. Six actual physical jars are bought, preferably glass jars, and the labels are stuck on them. Each month when paid a salary the individual puts his money into each of the jars in the exact same percentage. As an alternative you could open a 'jam jar bank account' that lets you divide your money into different pots with the same headings. Clearly the percentages to be paid into each metaphorical jar will differ from person to person but the advantage of this approach is that it can produce a disciplined approach to money management.

ACTIVITY 5.3

Read the following case study and answer the questions that follow.

Case study: John is aged 21. He has recently graduated and started a career as a financial paraplanner. He aspires to qualify as a Chartered and/or Certified Financial Planner and become an adviser. He shares an apartment with his girlfriend Sandra, a trainee solicitor, which they rent. They both live close to where they work. On a monthly basis, their main living expenses are as follows:

- Rent £850
- Food £400 (including £50 on takeaways)
- Council tax £100
- Electricity £60

- Car expenses £350 (John £200 and Sandra £150)
- Telephone £30
- Personal loan £125 (John – 17 months' instalments remaining)
- Entertainment, clothing, hobbies £375
- Saving £50 (Sandra)

They have little in the way of savings. Sandra has £500 in a Cash ISA and John has £250 in a bank deposit account. John's car is worth £1,000 and Sandra's £1,500.

1. Create a cashflow statement for John and Sandra.
2. Comment on John and Sandra's financial situation and opportunity for saving.
3. Divide John and Sandra's expenses into fixed, variable, periodic and discretionary.
4. They want to save £500 a month to buy their first property. Suggest three ways they can do this.

There are also a wide variety of apps to help you manage your personal finances. You can download these apps onto your phone and they should help you track your expenses with ease.

It is essential to review expenditure regularly, certainly at the very least annually but preferably every quarter by comparing actual cashflow with your budget. Staying in control allows you to avoid debt, develop money discipline, and have peace of mind and financial confidence.

5.2.3 Increasing your income

Besides reducing your expenses, you can also find ways to increase your income.

- *Rent out your drive/ parking space*: monetise personally owned assets by, for example, renting out a car (www.carclub.easycar.com), renting out a drive/ parking space (www.justpark.com). There are a number of companies that offer each of these services, all searchable online.
- *Rent a furnished room in your home* to a lodger and receive rental income (up to a limit) tax free. Alternatively take bookings from Airbnb (www.airbnb. co.uk), etc.
- *Get a part-time job* to supplement main income.
- *Work overtime* in a job if available.
- *Create a part-time business*, for example network marketing, online freelance work, eBay trading, etc. Think about what are the biggest frustrations and inconveniences people experience. Find a solution. Then start marketing it.
- *Increase marketability by becoming better educated*: Graduates during their working lives earn approximately 20 per cent more than non-graduates on average. If they have a Masters, a PhD and/or further professional qualifications these all increase their market value to an employer. If they are going to be better educated they

need to make sure they work hard and get the best possible grades too (ideally aim for at least a 2:1 for a bachelor degree).

● *Making oneself indispensable in a job by going the extra mile:* By always doing more than is expected eventually such people will be paid more for doing less. An employee should not ask what his employer can do for him, but instead ask what he can do for his employer.

In summary, living within one's means is crucial to your long-term financial security. A shortfall in income needs to be addressed by reducing your expenditure and finding ways to increase your income rather than turning to debt.

5.3 Importance of saving

The second pillar of wealth accumulation is saving. There are many reasons why people wish to save and John Maynard Keynes (1936) listed eight motives:

1. Uncertainty (precaution) – 'to build up a reserve against unforeseen contingencies', e.g. emergency fund.
2. Foreseen changes in income in relation to anticipated needs (foresight/ the life cycle motive), e.g. saving for retirement.
3. Time preference ('calculation') – 'to enjoy interest and appreciation'.
4. To enjoy a gradually increasing expenditure (improvement).
5. To enjoy a sense of independence – (independence).
6. To carry out speculative or business projects (enterprise).
7. To provide a large inheritance (ostentation/bequest motive).
8. Preference for frugality (miserliness, avarice).
9. To accumulate deposits to buy a house, cars and other durables (the deposit motive) (Browning and Lusardi, 1996).

Nowadays, saving for a house deposit is an important incentive for saving and so motive 9 has been added. In the UK, people also save for a variety of purposes: weddings, home improvements, big purchases such as electrical goods or a car. However, according to research by Birmingham Midshires (UK lender), people in Britain are saving £27 billion a year too little. In addition, the percentage of people who are not saving is rising to 32 per cent (from 22 per cent 12 months ago). Birmingham Midshires believes that low interest rates, combined with high levels of debt and increased National Insurance contributions, were putting people off saving (Mail Online, 2016). The saving ratio (saving expressed as a percentage of disposable income) as a consequence has declined, as can be seen in Figure 5.7 and Table 5.5.

Decline in saving is a common trend and global household saving shows some interesting trends, as can be seen in the table below. Table 5.5 shows three striking features: rising levels of saving in many countries after the financial crisis of 2008, the extraordinary level of saving in China, and decline in saving after 2012. Research shows that levels of saving are influenced by several economic, social and demographic factors (Browning and Lusardi, 1996; Kirsanova and Sefton, 2006):

Figure 5.7 Savings as percentage of household income in the UK
Source: www.tradingeconomics.com/united-kingdom/personal-savings.

Table 5.5 Household saving as a percentage of disposable income around the world, 2000–15

Countries	2000	2002	2004	2006	2008	2010	2012	2014	2015
Australia	2.33	0.03	1.62	1.73	9.85	10.07	10.17	9.23	–
Canada	5.3	3.0	2.57	2.6	3.35	4.39	4.82	3.98	4.3
China	28.25	27.21	30.57	34.35	37.32	38.99	38.11	–	–
Denmark	−5.99	1.18	−2.23	−1.73	−4.18	2.13	0.74	−2.76	4.97
France	10.04	11.63	10.95	9.38	9.46	10.35	9.46	8.75	8.89
Germany	9.0	9.63	10.11	10.08	10.48	9.97	9.29	9.38	9.67
Greece	−1.43	−2.01	1.15	−0.05	−3.84	−6.9	−10.91	−17.28	–
Ireland	−3.79	−0.7	0.27	−1.99	3.94	6.4	3.48	−0.4	–
Japan	6.98	3.29	2.31	1.31	0.56	2.15	1.36	−0.47	–
Russia	–	–	–	–	–	–	2.75	3.91	–
Switzerland	15.31	15.29	13.7	15.8	16.67	17.01	18.52	20.09	19.0
UK	4.26	3.55	0.51	−1.06	−0.81	5.67	2.68	0.51	−0.22
USA	4.33	5.2	4.72	3.44	5.09	5.82	7.89	5.77	6.0

Source: OECD data (https://data.oecd.org/hha/household-savings.htm#indicator-chart).

- **Demography:** The age structure of the population (proportion between working and non-working population) will influence saving rate. It is expected that people save more when they are working and less when they do not work. In countries with a higher working population, a higher rate of saving is expected.
- **The welfare state:** If the welfare system is generous and looks after people when they are old, sick and unemployed, then saving will be lower as people feel less need to save as they have a buffer. In countries where there is no provision of healthcare or income, people will face much uncertainty and so will save more.
- **Retirement behaviour:** Saving will be influenced by when people retire and whether they expect to work beyond retirement age.
- **Constraints on borrowing:** Saving will be affected by the ease of borrowing. In countries where it is difficult to borrow money, saving rates are expected to be high, and saving will be lower where access to credit is easy.

- **Income uncertainty**: In countries (or periods) where people face income uncertainty and where borrowing is difficult, people will save more to protect themselves against the unexpected and so saving will increase.
- **Changes in wealth**: Changes in consumers' wealth, known as the wealth effects, can affect the saving rate. When people's wealth increases as a result of gains on property and investments, they will feel richer and more confident so they will save less. Conversely, they save more when they feel less wealthy.

The above factors will help us understand the higher levels of saving in the aftermath of the financial crisis, the high level of saving in China, and changes in saving in the UK. In the immediate aftermath of the financial crisis in 2008, UK borrowing became more difficult, people faced higher income uncertainty as the economy plunged into a recession and unemployment increased, and people felt poorer as their house value and investments fell. All these made people more frugal and less willing to spend. Figure 5.8 below shows unsecured loans and credit card borrowings fell dramatically in 2009.

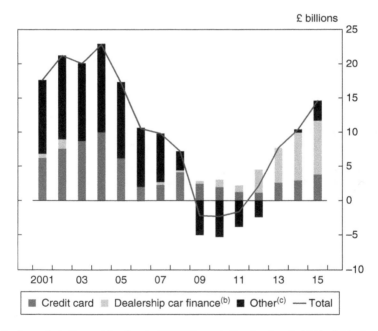

(a) Annual sterling net lending by UK MFIs and other lenders to UK individuals excluding student loans. Non seasonally adjusted.
(b) Dealership car finance net lending is estimated using change in outstanding stock rather than net lending. Net lending may therefore reflect breaks in the series as well as underlying flows.
(c) Other is estimated as total consumer credit lending minus dealership car finance as provided by the Finance & Leasing Association and credit card lending.

Figure 5.8 Net consumer lending flows in the UK (£bn)
Source: Bank of England (2016).

❖ BOX 5.2 SAVING IN CHINA

In China, the one-child policy, combined with the 1997 pension reform and the rise in income uncertainty, are believed to account for the extraordinarily high level of saving. The numbers are quite impressive because the per capita annual income is relatively low in China: $4,800 for urban areas and $1,500 for rural areas (expressed in 2010 purchasing power parities) (Cristadoro and Marconi, 2011, pp.15, 19, 21; see also Chamon et al., 2013). The one-child policy affected the saving behaviour in two ways: reducing consumption needs for families with children, and removing a substitute for saving for retirement. In China and other Asian countries, children have the obligation to look after their elderly. In rural areas, where government support was not in place until recently, the elderly traditionally relied on their children. However, the movement of the young generation to the cities in search of work and the subsequent changes in social norms have weakened this extended-family arrangement.

Changes in the pension system have also induced higher saving for foresight motives. The pension reforms have led to a reduction in pension replacement income relative to average wages for workers retiring after 1997. This has resulted in rising saving, particularly for older workers, who have less time to adjust to the changes. The workers in state-owned enterprises (SOEs) are lucky as they are covered under the new pension system. However, others (those in private enterprises) receive less and those self-employed and workers without labour contracts do not get any entitlement to pension. These last two categories, accounting for about 60 per cent of total employment in urban areas and composing largely of immigrants, then need to save to enable them to self-insure for old age and to have money to send home to relatives in the countryside.

Healthcare expenditures also present a major source of uncertainty for Chinese. Like the pension system, the healthcare system is also managed locally. Medical insurance is based on local schemes and insured patients can only access healthcare in the area of residency. As a consequence, migrant workers in the city have no coverage. Medical care expenses have increased in recent years affecting both the uninsured and insured. Even for the insured, they still have to pay 45 per cent of their own medical expenses (Cristadoro and Marconi, 2011).

Many Chinese households also save so that they can send their only child abroad for education. Since China opened up in 1978, it is estimated that more than 3.5 million students have gone abroad to study with popular destinations including the USA, UK, Australia, Japan and France. In 2014 alone, 459,800 Chinese students went abroad and 423,000 (92 per cent) were self-funded. Of these, nearly a fifth went to the UK (89,540 students or 19.5 per cent in 2014–15, a 6.8 per cent increase from 2012–13 when 83,790 students went there) (see ICEF Monitor, 2015; UKCISA, n.d.). The cost of an overseas education is estimated at \$165,000–\$330,000. The biggest increase came from lower middle class families. In 2009, students from lower class families made up 2 per cent of students going overseas, but by 2010 the proportion had increased to 34 per cent (*Financial Times*, 2013). The high rate of saving in China, then, has a strong educational element.

Saving in the UK has been declining steadily but plunged in 2012, and, according to OECD data, the current saving rate is negative. The demographic factor is likely to have an influence on the changes in the saving rate because those who reach retirement tend to dis-save rather than save. In the UK, many baby boomers (those born between 1946 and 1964) reached their retirement from 2011 onwards. In 2011, 726,069 people reached their retirement age (169,000 more people than the previous year), and in 2012 720,226 people. It is expected that 600,000 people will retire a year until 2018 and 3.3 million people in the UK will hit their state pension age in five years (The Telegraph, 2012). Miles (1999) projected a fall in the UK national saving rate of 8 percentage points as a consequence of ageing (quoted in Young, 2002). The OECD data seem to support this, as the saving rate in the UK fell from 5.67 per cent in 2010 to −0.22 per cent in 2015 (OECD, 2016). This fall has not been compensated by the accompanying rise in savings among those working.

To achieve long-term financial success, it is generally recommended to save at least 10 per cent of income and the only way to do this is if you *pay yourself first*, that is *save* before *spend*. The average salary in the UK is £26,500 a year. After deducting Income Tax and National Insurance that leaves an individual with net pay of £1,736 per month. If an individual were to save 10 per cent of his/her net pay, i.e. £173 per month and make a return of 10 per cent p.a. over a period of 40 years (a typical career length) his/her investment would have grown to £1,097,860!

Alternatively, you can pay 10 per cent of your gross income as with a pension fund. If you do this, in the UK you will usually receive a contribution from your employer and a contribution from the government in the form of tax relief (see Chapter 10). Let's assume that you earn £26,500 and choose to put 10 per cent into your pension fund. Your gross monthly pay is £2,208 and so 10 per cent is £220. If you contribute £220 into a pension fund, and you qualify for 20 per cent tax relief, you will either pay £44 less in tax or an extra £55 will be added to your pensions scheme, depending on how the tax relief is given. Suppose, under the 'relief at source' system (see Chapter 11, Section 11.2.3) £55 was added so that £275 went into your pension fund every month. Imagine if you invest your contributions for 40 years and the net-of-inflation growth on your investments is 5 per cent per year, your pension fund will be worth **£409,000**.

Now, imagine that your employer also contributes 5 per cent into your pension fund, and so now you have £220 from you, £110 from your employer, £55 from tax relief, giving a total of £385 per month. After 40 years at 5 per cent net-of-inflation investment growth, you could accumulate a pension fund of **£573,000**. Your net pay will decrease to £1,516 per month, a difference of £220 per month, but you will get £385 per month in your pension fund. Though difficult at first, studies show that people do adjust to the new situation and tend to respond to reduced income by cutting their spending. Spending on non-essentials such as luxuries, vacations, eating out and home furnishings are reduced first. Achieving financial security in the long term requires discipline and short-term sacrifice but the peace of mind afforded by knowing that you are on track to achieve your goal makes the effort worthwhile.

5.4 Compound interest

Compound interest is a powerful force in building wealth. When we invest money, we receive interest on the original amount we invest (known as the principal). If we choose to add the interest to the principal (rather than withdraw and spend it), it also earns interest along with the interest paid on the principal. This is known as **compounding**. It is an important concept to understand because it shows the importance of investing early and the power of reinvesting the interest earned. Money subject to compound interest will grow to a large sum over a long period of time. Compound interest is particularly important when it comes to deciding whether to postpone saving; if individuals delay, they may not enjoy the full benefits of this powerful force.

Suppose that you invest £1,000 at 10 per cent interest. At the end of the first year, you will receive £100 interest on your £1,000 investment. If you reinvest the interest, the £100 interest is added to your original investment of £1,000 and so your investment at the start of the second year is now £1,100.

In the second year, the interest on your investment is £110 (10 per cent of £1,100), and you earn £10 more interest because your investment is £100 more than the amount in the first year.

In the third year, your investment will grow to £1,210 and the interest earned is £121. With compounding, the interest earned grows with time – £100 in the first year, £110 in the second year and £121 in the third year. Consequently, the value of your investment grows exponentially with the passage of time. The money value of the increase is not so much in the early years, but is very large in the latter years.

In contrast, if you choose not to reinvest the interest, your original principal will earn *simple* interest of only £100 each year. A £1,000 investment will grow by just £100 each year. After two years, you will have had only £1,200 (compared to £1,210 with annual compounding). However, over a long period of time the differences between simple and compound interest can be enormous. Another simple example can demonstrate this: at 15 per cent simple interest, £100 grows to £550 in 30 years,

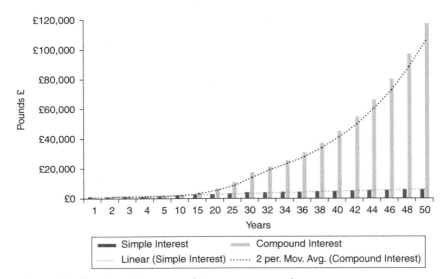

Figure 5.9 Simple and compound interest compared

while at 15 per cent interest compound annually, £100 grows to £6,621 in 30 years, a difference of £6,071.

The frequency of adding interest can affect the amount of interest accrued. Interest can be added more frequently than once a year – it can be monthly, quarterly, semi-annually or annually. This is known as compounding frequency. The greater the frequency, the higher the amount of interest earned. For simplicity, the examples here use nominal interest rates, but when planning over long periods you will need to take inflation into account.

Suppose two banks offer two interest options: bank A pays interest monthly and bank B pays interest annually. With interest added monthly, £1,000 at 10 per cent will give you £104.71 of interest in year 1, while £1,000 at 10 per cent with interest added annually will give you £100 of interest, a difference of £4.71. However, over 30 years this can lead to a huge difference: adding interest monthly grows to £19,837 while adding it annually grows to £17,449, a difference of £2,388.

Compound interest richly rewards those who invest early. The benefit of investing early can be illustrated by the story of twins: Samantha and Lizy. Samantha started work after leaving university at the age of 21 and began investing £1,000 per annum with compound interest of 8 per cent per year. Lizy also left university and started work at the same time, but she failed to set up a saving plan because she liked to party and buy clothes. Samantha stopped saving at age 30 when she left her job to have a baby. She left her savings to grow but did not invest any more. Lizy, on the other hand, started saving £1,000 per year at age 30 earning 8 per cent compound interest per year.

By the age of 65, Samantha has accumulated a bigger pot of savings. Although she has only paid in £10,000 over 10 years, her investment is now worth £231,324 because her investment has had 44–45 years of growth. Although Lizy has paid a total of £35,000 over the 35-year period, her investment is now worth less than Samantha (£186,102) because of the shorter period of investment. The lesson is clear – the sooner you start saving, the better.

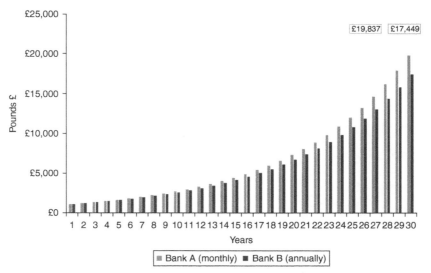

Figure 5.10 Effect of saving monthly or yearly compared (assuming 10% p.a. growth)

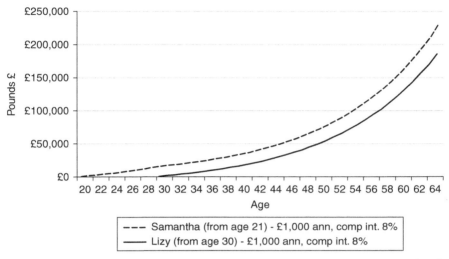

Figure 5.11 The importance of starting to save early (nominal amounts for simplicity)

People often think that investing only makes sense if you have a lot of money to begin with. This is not true and compounding works on any starting sum. Whether it is on a large or small sum, compounding works its magic and gives the same impressive percentage increase.

While compound interest can work miraculously when you save, it can have a ruinous effect when you borrow. For example, if you borrow £1,000 over 30 years at 10 per cent per annum, the total amount you will have to repay is £17,449, which is more than 17 times the original amount borrowed.

Here, it might be worthwhile to distinguish between good and bad debt. People often borrow money to buy property because this is perceived as a good debt as its value is likely to grow over time. Although borrowers will have to repay back more than the amount they owe, they take the risk in the hope that their asset will grow more in value and they can still make a profit. Bad debt, on the other hand, refers to assets whose value depreciates over time (e.g. paying off other debts), and so money borrowed for these purposes will not enable individuals to accumulate wealth.

Compound interest, then, is a double-edged sword: it can help those who invest early to build a significant sum of money over a long period of time, and it will punish those who borrow money for a lengthy period. The lessons are clear: when it comes to saving, save early and leave your money to grow as long as possible. When it comes to borrowing, borrow as little as possible and repay with speed.

5.5 Importance of investing

The third pillar of wealth accumulation is investing, often seen as the engine of financial growth. It is different from saving because its long-term strategy is growth and

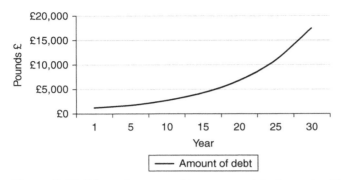

Figure 5.12 Effect of compound interest on debt (assuming 10% p.a. interest)

investing entails potentially higher risks and returns. You will study the principles of investment in Chapter 9. However, next, we consider a particular form of financial planning that can affect savings and debt: insuring risks.

5.6 Conclusion

This chapter has shown the importance of living within your means, so that you can avoid debt, have surplus income to save and invest, and build a financially secure future. To be successful, you need to be committed to the cause and to exercise discipline through budgeting and regular monitoring of your financial affairs. Living within your means will also help you maintain a good credit history – your main source of financial capital when starting out. With discipline, determination, a clear plan and an excellent credit history, you will be able to travel with a greater speed to your destination of financial success.

End of chapter test

1. Give five non-financial benefits of financial independence.
2. Give three reasons for a poor credit score.
3. Why is the controlling of your expenditure so important?
4. Name five ways you can increase your income in your spare time.

Note

1   Many people in the UK will have a lower take-home pay. The average salary is £26,500 per year. After deducting Income Tax and National Insurance contributions, an individual is left with net pay of £1,736 per month.

References

The AA (2016), 'Depreciation: The biggest cost after fuel purchase', available at www.
theaa.com/motoring_advice/car-buyers-guide/cbg_depreciation.html (Accessed
11 June 2016).

Aviva (2015), 'The Aviva Family Finances Report', August, available at https://www.
aviva.com/media/upload/Family_Finances_Final_August_2015.pdf (Accessed 6
June 2016).

Aviva (2016), 'Family debt jumps by 42% to 2½ year high as incomes and saving habits
stall', 13 January, available at www.aviva.com/media/news/item/uk-family-debt-
jumps-by-42-to-212-year-high-as-incomes-and-saving-habits-stall-17578/
(Accessed 18 October 2016).

Bach, D. (2004), *The Automatic Millionaire: A powerful one-step plan to live and finish rich*
(New York: Broadway Books).

Bank of England (2016), 'Credit conditions review: 2016 Q2', Bank of England, available
at www.bankofengland.co.uk/publications/Documents/creditconditionsreview/
2016/ccrq216.pdf (Accessed 31 October 2016).

BBC (2016a), 'Household debt at highest for 5 years', 8 January, available at www.bbc.
co.uk/news/business-35261373 (Accessed 11 June 2016).

BBC (2016b), 'UK new car registrations at all-time high in 2015', 7 January, available
at www.bbc.co.uk/news/business-35249044 (Accessed 11 June 2016).

Browning, M., and Lusardi, A. (1996), 'Household saving: Micro theories and micro
facts', *Journal of Economic Literature*, XXXIV, 1797–1798.

Butler, S. (2015), 'Soaring sales at Aldi and Lidl push market share to 10%', available
at https://www.theguardian.com/business/2015/nov/17/soaring-sales-at-aldi-
and-lidl-drive-market-share-to-10-percent (Accessed 11 June 2016).

Chamon, M., Liu, K. and Prasad, E. (2013), 'Income uncertainty and household savings
in China', *Journal of Development Economics*, 105, 164–177.

China Household Finance Survey (n.d.), 'Expenditure and income', available at www.
chfsdata.org/detail-19–30.html (Accessed 8 June 2016).

The Clergy Journal (2004), 'Maximize good debt and minimize bad debt', *The Clergy
Journal*, September, 80, 9, 23.

Cristadoro, R., and Marconi, D. (2011), 'Households' savings in China', Banca D'Italia
Eurosistema, Temi di discussion (working papers), Number 838, pp.15, 19, 21.

Financial Ombudsman (2014), Service Insight Report, 'Payday lending: Piece of the
picture', available at www.financial-ombudsman.org.uk/publications/policy-
statements/payday_lending_report.pdf (Accessed 11 June 2016).

Financial Times (2013), 'Chinese parents count cost of sending children to overseas
universities', 29 December, available at www.ft.com/cms/s/0/98c4a5ac-63c1-
11e3-b70d-00144feabdc0.html#axzz49BN5AI3B (Accessed 11 June 2016).

Financial Times (2014), 'Can you resist instant gratification for your finances?', 26
September, available at www.ft.com/cms/s/0/8bc0b116-43fe-11e4-8abd-
00144feabdc0.html#axzz48wXco6R4 (Accessed 11 June 2016).

Foster, A.C. (2015), 'Consumer expenditures vary by age', *US Bureau of Labour
Statistics*, 4, 14.

ICEF Monitor (2015), 'Number of Chinese outbound students up by 11 per cent in
2014', 31 March, available at http://monitor.icef.com/2015/03/number-of-chinese-
outbound-students-up-by-11-in-2014/ (Accessed 11 June 2016).

IMF (2012), 'Dealing with household debt', available at https://www.imf.org/external/
pubs/ft/weo/2012/01/pdf/c3.pdf (Accessed 11 June 2016).

Insley, J. (2010), 'Debt problems "impact negatively people's health" ', 21 July, available at www.theguardian.com/money/2010/jul/21/debt-problems-impact-health (Accessed 11 June 2016).

The Institute of Economic Affairs (2015), 'The problem with high household debt and what to do about it,' available at www.iea.org.uk/blog/the-problem-with-high-household-debt-and-what-to-do-about-it (Accessed 11 June 2016).

Intelligent Environments (2016), 'World's first Internet of Things bank, launched by Intelligent Environments, helps you take control of finances', available at www.intelligentenvironments.com/info-centre/intelligent-environments-launches-world-s-first-internet-of-things-bank-today (Accessed 11 June 2016).

Keynes, J.M. (1936), 'The General Theory of Employment, Interest and Money', available at https://ebooks.adelaide.edu.au/k/keynes/john_maynard/ (Accessed 11 June 2016).

Kirsanova, T., and Sefton, J. (2006), 'A comparison of national saving rates in the UK, US and Italy', available at www.niesr.ac.uk/pubs/DPS/dp278.pdf (Accessed 11 June 2016).

Mail Online (2016), 'One-in-three do not save money', 18 May, available at www.dailymail.co.uk/news/article-183718/One-save-money.html (Accessed 11 June 2016).

Miles, D. (1999), 'Modelling the impact of demographic change upon the economy', *Economic Journal*, January, 109, 452, 1–37.

The Money Charity (2015), *Money Statistics*, December, available at http://themoneycharity.org.uk/media/December-2015-Money-Statistics.pdf (Accessed 11 June 2016).

The Money Charity (2016a), *Money Statistics*, June, available at http://themoneycharity.org.uk/money-statistics/june-2016/ (Accessed 31 October 2016).

The Money Charity (2016b), *Money Statistics*, October, available at http://themoneycharity.org.uk/money-statistics/october-2016/ (Accessed 1 November 2016).

OECD (2016), 'Household savings (indicator). doi: 10.1787/cfc6f499-en, available at https://data.oecd.org/hha/household-savings.htm#indicator-chart (Accessed19 December 2016).

Office for National Statistics (2015), 'Household expenditure', available at www.ons.gov.uk/peoplepopulationandcommunity/personalandhouseholdfinances/incomeandwealth/compendium/familyspending/2015/chapter1overview (Accessed 11 June 2016).

Pettinger, T. (2015), 'UK house price to income ratio and affordability', available at www.economicshelp.org/blog/5568/housing/uk-house-price-affordability/ (Accessed 11 June 2016).

Pitas, C. (2013), 'Intimidating debt collectors push Britons to suicide', 23 January, available at http://uk.reuters.com/article/uk-debt-suicides-idUKLNE90M00120130123 (Accessed 11 June 2016).

Pompian, M. (2012), *Behavioural Finance and Wealth Management: How to build optimal portfolios that account for investor biases* (Hoboken, NJ: Wiley).

Sheffield, H. (2016), 'More than 40% of young people use payday loans or pawnshops', 8 January, available at www.independent.co.uk/news/business/news/more-than-40-of-yoing-people-millennials-use-payday-loans-or-pawnshops-a6802206.html (Accessed 11 June 2016).

Shipman, L. (2007), 'Good debt vs bad debt', *RN*, 70, 11, 57–58.

Shoda, Y., Mischel, W. and Peake, P.K. (1990), 'Predicting adolescent cognitive and self-regulatory competencies from preschool delay of gratification: Identifying diagnostic conditions', *Developmental Psychology*, 26, 6, 978–986. Also available at www.webcitation.org/62C0yfhcJ.

Strauss, R. (2016), 'Household debt binge hits pre-crisis levels as Britons go mad for new cars and cheap loans, Bank of England warns', available at www.thisismoney.co.uk/money/cardsloans/article-3539847/Household-debt-binge-hits-pre-crisis-levels-says-Bank-England.html (Accessed 11 June 2016).

The Telegraph (2012), 'Record numbers reach retirement age as baby boomers reach 65', 25 September, available at www.telegraph.co.uk/finance/personalfinance/pensions/9563647/Record-numbers-reach-retirement-age-as-baby-boomers-turn-65.html (Accessed 11 June 2016).

The Telegraph (2015), 'Average British family to spend £800 on Christmas: Charity research suggests families are under pressure to overspend', 8 December, available at www.telegraph.co.uk/finance/personalfinance/household-bills/12038620/Average-British-family-to-spend-800-on-Christmas.html (Accessed 11 June 2016).

UKCISA (n.d.), 'International student statistics: UK higher education', available at www.ukcisa.org.uk/.

Walker, C., Cunningham, L., Hanna, P. and Ambrose, P. (2012), 'Responsible individuals and irresponsible institutions? A report into Mental Health and the UK credit industry', University of Brighton, December, p.5, available at https://www.brighton.ac.uk/_pdf/research/ssparc/debt-and-mental-health-report.pdf (Accessed 11 June 2016).

Which? (2012), 'Christmas on credit – blown out finances or under control?', available at https://conversation.which.co.uk/money/christmas-debt-2012-credit-cards-spending-presents-festive-food/ (Accessed 11 June 2016).

Young, G. (2002), 'The implications of an ageing population for the UK economy', Bank of England report, p.14, available at www.bankofengland.co.uk/archive/Documents/historicpubs/workingpapers/2002/wp159.pdf (Accessed 15 May 2016).

Chapter 6

Insuring risks

Lien Luu

❖ CONTENTS

Many people see insurance as a waste of money. This chapter proposes a new way of looking at insurance: as a means of wealth preservation. It examines the importance of human capital, the risks we face, and the ways to mitigate these risks.

This chapter will explore the range of insurance/assurance products and schemes now available, and consider how such policies can be used as possible investment and wealth preservation vehicles.

Learning outcomes

By the end of this chapter you will:

- understand the different types of risks individuals face;
- be able to understand the difference between human and financial capital;
- understand different types of products to mitigate risks;
- become aware of how behavioural traits can hinder risk management.

6.1 The importance of protection

Many people believe that they only need to consider protection once they have built assets. This is a misconception. Protection, in fact, is the foundation of wealth accumulation. We need to protect not only our assets but, more importantly, our human capital and our loved ones from misfortunes. The pyramid below shows an approach to financial priorities within a four-stage model of financial planning. By providing peace of mind and financial security, protection is a building block of a financial plan.

Figure 6.1 Financial planning pyramid
Source: adapted from financialguide101.com.

6.1.1 Human capital versus financial capital

Human capital is arguably the most important irreplaceable asset that needs protection. Economists define this simply as the **present value** of lifetime earnings. With more years to earn a living, human capital therefore peaks in the early years and diminishes over time. From this point of view, protection need is highest in early years. Financial capital, on the other hand, moves in the opposite direction and rises over time, as human capital is assumed to transform into financial capital through savings and investments as you can see in Figure 6.2.

Available data shows that many people do not protect their most important asset – their human capital. In the UK (see Figure 6.3), for example, a high proportion of households buy contents, buildings and motor insurance, and a much lower proportion buy income protection and life insurance (including both term and whole of life). Many households buy buildings and motor insurance partly because this is compulsory in the UK. Mortgage lenders insist on buildings insurance (and contents insurance is often bought together with buildings insurance), while the government requires all drivers to take out car insurance.

Yet, individuals face many personal risks that could affect their ability to earn money, or their human capital, leading to the loss or reduction of income, extra expenses, and the depletion of financial resources. There are three major personal risks that individuals face:

- risk of premature death;
- risk of poor health;
- risk of unemployment.

As Figure 6.3 also shows, few households have a personal pension. Individuals in the UK thus face another risk – insufficient income in retirement.

Different risks have different levels of financial impact and frequency (see Figure 6.4). Some risks have low frequency and low impact (kettles or toasters breaking down during their guarantee period), others have high frequency and low impact

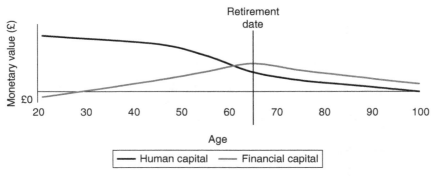

Figure 6.2 Human and financial capital over lifetime (£)

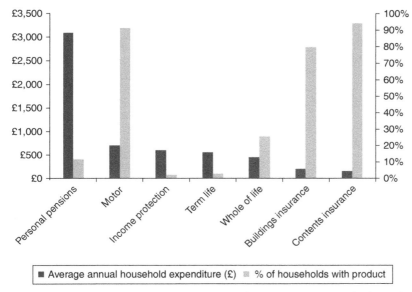

Figure 6.3 Types of insurance purchased and annual expenditure by households in the UK, 2013
Source: ABI (2015).

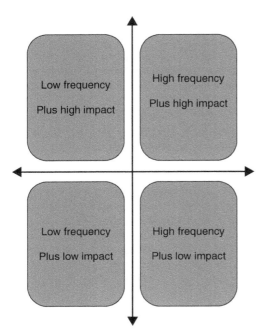

Figure 6.4 Frequency and impact matrix
Source: Chartered Institute of Insurance (CII) (2015).

(losing your umbrella). Other risks have low frequency but high impact (house burnt down), and high frequency and high impact (unemployment, reaching retirement with inadequate income). Insurance has an effective role to play in the low frequency and high impact risks.

There are three possible ways to deal with these risks: ignore, reduce or eliminate, and self-insure (Callaghan et al., 2012). Ignoring these risks can have devastating financial consequences and so the real choice is between risk reduction/elimination through buying insurance and self-insurance. The chapter will now examine the importance of human capital, each of these risks in turn and compare different mitigation strategies.

6.1.2 Importance of human capital

Human capital represents the most valuable and invisible asset. The Office for National Statistics defines it as a measure of an individual's skills, knowledge, abilities, social attributes, personality and health attributes, and is valued in monetary terms as the total potential future earnings. As a measure of earning, human capital takes many different forms: earnings derive from employment or self-employment, and income from owning a business or running a business as a manager or executive. Human capital can be distinguished from traditional financial assets because it is illiquid. Future earnings cannot normally be sold for immediate consumption, but can only be realised over time. Second, earnings from employment or business are often tied to the fortunes of a sector or industry. Third, unlike explicit assets such as financial capital and property, the value of human capital (or implied assets) is much more difficult to quantify. Estimating the value of human capital is fraught with difficulties, as this involves identifying not only our current salary, but also making key assumptions about future education, training and earnings growth, the period of earnings, and the volatility of future cash flows. The growth rate used is critical in determining the value of human capital. For a teacher, the growth of human capital may follow a *bond-like* pattern, while for an investment banker it is more like volatile stock (Johnson and Horan, 2013).

For most individual investors, human capital is believed to dwarf financial capital. In the United States, for example, it represents 90 per cent of total assets (including home equity and private businesses) for investors under the age of 30.

Over time with career progression, human capital is transformed into financial capital through savings. Even for investors in their 50s, it is thought that human capital still represents at least half of their total wealth. Human capital decreases when we reach 60 years old and so it is imperative that we have other capital to compensate for this.

In the UK, the value of employed human capital was estimated at £18.22 trillion in 2014, while the value of the UK's full human capital stock (including the unemployed) was £18.95 trillion. By 2015, the value of employed human capital had increased to £19.23 trillion and the value of the UK's full human capital stock to £19.90 trillion. The value of human capital is much higher than the value of financial capital in the UK (estimated at £11.1 trillion, see Chapter 1).

In the UK, the average employed human capital stock per head of working age population was £448,358 in 2014. By 2015, the average employed human capital stock per head had increased by 3.9 per cent to £471,000 (see Figure 6.7).

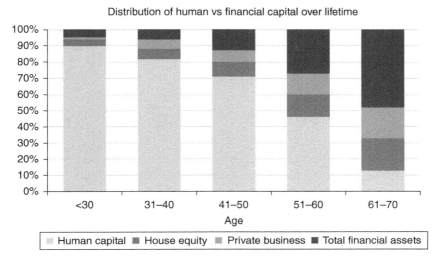

Figure 6.5 Magnitude of human capital
Source: adapted from Johnson and Horan (2013).

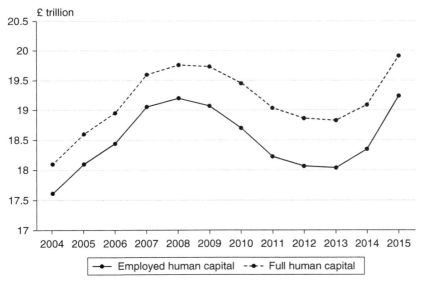

Figure 6.6 Human capital in the UK, 2004–2015
Source: Office for National Statistics (2015).

Figure 6.8 shows that the stock of human capital is disproportionately concentrated in younger workers. For example, 41.3 per cent of the working age population are aged between 16 and 35 but this group accounts for 65.8 per cent of the human capital stock. For example, a 25 year old who earns £30,000 a year and plans to retire

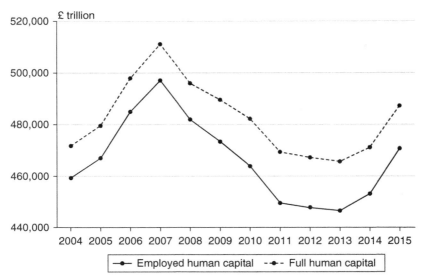

Figure 6.7 Human capital per head
Source: Office for National Statistics (2015).

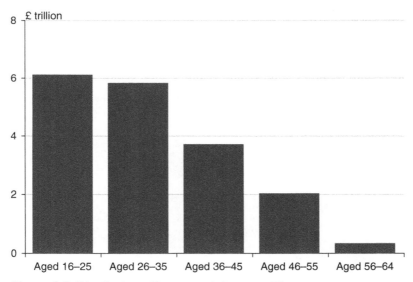

Figure 6.8 Distribution of human capital among different age groups
Source: Office for National Statistics (2015).

at the age of 65 has the earning potential of £1.2 million (without earnings growth), while a 50 year old who also earns £30,000 and plans to retire at 65 has the earning potential of £450,000.This indicates that being relatively young and having more years of paid employment more than offsets the effect of having higher earnings but being older and having fewer years to work. Despite the common perception, this also confirms that the young, not the old, have the greatest protection need.

6.2 Risk of premature death

The greatest threat to human capital is premature death, defined as the death of a breadwinner with financial obligations, normally before the age of 75. These obligations include the need to support dependants, pay the mortgage and maintain school fees. The death of the breadwinner can create financial difficulties for the surviving family members if they do not have financial resources to replace the lost income or their replacement income is lower than what they have been used to.

Though rare, there are many causes of premature death. Recent research shows that poor diet is the biggest contributory factor to premature death around the globe. Smoking cigarettes is still one of the highest risk factors of premature death in the UK, followed by high blood pressure and obesity. But the Institute of Health Metrics and Evaluation (IHME), based in the USA, finds that a combination of dietary factors (eating too few fruits and vegetables, nuts and whole grains, too much sodium and cholesterol) is inflicting high casualties in the UK and across the globe.

The IHME's study found that the biggest contributor to early death globally is high blood pressure. They argue that, although this is influenced by age and family history, other factors such as obesity, smoking, excessive salt consumption, lack of exercise and drinking large amounts of alcohol also play a large part. The study looked at 14 dietary risk factors and concluded that cumulatively, unhealthy eating (including diets low in fruit, whole grains and vegetables, and diets high in red meat and sugar-sweetened beverages) contributed to more deaths than any other factor, causing ischemic heart disease, stroke and diabetes (IHME, 2016).

In the UK, a government report, *Living Well for Longer*, blames the top five killers for more than 150,000 deaths a year among under 75s in England, and the Department of Health estimates that two-thirds (100,000) are avoidable. This is because many of these premature deaths are believed to result from an unhealthy lifestyle: smoking, drinking too much alcohol, poor diet, lack of physical activity and being overweight. Leading a healthier life, then, can increase our life expectancy.

Table 6.1 Risks associated with the highest number of deaths, 2013

Risk rating	Global health risk rating	UK health risk rating
1	High blood pressure	Smoking
2	Smoking	High blood pressure
3	High body mass index	High body mass index
4	Diabetes	High total cholesterol
5	Diet high in salt	Low physical activity
6	Diet low in fruits	Diet low in fruits
7	Ambient air pollution	Diabetes
8	Household air pollution	Kidney diseases
9	High cholesterol	Alcohol use
10	Alcohol use	Diet low in vegetables

Source: IHME (2016).

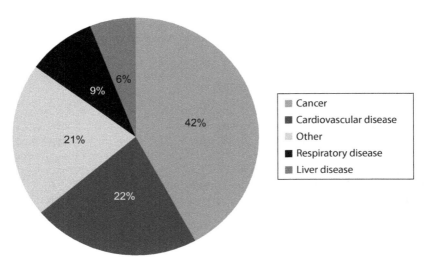

Figure 6.9 Major diseases in the UK
Source: Department of Health (2014).

Premature death can have significant financial impact on survivors. First, the human life value of the breadwinner is lost forever. This loss can be substantial. Imagine someone who earns £30,000 a year with no financial assets and dies at the age of 25; that is a loss of more than £1.2 million assuming that salary keeps pace with inflation (100 per cent of total wealth), assuming the same salary for the next 40 years. In reality, the loss is greater as salary usually rises faster over time. Imagine another example: a 35-year-old person earning £40,000 per year and having financial assets worth £50,000. If we combine that person's financial capital with human capital, the true net worth is £1.25 million. Without life insurance, a person's total wealth is not protected and in this example the family would lose 96 per cent of the total wealth in the event of death (Gordon and Leahy, 2010).

Second, additional expenses may be incurred because of funeral expenses, probate and estate settlement costs, and inheritance taxes for larger estates. According to a report by Royal London, the average cost of a basic funeral in the UK in 2015 was £3,700. The cost rises to £6,000 if extra expenses such as flowers, a reception and a headstone are included. Many people cannot afford the cost. Those on low income can apply to the government's Social Fund Funeral Payment to help meet the cost of a funeral. In 2014, 32,000 people received payments costing the taxpayers £44 million (BBC, 2015).

Third, some families might struggle to make ends meet due to insufficient income. Some may even lose their homes if they cannot afford to pay mortgage payments. Finally, certain non-economic costs are also incurred, such as emotional grief, loss of a role model and absence of a partner to bring up children.

The financial impact of premature death can be mitigated in two ways – self-insure through precautionary saving or take out life insurance. The main benefit of taking up an insurance policy is the immediate access to capital value (i.e. the sum assured). This is a clear advantage over precautionary saving which requires time to build up the required savings/capital, and exposes individuals to insufficient funds in

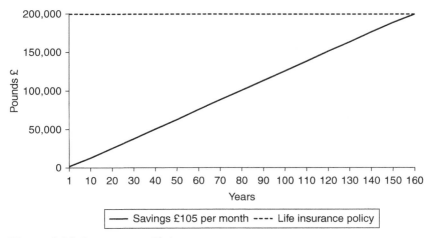

Figure 6.10 Saving versus life insurance

the meantime (Diacon and Mahdzan, 2008). Let's assume that the individual takes out a life insurance policy with a sum assured of £200,000. In the event of death, the family would receive a payment of £200,000. Imagine that the individual decides to go for precautionary saving; it would take 20 years to build up a sum of £200,000, requiring a saving of £10,000 per year or £833 per month, an unrealistic sum for many. In the UK, households save on average £105 per month and so it would take 160 years to save £200,000, as illustrated in Figure 6.10.

Self-insuring through precautionary saving, however, does have its advantages. First, the risks to be covered do not need to be specified in a formal contract. Insurance only covers risks defined in the insurance contract. Second, there might be high costs involved in getting insurance policies as individuals might need several to cover different types of risks, whereas the costs for precautionary saving are quite low. One saving account might be sufficient. Third, unused precautionary savings can be used for alternative consumption or for any purpose if the risk decreases, whereas any unused premiums are usually lost (Diacon and Mahdzan, 2008).

The process of taking out a life insurance policy is also much more complex than precautionary saving and requires many decisions at the start of the policy. There are many issues to consider: who needs to be insured; how much cover; how long is the term; what type of policy – level, decreasing or increasing term; whole of life or term insurance; should the policy be single or joint; and which insurance provider. The most

Figure 6.11 Factors to take into account in life insurance purchase

important decision is deciding how much cover to buy and for how long. This will depend on several needs:

- **Capital needs**: this is the amount needed to pay off any mortgage and any other loans, set up an emergency fund, legacies and any inheritance tax liability.
- **Short-term capital needs**: this is the amount needed to take care of costs such as funeral expenses.
- **Income needs**: this is the amount required to replace the loss of income and may include the provision for income to support the children's education and upbringing, and income required to support a dependent relative or a partner. This is an important consideration because without an income, surviving family members may live in impoverishment. The insurance industry uses the widow story to illustrate the problem. A widow received a life insurance policy payout to pay off the mortgage but was forced to sell her home as she had no source of income.

Experts believe that families should insure a lump sum amount worth between five and ten times someone's annual salary. For example, for someone with a salary of £20,000, a £200,000 life insurance is recommended. In the USA, the recommended amount is higher. US households are believed to need $800,000 to maintain the living standards of survivors (Schanz and Wang, 2014).

There is a big life insurance gap in the UK. The ABI (2015) report shows that people buy two main types of life insurance in the UK – term insurance or whole of life. A term insurance contract provides coverage for a limited period, normally set up to age 65, and benefits are paid only if death occurs in this period. For this reason, term insurance is relatively cheap because it provides pure insurance coverage and nothing is paid in the event of survival. In addition, the chances of death before 65 are low. Few households in the UK have a term life insurance policy. In 2013, for example, only 0.6 million households (or 2.2 per cent) of the total 26.7 million households had one (ABI, 2015).

A higher proportion of households in the UK buy whole of life insurance (approximately 23 per cent). This is more expensive than term life insurance because there are two elements to the policy: investment and insurance. The policy has no expiry date, and the policy pays out whenever death occurs. As the policy has an investment element, it might have a value when the policyholder decides to cancel the policy. Term life insurance, however, has no cash in value if the policy is cancelled. A whole of life policy is often taken out to cover an anticipated inheritance tax. In addition, 3.2 million UK households have life insurance dedicated to paying off their mortgage on death.

Many employers in the UK offer life insurance as part of employee benefits and this may partly explain why many households do not buy a personal policy. It is estimated that 9.4 million employees have a death-in-service benefit. However, it is estimated that in the UK, one in four breadwinners (or 8.5 million adults with dependants) do not have life insurance. Just 45 per cent of male and 38 per cent of female breadwinners have cover (Rutt, 2016). This is compared with over 80 per cent of households in Japan who have a life insurance policy (Obara and Inakura, n.d.).

The life insurance gap, in the UK and globally, is huge. Swiss Re estimated the global life insurance gap to be $86 trillion, or 116 per cent of the world's GDP, in 2013 (Schanz and Wang, 2014). For the UK, Swiss Re estimated that the gap was £2.3 trillion in 2006. It appears that £4.2 trillion worth of cover was needed to cover the expenses of all UK families (including any ongoing mortgage payments and basic family expenses), but only £1.8 trillion protection cover was in place. By 2011, the protection gap in the UK had risen to about $4 trillion, or £2.6 trillion (Schanz and Wang, 2014). Experts believe that the low uptake of life insurance is due to the fact that many families see it as an additional and unnecessary expense (The Telegraph, 2005).

❖ CASE STUDIES 6.1, 6.2 AND 6.3

- A 38-year-old woman died from breast cancer. Unfortunately she did not have life insurance as it was thought she did not need a life insurance policy as she was a housewife. She used to stay at home looking after her 2-year-old child. Her death meant that her husband now had to find someone to take care of their son.
- A 50-year-old man died in a car crash. Luckily, he had a life insurance policy for £200,000. His widow received a payout, enabling her to buy a house in a better area. They had four children. Working part-time as a nurse earning £20,000 a year, she found it difficult to support the children.
- A self-employed gardener died leaving his wife and three boys. They only had a life insurance policy of £100,000 but the mortgage was £500,000. The widow was forced to sell her home, as she was unable to support the mortgage.

In the USA, the life insurance gap is also massive, estimated at $15.3 trillion as many Americans also do not have life insurance (Dahl et al., 2013). According to research, the most common reason given is that they have competing financial priorities. The second most common reason is that they think they can't afford it. Yet, it is reported that 70 per cent of US households with children under 18 would have trouble meeting everyday living expenses within a few months if a primary wage earner were to die today. Four in ten households with children under 18 say they would immediately have trouble meeting everyday living expenses.

The massive life insurance gap has prompted much academic interest in the factors that affect the demand for life insurance. In an article on the determinants of demand for life insurance in European countries in 2009, four social and economic variables have been identified: income, education, population and inflation. Studies show that there is a significant and positive relationship between level of income and demand for life insurance. When household income goes up, we can expect the demand for life insurance to go up. A recent study of life insurance in the USA during the recession 2007–2009 shows that the demand for life insurance decreased due to a deterioration in household financial status and increases in unemployment (Peaslee, 2014). Education is also positively related to the demand for life insurance. If education is high, people are aware of types of life insurance and seek to protect themselves and their dependants by using them. Population also has a positive impact on the demand for insurance. As population increases, we would expect the demand for life insurance to increase too. Inflation, however, is negatively related to demand for life insurance. When inflation rises, the demand for life insurance falls. In a study of demand for life insurance in China, the author argues that besides personal disposable income, inflation, education level and the level of population, there are other factors affecting demand including dependency ratio, death rate, social security benefits, and price of life insurance as well as interest rates (Celik and Kayali, 2009).

Another research shows that the demand for life insurance is influenced by the wife's human capital. It is argued that households often purchase life insurance on the husband on the assumption that the wife will face financial difficulties if the husband dies before retirement. However, if the wife possesses high human capital allowing her to enter the labour market, there may be no need for life cover and it is believed that she might discourage the purchase of insurance on the husband (Goldsmith, 1983). These factors probably contribute to the short-term fluctuations in demand for life insurance but there are also fundamental behavioural factors. These will be examined later in Section 6.7.

6.3 Risk of poor health

Poor health is another major risk individuals face. Illness or accident can result in taking time off work, leading to a loss of earnings and financial problems. In some countries such as the USA, poor health results not only in a loss of earned income but also high medical bills. It is generally accepted that the risk of being off work due to illness or accident is much higher than death. In the UK, for every individual of working age who dies, it is believed that 14 have been off work for more than six months. There is also the risk of a critical illness, which is life-threatening and full recovery may not be possible. This includes heart attacks, strokes and cancer. A study by Macmillan Cancer Support shows that there were an estimated 2.5 million people in 2015 living in the UK with cancer, and the number is expected to rise to 4 million by 2030 (Macmillan, 2015).

Figure 6.12 gives a simple illustration to demonstrate the impact of disability on lifestyle. With the advent of disability/illness, income drops drastically while expenses rise, resulting in a growing debt. In the UK, there are some state benefits but there is still a gap between the amount received in benefits and expenditure. A private insurance policy (e.g. income protection) narrows the gap between income and expenditure.

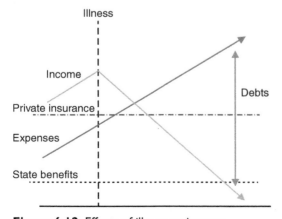

Figure 6.12 Effects of illness on income

A report by PCW (2015) shows that each year one million workers suddenly find themselves unable to work due to serious illness or injury. The same report estimates that 10.8 million households – more than 60 per cent of working families – would experience a drop in income by more than one-third if the main earner had to stop work due to ill health, and they have no insurance to give them a financial safety net if this happens. Forty per cent of working families would see their income fall by more than half without insurance to provide a safety net. Despite these facts, millions of UK households relying on income from employment have not put in place an adequate safety net (All Party Parliamentary Group, 2015).

A survey by Aviva in 2011 showed that over half (58 per cent) of employees worried whether their family or themselves would be able to survive financially if they went on long-term sick leave. One in five (21 per cent) would be concerned about paying their mortgage (Barton, 2011).

This is not surprising as savings are low in the UK. A survey by the Money Advice Service has found that four in ten adults in the UK do not have £500 or more in savings. Another by ING bank suggests 28 per cent of UK adults have nothing at all in the bank (BBC, 2016). Among those who do save, according to Halifax, the average amount people had stored away was £5,582. People between the ages of 35 and 54 have on average £8,138, while over-65s have more than twice this amount with almost £18,000 set aside (The Children's Mutual, 2016).

Saving rate in the UK is much lower than elsewhere. According to Lloyds TSB, a typical British household in 2012 had £5,000 in savings and investments and saved 7 per cent of their disposable income. This compared to over £19,000 in China, where the saving rate was estimated at 47 per cent. The bank believes that the absence of a 'social safety net' in China, such as state pensions and benefits, means that families must provide for themselves financially' (Hall, 2012). Although the OECD's data shows a lower saving rate (38 per cent for China and 2.68 per cent for the UK in 2012), it is indisputable that China has one of the highest saving rates in the world (OECD, 2016).

In the UK, the provision of the welfare state provides a cushion. The NHS provides free at the point of use healthcare and individuals between the ages of 16 and 64 suffering from disability can claim benefits (such as Personal Independence Allowance payment in 2015–16 and Employment Support Allowance (ESA)) to live on – although the amounts are low. Individuals with disability might be able to claim up to £239.75 per week or £1,038 per month in 2016–17. However, surveys show the average UK household spending per week is £517 or £2,240 per month (ONS, 2015). Even if individuals can claim the maximum amount available for those who suffer disability, the amount is less than half the amount needed. There is likely to be a shortfall between what they need and what they receive.

The financial impact of poor health can be mitigated through precautionary saving or a suitable insurance policy. Again, precautionary saving is much more flexible than an insurance policy. However, the risk of poverty or depletion of wealth is high when the illness is prolonged and the individual is unable to work again. In addition, given the low saving rates in the UK, many households do not have a sufficient buffer. An insurance policy might be a more suitable option.

In the UK, there are three different types of insurance. First, there is a short-term policy, known as Accident and Sickness, providing cover for up to two years. The benefit is normally a fixed sum not related to earnings. Second, there is a critical illness policy, paying a lump sum or an income. This can be combined with life insurance or stand-alone. A critical illness policy often requires 30 days' survival before payout. Death before 30 days often results in non-payment. It is therefore often recommended to combine critical illness with life insurance.

❖ CASE STUDIES 6.4 AND 6.5

- A man in his late 40s suffered a heart attack and survived. He had a critical illness policy and received a lump sum. This enabled him to pay off the mortgage and allowed him to take a less stressful job after his recovery. He thought critical illness insurance was the best thing he had.
- A 50-year-old man suffered a stroke. Although he recovered, he lost his speech and is now taking speech therapy. He worked for a small firm and unfortunately did not have critical illness cover or income protection. Luckily, his wife earned a good salary.

Third, there is income protection or permanent health insurance. Income protection is designed to provide cover for long-term disability as it provides payment until the insured gets better or retires. Potentially, cover is provided for a period of more than 45 years. Income protection insurance allows the insured to protect a large percentage of their income – up to 75 per cent – which is paid out tax-free. Income protection is good for high earners as it provides cover based on *income*, rather than *expenses*. (Some other insurances, such as mortgage payment protection, for example, only pay for the costs of the mortgage and bills, and not living costs.)

Yet, the purchase of income protection is very low. In 2013, only 2–3 per cent of UK households bought an income protection policy (ABI, 2015). A lack of awareness as a result of the distribution channel may explain this. Banks do not sell income protection, but instead sell payment protection policies. The other possible reason is that some employers provide this benefit. It is estimated that 2.6 million are members of group income protection and group critical illness schemes. Swiss Re estimated that in 2005 the income protection gap in the UK amounted to £175 billion of annual benefit (Diacon and Mahdzan, 2008). The gap is likely to be much bigger now. It is also possible that the low take-up of income protection is due to the complexity of the product and the fact that the premium can be too high for the people most in need, such as those in poor health (Callaghan et al., 2012).

ACTIVITY 6.1

Read the following case study and discuss the types of insurance he could have purchased to help him deal with the financial consequences of disability.

Case study: A young trainee accountant aged 22 years old was looking for a property to move in with his girlfriend. One day returning from work, he crossed the road and was hit by a truck, leaving him paralysed. His life changed irrevocably. His mum had to leave her job to stay at home and look after him.

In countries such as the USA, there is no free healthcare. Individuals need to have private healthcare. However, it is estimated that 20 million people have no health insurance, and that in 2012 80 million people in the USA (around a quarter of the population) reported that, during the past year, they did not go to the doctor when sick or did not fill a prescription because of cost (O'Hara, 2015). Although some can claim some benefits to help them cope, it is well known that ill health can bring severe financial difficulties and even bankruptcy in the USA.

Ill health then brings two potential problems: payment of medical bills, and the loss of earnings due to the inability to work. In the UK, it is possible to insure both of these risks. A private medical insurance policy will enable individuals to access private healthcare in times of need. Although the NHS provides free at the point of use healthcare, there might be a long waiting period for treatment and the quality might not be as good as private care (e.g. individuals do not get a private room). People in the UK therefore buy private medical insurance to enable them to access better quality and faster service. In the UK, a small proportion of the population (5.1 million people) has private healthcare insurance (ABI, 2015).

6.4 Risk of unemployment

Loss of employment poses another threat to financial security. Unemployment can result from business cycle downturns, seasonal factors, structural and technological changes in the economy as well as imperfections in the labour market.

Prolonged unemployment can cause financial difficulties in a number of ways. First, individuals lose their earned income and benefits associated with their employment. They may lose their car if that has been provided by work. Second, they may apply only for part-time jobs due to the economic climate. Third, savings may be depleted as individuals dip into these to fund lifestyle. Unemployment can exert a heavy toll on the individuals, sapping their self-confidence, self-esteem and straining relationships (Rejda, 2011).

Figure 6.13 shows unemployment in the UK between 1971 and 2016. Unemployment peaked in the early 1980s, dipped in 1990 but rose again in 1993. Since 2000, unemployment fluctuated between 5 and 8 per cent. In 2015, the unemployment rate fell to 5 per cent.

Figure 6.13 masks the age dimension of unemployment. Those aged between 16 and 24 experience a much higher rate of unemployment.

As can be seen in Figure 6.14, the lowest rate for youth unemployment is nearly 12 per cent, and the highest is nearly 23 per cent in 2011. In 2015, when the national average of unemployment was 5 per cent, youth unemployment stood at around 14 per cent. Between November 2015 and January 2016, 630,000 young people aged 16–24 were unemployed, giving an unemployment rate of 13.7 per cent (Delebarre, 2016), in comparison to 3.9 per cent unemployment rate among graduates in 2015.

Youth unemployment in the UK pales in comparison to other European countries. Greece and Spain, for example, have a staggering youth unemployment rate of more than 48 per cent and 46 per cent, respectively – see Table 6.2. Germany has the lowest youth unemployment in Europe – 7 per cent – thanks to its high emphasis on high quality vocational courses, apprenticeships and links with industry (The Economist, 2013). However, with more than a million unemployed in 2011, the UK is believed to have the

BUILD A SECURE FOUNDATION

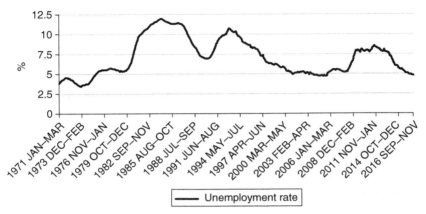

Figure 6.13 Unemployment rate in the UK, 1971 to 2016
Source: Office for National Statistics (2016).

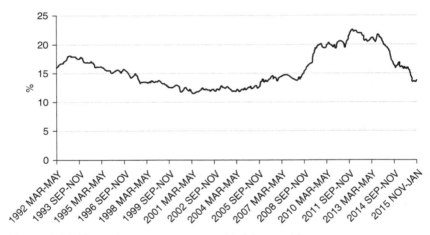

Figure 6.14 Unemployment rate among 16–24 year olds
Source: Office for National Statistics (2014).

largest absolute number of unemployed young people of all EU member states. Young people in the UK find it harder to compete with older and more experienced workers than other countries. A young person in the UK is currently more than three and a half times more likely to be unemployed than an 'adult' (i.e. someone aged over 25). This is a relatively high ratio when compared to other European countries, such as Greece, Ireland, Spain and Portugal, where young people are about two and a half times more likely to be unemployed than adult workers. In Germany, a young person is only one and a half times more likely to be unemployed than an adult worker.

Table 6.2 Youth unemployment rate in the EU as of December 2015

European countries	% youth unemployment	European countries	% youth unemployment
Greece	48.6	Great Britain	13.5
Spain	46	Netherlands	11.2
Italy	37.9	Austria	11.2
Portugal	31	Denmark	10.3
France	25.9	Germany	7
Belgium	22.7		
Euro area	22		
EU	19.7		
Ireland	19.2		
Sweden	18.8		
Luxembourg	0.147		

Source: www.statista.com (2015).

Youth unemployment is a massive, global problem. The International Labour Organisation estimates that there are 75 million 15–24 year olds looking for work across the globe. However, this figure does not include a large number of young people who do not participate in the labour market at all. Among 34 members of the OECD, it is estimated that there are 26 million youths not in education, employment or training (known as NEETs). The World Bank estimates that there are 262 million such youths in developing countries. Add these together, there are as many as 290 million 15–24 years old not participating in the labour market – almost a quarter of the world's youth (The Economist, 2013).

Research shows that young people with low or no qualifications make up a high proportion (39 per cent) of all young people unemployed and not in education. Even before the post-global-financial-crisis recession began, across the OECD, young people with low or no skills were three times more likely to be unemployed than those with higher skills (BIS Research Paper, 2013).

Traditionally, youth unemployment in the UK is blamed on several factors: skill deficiencies, a lack of work ethic among young people and the failure of the education system to produce 'job-ready' young workers. However, it is now increasingly recognised that young people face a tough job market and there is a lack of support during the transition from school to work. A recent study argues that the key lesson from countries with low rates of youth unemployment is the need to develop strong transition systems, including high quality initial vocational education and training that brings real opportunities in the labour market. It concludes that resources should be focused on increasing the number of diverse and high quality vocational education and training programmes, and on encouraging more employers to provide work experience and training, preferably as part of formal college-based vocational programmes (Lanning and Rudiger, n.d.).

The risk of unemployment can be mitigated by insurance. Unemployment insurance provides individuals with protection for a period of up to two years. However, this is not designed to deal with youth unemployment. For the young, the best insurance against unemployment is probably qualifications and skills, as those with higher qualifications earn more and face a lower risk of unemployment (BIS Research Paper, 2013).

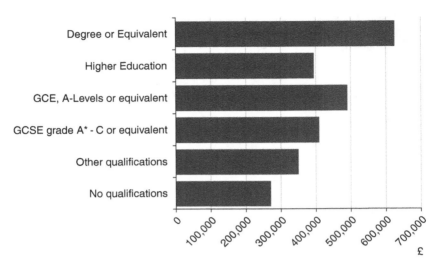

Figure 6.15 Qualifications and human capital
Source: Office for National Statistics (2014).

Figure 6.15 shows the link between qualifications and human capital. In 2015, those with a degree or equivalent had human capital valued at £628,000, £136,000 more than those with GCE A-Levels or equivalent (£492,000 per head). Those with no qualifications had a human capital of £274,000.

In 2015 graduates typically earned £31,200 per year, while non-graduates were paid £22,100, a gap of £9,100. The employment rate of graduates is also much higher – some 87.5 per cent of working-age graduates were employed compared with 69.3 per cent for non-graduates. However, many argue that the prospects for graduates are worsening. Although they have a higher rate of employment, many are saddled with student debt and are doing a non-graduate job, taking on lower skilled and lower paid jobs, and in the process pushing those without a degree out of the job market (Burns, 2015). Youth unemployment, then, could result from a displacement effect, as graduates take on non-graduate jobs and push those without formal qualifications out of the job market.

6.5 Other types of insurance

Besides life insurance and health insurance, many people also buy other types of insurance to protect themselves against a spike in expenditure. These include:

- **Boiler insurance**: a boiler can be costly to replace and repair and so with an insurance policy in place, households have peace of mind that they are covered in the event of a breakdown.
- **Holiday/travel insurance**: people on holiday can face unexpected medical expenses if they fall ill while on holiday abroad. This insurance can help ensure that they have access to medical care without worrying about the costs.

- **Liability insurance**: professional liability insurance provides protection against negligence claims arising from mistakes or failure to perform. Doctors, dentists and surgeons, for example, need liability insurance in the event of a claim from patients for negligence. Financial advisers also need liability insurance in the event of a claim for unsuitable advice.
- **Business insurances**: businesses need to buy employer liability insurance to protect against claims from employees who get injured, sick or die as a result of their work. If a business sells products, it also needs to buy product liability insurance to deal with lawsuits for damages from its products.
- **Legal costs insurance**: the cost of taking legal action (e.g. unfair dismissal at work, claim compensation, disputes) can be expensive and this insurance can help meet the cost of a claim.

6.6 Risk of inadequate retirement income

While the young confront difficulties in entering the job market, those reaching retirement face a major risk of insufficient income in retirement. The vast majority of workers in the West retire at 65 or older and when they retire, they will lose their earned income. Retirees will face financial impoverishment if they do not have financial assets or have access to other sources of income.

The life cycle theory of saving stipulates that, in a rational world, individuals save when they are working. When retirement sets in, individuals will use their savings to fund lifestyle in retirement.

The reality is quite different. It is accepted that there is a retirement crisis in the UK, as individuals have insufficient savings to fund their increasing period of time in retirement. Research by True Potential shows that savers are only saving a fifth of the amount they need to secure a comfortable retirement. Their data from over 12,000 pension savers shows that the majority of people believe that an annual income of £23,457 is the minimum required to fund a comfortable retirement. To produce this income, savers need a pot of £469,140 by retirement assuming a 5 per cent annuity rate. Yet, for someone starting saving at 35 and retiring at 60, they are likely to have a pot of £86,450, which is a small proportion of the £469,140 required.

Starting to save early is the key – see Chapter 5, Section 5.4. For those starting to save at 35 and stop work at 60, they need to save £463 per month assuming 7 per cent investment growth. However, if they start saving at age 20 and stop work at 65, giving them 45 years to save, they only need to save about £78 per month assuming the same growth rate. Due to compound interest, it is important to start saving early.

In the past, retirees in the UK have sought to reduce longevity risk by taking out an annuity. This allows individuals to exchange a lump sum for a guaranteed income for life, thereby reducing the risk of running out of money. However, recent reforms have removed the need for annuitisation and individuals are now allowed to take their pension pots as lump sums. Individuals who have bought an annuity already can also cash in their annuity for a lump sum. With increasing life expectancy and low financial literacy in the UK, this freedom, by removing some of the built-in guarantees, may result in an undesirable outcome for many in retirement.

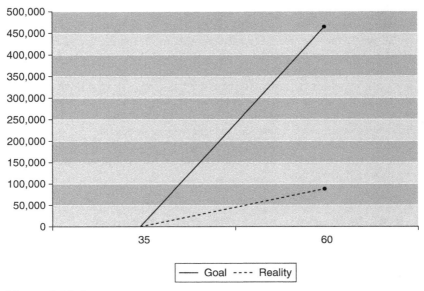

Figure 6.16 Savings gap
Source: True Potential (2015).

6.7 Behavioural issues in the protection gap

Individuals in the UK, and indeed across the globe, are grossly under-insured. Social and economic variables such as disposable income and education do not adequately explain the low up-take of insurance. There are more fundamental reasons. The first concerns the nature of insurance products. An insurance contract promises an intangible future benefit, which may not be realised, but the cost is incurred now. This seems to run against the culture of 'buy now, pay later'.

Second, there is a lack of 'insurance literacy'. Findings from a survey carried out in August 2007 by the Association of British Insurers seem to support this. The survey interviewed 2,000 households and explored the respondents' attitudes to protection. The Association (cited in Diacon and Mahdzan, 2008) observed that participants tended to:

- misunderstand what insurance covers, and the types of insurance contracts;
- have a lack of confidence in seeking information on insurance;
- over-state the benefits provided by their employer's sickness schemes;
- underestimate the impact of long-term illness;
- not consider covering the second adult in two-parent households;
- show a lack of awareness of the benefits insurance provides.

Third, in making a decision to buy an insurance product, consumers are affected by several behavioural biases. One is *loss aversion*, as people tend to frame outcomes in terms of changes from a reference point rather than the impact on

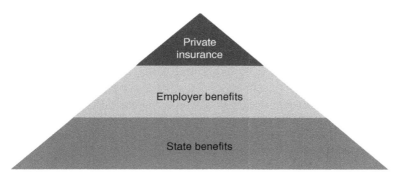

Figure 6.17 Different levels of insurance

their resulting state of wealth, and then weigh losses more heavily than gains. Kunreuther (1996) demonstrated that people usually fail to insure themselves against 'low probability, high loss' risks, even when the terms and premiums are favourable. The 'loss' of premium is seen to outweigh the 'gain' of any insurance recovery because the premium loss is exaggerated. This results in a lack of appreciation of the benefits of insurance. For example, an individual pays £100 per month for a life and critical illness policy for a sum assured of £100,000. Loss aversion means that the loss of premium of £100 per month causes more pain than the potential gain of £100,000 in the event of a claim. The pain arises partly because an insurance policy promises a future benefit (one that may never materialise), while premiums are a current cost.

Heuristics is another useful concept providing insights into the behavioural issues regarding the purchase of insurance. This refers to decision-making processes based on mental shortcuts or rules of thumb. The best-known heuristic is the concept of *availability* – where a person's decision making is influenced by their ability to conceptualise, relate or recall similar incidents. For example, a study conducted in California by Kunreuther (1996) found that before an earthquake in 1989, 34 per cent of uninsured homeowners thought earthquake insurance unnecessary. After the tragedy, only about 5 per cent gave the same response and one-third of the previously uninsured homeowners decided to insure their properties against earthquake. This concept of *availability* helps explain the low demand for life insurance, income or critical illness insurance: individuals do not buy insurance because they do not think it is necessary as they cannot relate to the risks and may believe that these 'will never happen to me'.

The existence of the welfare system in the UK also acts as a disincentive for some individuals to take out private insurance. Whatever happens, individuals in the UK know that there is someone to take care of them: the government. Though the amount might not be high, individuals can claim benefits for unemployment, disability and incapacity, and their dependants can claim some financial aid in the event of death. They also receive benefits from employers: many employers offer death-in-service, but some also offer income protection and critical illness cover, as well as private medical insurance. For some individuals, the existence of these two pillars of support (see Figure 6.17) negates the need to purchase private insurance.

6.8 Conclusion

Individuals face many risks including premature death, ill health and unemployment, threatening the full realisation of human capital and the enjoyment of life. Contrary to common perception, it is the young, not the old, who have the greatest protection need due to the concentration of their assets in human capital at a young age. A lack of literacy, combined with behavioural biases (loss aversion, and availability heuristic) may prevent us from making an informed decision. Greater knowledge about insurance and the potential benefits derived as well as a greater awareness of our behavioural biases may help us make a more rational choice.

End of chapter test

1. Explain the different types of risks individuals face.
2. Explain how these risks can be mitigated.
3. Compare and contrast the different types of insurance available.
4. Can you give some more examples of how behavioural biases can affect the purchase of insurance?

References

ABI (2015), 'UK insurance and long term savings: Key facts 2015', available at https://www.abi.org.uk/~/media/Files/Documents/Publications/Public/2015/Statistics/Key%20Facts%202015.pdf (Accessed 19 October 2016).

All Party Parliamentary Group on Insurance and Financial Services (2015), 'Income protection insurance', February, available at www.postonline.co.uk/digital_assets/8657/APPG_-_note_of_meeting_(Income_Protection_Insurance)_v2_240215.pdf (Accessed 19 October 2016).

Barton, T. (2011), 'Aviva UK Health research: Long-term absence has major impact on morale', 15 July, available at https://www.employeebenefits.co.uk/aviva-uk-health-research-long-term-absence-has-major-impact-on-morale/ (Accessed 11 June 2016).

BBC (2015), 'Cost of a funeral soars to £3,700 – but what do you get?', 4 October, available at www.bbc.co.uk/news/business-34424586 (Accessed 19 October 2016).

BBC (2016), 'How much of a savings buffer do people need?', 15 March, available at www.bbc.co.uk/news/magazine-35801951 (Accessed 11 June 2016).

BIS Research Paper 101 (2013), 'Youth unemployment: Review of training for young people with low qualifications', Department for Business Innovation and Skills, February, available at https://www.gov.uk/government/uploads/system/uploads/attachment_data/file/70226/bis-13-608-youth-unemployment-review-of-training-for-young-people-with-low-qualifications.pdf (Accessed 19 October 2016).

Burns, J. (2015), 'Graduates are earning less but more are in work', available at www.bbc.co.uk/news/education-33069312 (Accessed 19 October 2016).

Callaghan, G., Fribbance, I. and Higginson, M. (2012), *Personal Finance* (Oxford: Oxford University Press).

Celik, S., and Kayali, M.M. (2009), 'Determinants of demand for life insurance in European countries', *Problems and Perspectives in Management*, 7, 3, p.34.

Chartered Institute of Insurance (CII) (2015), *Financial Protection* (R05), available at www.cii.co.uk/qualifications/diploma-in-regulated-financial-planning-qualification/unit-financial-protection-(r05)/ (Accessed 31 October 2016).

The Children's Mutual (2016), 'UK adults have savings that are 21% of average annual earnings', available at www.thechildrensmutual.co.uk/family-articles/savings/uk-adults-have-savings-that-are-21-of-average-annual-earnings/ (Accessed 11 June 2016).

Dahl, C., Anderson, B. and Gilbert, B. (2013), 'The shocking statistics behind the life insurance coverage gap', available at www.lifehealthpro.com/2013/08/30/the-shocking-statistics-behind-the-life-insurance?t=life-sales-strategies (Accessed 11 June 2016).

Delebarre, J. (2016), 'Youth unemployment statistics', Briefing paper 5871, 16 March, House of Commons Library, available at http://researchbriefings.parliament.uk/ResearchBriefing/Summary/SN05871 (Accessed 6 April 2016).

Department of Health (2014), 'Living well for longer: National support for local action to reduce premature avoidable mortality', available at https://www.gov.uk/government/uploads/system/uploads/attachment_data/file/307703/LW4L.pdf (Accessed 6 June 2016).

Diacon, S., and Mahdzan, N.S.A. (2008), 'Protection insurance and financial well-being: A report for the Financial Services Research Forum', June, available at https://www.nottingham.ac.uk/business/businesscentres/crbfs/documents/researchreports/paper55.pdf (Accessed 6 April 2016).

The Economist (2013), 'Why is youth unemployment so high?', 8 May, available at www.economist.com/blogs/economist-explains/2013/05/economist-explains-why-youth-unemployment-so-high (Accessed 19 October 2016).

Goldsmith, A. (1983), 'Household life cycle protection: Human capital versus life insurance', *Journal of Risk and Insurance*, 50, pp.473–486.

Gordon, M.J., and Leahy, T.J. (2010), 'Human capital: Painting a more complete picture of the role of life insurance', *Life Insurance Selling*, September, 85, 9, pp.26, 28.

Hall, J. (2012), 'Chinese save four times as much as Britons: The average household in China has four times more savings than the average household in the UK, new research shows', 3 February, available at www.telegraph.co.uk/finance/personalfinance/savings/9057328/Chinese-save-four-times-as-much-as-Britons.html (Accessed 19 October 2016).

IHME (2016), 'Avoidable risk factors take an increasing toll on health worldwide', available at www.healthdata.org/news-release/avoidable-risk-factors-take-increasing-toll-health-worldwide (Accessed 11 June 2016).

Johnson, R.R., and Horan, S.M. (2013), 'Human capital and behavioral biases: Why investors don't diversify enough', *The Journal of Wealth Management*, 16, 1, pp.9–21.

Kunreuther, H. (1996), 'Mitigating disaster losses through insurance', *Journal of Risk & Uncertainty*, May, 12, 2, pp.171–187.

Lanning, T., and Rudiger, K. (n.d.), 'Youth unemployment in Europe: Lessons for the UK', available at https://www.researchonline.org.uk/sds/search/download.do%3Bjsessionid=8EB0BC2ACB09A1B9DD9ED6AA24C78047?ref=B27130 (Accessed 6 April 2016).

Macmillan Cancer Support (2015), 'Statistics factsheet', available at www.macmillan.org.uk/documents/aboutus/research/keystats/statisticsfactsheet.pdf (Accessed 1 November 2016).

Obara, K., and Inakura, N. (n.d.), 'Empirical evidence on households' life insurance holding behavior in Japan: Is it excess or deficient?', available at https://www.yu-cho-f.jp/research/old/research/repo/obara_inakura0615.pdf (Accessed 19 October 2016).

Office for National Statistics (2014), 'Family spending, 2014', available at www.ons.gov.uk/ons/rel/family-spending/family-spending/2014-edition/index.html (Accessed 11 June 2016).

Office for National Statistics (2015), 'Human capital estimates: 2015', available at www.ons.gov.uk/peoplepopulationandcommunity/wellbeing/articles/humancapitalestimates/2015 (Accessed 11 June 2016).

Office for National Statistics (2016), 'Unemployment rate', available at www.ons.gov.uk/employmentandlabourmarket/peoplenotinwork/unemployment/timeseries/mgsx/lms (Accessed 31 October 2016).

O'Hara, M. (2015), 'US style healthcare: Where being ill could cost everything you have', 27 January, available at www.theguardian.com/society/2015/jan/27/us-healthcare-being-ill-cost-everything-nhs (Accessed 11 June 2016).

PCW (2015), All Party Parliamentary Group on Insurance & Financial Services, available at www.postonline.co.uk/digital_assets/8657/APPG_-_note_of_meeting_(Income_Protection_Insurance)_v2_240215.pdf (Accessed 6 May 2016).

Peaslee, C. (2014), 'Life insurance holdings in the Great Recession', available at http://digitalcommons.colby.edu/cgi/viewcontent.cgi?article=1006&context=economics_honors (Accessed 6 May 2016).

Rejda, G.E. (2011), *Principles of Risk Management and Insurance* (Boston: Pearson).

Rutt, R. (2016), 'One in four breadwinners don't have life insurance leaving their families with a cover gap of £263 billion', available at www.thisismoney.co.uk/money/news/article-3387027/One-four-UK-breadwinners-not-life-insurance-buy-life-cover.html#ixzz44x57Ft2N (Accessed 11 June 2016).

Schanz, K., and Wang, S. (2014), 'The Global Insurance Protection Gap Assessment and Recommendations: A Geneva Association research report', November, p.25, available at https://www.genevaassociation.org/media/909569/ga2014-the_global_insurance_protection_gap.pdf (Accessed 19 October 2016).

The Telegraph (2005), 'Life cover: Mind the gap', 14 December, available at www.telegraph.co.uk/finance/personalfinance/insurance/2928295/Life-cover-mind-the-gap.html (Accessed 19 October 2016).

True Potential (2015), 'Tackling the savings gap: Consumer savings and debt data Q1 2015', available at www.tpllp.com/wp-content/uploads/2015/05/Tackling-the-Savings-Gap-Q1-2015.pdf (Accessed 19 October 2016).

Part III

Multiply your wealth

Chapter 7

Residual income

Lien Luu

Many people aspire to get a job and receive a wage because it provides a sense of security as wages are paid on a regular and predictable basis. Yet, this source of income is fragile because it depends on your ability to work. When you do not want to work or are not able to do so due to health reasons, this source of income stops. It is therefore important to create a source of income that is independent of you and your ability to work. This chapter explores the importance of **residual income** and different methods of creating it.

Learning outcomes

By the end of this chapter you will:

- be aware of the differences between different types of income;
- understand why passive and residual income is important;
- be able to explain what passive income is;
- be able to describe different ways to create passive and residual income.

7.1 Earned versus residual income

Residual income is seen as the key to wealth and financial independence because it is not dependent on one's *continuous* efforts. This frees us from working for a living and gives us the time to pursue other interests. It is generally recognised that there are two types of income: **active income** (also known as *earned income*, or linear income) and *residual or recurring income*.

Active income requires one to work continuously to earn money. It is believed that 95 per cent of people around the world are dependent on active income. This requires trading time for money and for that reason it is difficult to become financially independent. Active or linear income means you receive a pay cheque based on how much work you do. You need to put in a certain number of hours every week, and in effect means that you are exchanging time for money. When you stop working, your income stops. Linear income requires continued work and it is based on your time and efforts alone. This means that you can only have one or two (if you take another job) sources of linear income. Although some people can earn a lot of money from linear income (Richard Eisner of Disney Corporation received a $126 million dollar bonus in a single year, Lee Iacocca of Chrysler Corporation was paid $26.7 million dollars as a bonus in a single year), the ability to amass a fortune from earned income alone is limited for many. In addition, it is only possible to have earned income when you work. When you stop work, this source of income stops. It is for this reason that many seek residual income.

Residual income is regarded as a more powerful and profitable source of income, because it keeps coming in on a regular basis, from work you do once – meaning that you can earn a lot of money even when you are not working. Residual income requires effort, determination and time especially in the beginning but after that these will produce a regular stream of residual income. As residual income is not dependent on your time and efforts, you can have multiple sources of income. Only 5 per cent of the world population is believed to have residual income (Kiyosaki, 2002).

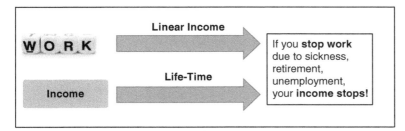

Figure 7.1 Celebrities and linear income
Source: Telegraph (2008), *Forbes* (2013).

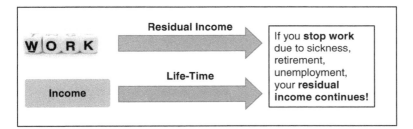

Figure 7.2 Residual income
Source: adapted from azam.biz/residual-income/ (2016).

Table 7.1 Celebrities and residual income

Names	Income	Year	Source
JK Rowling	£160 million	2007–8	Books
Stephen King	£24 million	2007–8	Books
Madonna	£125 million	2012–13	Music
Paul McCartney	£47 million	2012–13	Music
Michael Jackson	$160 million		Music

Source: Telegraph (2008), *Forbes* (2013).

Some of the world's richest people become rich due to residual income. Writers, for example, receive royalties from their books. They write a book once, and then they can sell an *unlimited* number of copies *indefinitely* if there is demand. Musicians also receive royalties from their music. They record a song once and every time their song is played, they receive money. What is also powerful is that this income is still paid to them (or their family) after their death. Reports suggest that Michael Jackson's estate has received more than $1 billion since his death. Fans mourned his tragic death around the world, resulting in more than 415,000 albums sold in the first four days in America alone – and 2.3 million songs downloaded across the world (Murray, 2010). Actors or actresses also receive residual income from their movies. After making a film, their initial efforts can be rewarded indefinitely.

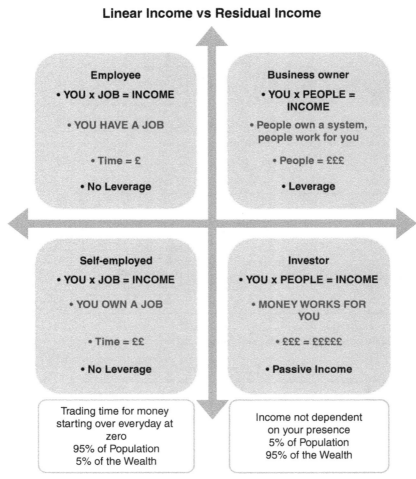

Linear Income vs Residual Income

Employee
- YOU x JOB = INCOME

- YOU HAVE A JOB

- Time = £

- No Leverage

Business owner
- YOU x PEOPLE = INCOME

- People own a system, people work for you

- People = £££

- Leverage

Self-employed
- YOU x JOB = INCOME

- YOU OWN A JOB

- Time = ££

- No Leverage

Investor
- YOU x PEOPLE = INCOME

- MONEY WORKS FOR YOU

- £££ = £££££

- Passive Income

Trading time for money starting over everyday at zero
95% of Population
5% of the Wealth

Income not dependent on your presence
5% of Population
95% of the Wealth

Figure 7.3 Different sources of income
Source: adapted from Kiyosaki (2002, p.176).

Income is derived from several sources. Robert Kiyosaki, the author of *Rich Dad Poor Dad*, classifies those sources into four categories: employment, self-employment, investments and business. On the left side of the quadrant, there is no leverage and he argues that the difference between employed and self-employed is that the former *has* a job while the latter *owns* a job. The self-employed exchange security for independence and both exchange time for money. Those in the investor quadrant receive residual income from investments and may have financial freedom but he believes it is those who own businesses who are really wealthy because they can leverage other people's time and skills and receive *passive income* in return. Passive income is often used interchangeably with residual income but a true passive income requires no involvement from you. Residual income, on the other hand, does require your active involvement at the beginning.

It is possible to be in several quadrants. A doctor may be employed in a hospital but carry out private work as a self-employed consultant. He may also invest in property and own shares and businesses (such as care homes). An accountant is employed but may also work on a self-employed basis. A teacher may be employed but also do private tuition on a self-employed basis, or he/she can set up an online tuition business allowing him/her to leverage other people's skills and time (see Section 7.8 below for an explanation of leverage).

The ability to navigate between quadrants requires a particular mindset, the mindset of an entrepreneur who is able to take risks and exploit opportunities. Many people believe that a job or a position offers financial security, but an entrepreneur sees having a job as very risky as your income is totally dependent on you. Robert Kiyosaki also believes that being self-employed is also very risky, as sickness, injury or death can adversely affect your income. Hard work, for example, can lead to physical, mental and emotional exhaustion and this in turn can affect health. Kiyosaki believes that being on the right side of the quadrant (investment and business) is more secure because it is not dependent on you. If you have a business employing other people, it can exist without you. Likewise, if you own rental properties, income should be generated without your daily involvement.

T. Harv Eker, the author of the *Secrets of the Millionaire Mind*, argues that the difference between the rich and the poor lies in the different mindset and mentality. He summarises the differences as shown in Box 7.1.

❖ BOX 7.1 DIFFERENCES BETWEEN RICH AND POOR

1. Rich people believe 'I create my life'. Poor people believe 'Life happens to me'.
2. Rich people play the money game to win. Poor people play the money game to *not* lose.
3. Rich people are committed to being rich. Poor people want to be rich.
4. Rich people think big. Poor people think small.
5. Rich people focus on opportunities. Poor people focus on obstacles.
6. Rich people admire other rich and successful people. Poor people resent rich and successful people.
7. Rich people associate with positive, successful people. Poor people associate with negative or unsuccessful people.
8. Rich people are willing to promote themselves and their value. Poor people think negatively about selling and promotion.
9. Rich people are bigger than their problems. Poor people are smaller than their problems.
10. Rich people are excellent receivers. Poor people are poor receivers.
11. Rich people choose to get paid based on results. Poor people choose to get paid based on time.
12. Rich people think 'both'. Poor people think 'either/or'.
13. Rich people focus on their net worth. Poor people focus on their working income.
14. Rich people manage their money well. Poor people mismanage their money well.

15. Rich people have their money work hard for them. Poor people work hard for their money.
16. Rich people act in spite of fear. Poor people let fear stop them.
17. Rich people constantly learn and grow. Poor people think they already know.

Source: Harv Eker (2005).

These statements suggest that rich people have certain personal qualities and skills that contribute to their financial success: proactiveness, commitment to success and personal development, being positive, risk taking, focus on asset building, and possessing money management skills.

ACTIVITY 7.1

1. Discuss the statements above on the differences between the rich and poor. Do you agree or disagree? Can you give any examples to support your arguments?
2. What do you think are the qualities needed for success?

7.1.2 Importance of assets

Building assets is the key to generating residual income. Assets can be tangible (such as property), or intangible (bonds, shares). T. Harv Eker believes that the true measure of wealth is 'net-worth', not working income. Net-worth is defined as the financial value of all assets owned less all liabilities. To work out your net-worth, add up everything you own (savings, investments, the value of your property, the value of your business, etc.) and deduct everything you owe (e.g. mortgage, loan, credit card).

Harv Eker (2005) argues that net-worth is determined by four factors:

1. *Income* – your net-worth is determined by whether you receive active or residual income. Many people focus on working income and end up with low or no net-worth.
2. *Savings* – saving is important because if you spend all your income, you have no savings and will not be able to accumulate wealth.
3. *Investments* – investments are significant in building net-worth because they generate higher returns than savings and allow you to accumulate wealth faster.
4. *Simplification* – refers to the cost of your lifestyle. The lower the cost, the more you will have to save and invest.

❖ CASE STUDY 7.1

Russell came as a refugee to the UK in the 1940s. He and his wife had no money and so they lived a frugal life. They did not think they could afford to have children and so did not have any.

As a frugal man, he was always looking for ways to save money. He would travel by Underground to his closest supermarket to buy food, even in his 90s, and he would always buy food on offer – those with expired sell-by dates.

He died leaving more than £1 million in his estate. In this example, although Russell was careful to build up assets by investing his income in property and shares, he never in fact benefited or enjoyed the benefits of his wealth. This underlines the importance of realising that wealth is a means not a goal in itself.

ACTIVITY 7.2

Read Case Study 7.1 and answer the following questions:

1. If you have assets of more than £1 million on your deathbed and there are no children and relatives, what would you do with the money?
2. What would be your greatest regret?

In terms of acquiring assets, Robert Allen, in his book *Creating Wealth*, offers five useful wealth principles (Allen, 2006, pp.22–38):

- **Invest in things that go up in value**: certain things we buy increase in value, while others depreciate. Assets such as cars, TVs, phones, clothes and boats are often referred to as *depreciating assets* as their value goes down over time rather than up. Other assets such as property, shares, rare coins, gold, precious metals and so on are classified as real assets as they tend to go up in value. As wealth accumulation depends on the acquisition of appreciating assets, it is important to ask several questions before you spend your money: what will this item be worth ten years from now? Will this item enhance my goal of retirement or will it detract? Is this item something I need, or it is merely something I want?
- **Don't diversify! Concentrate all of your eggs in the right basket**: this is interesting advice because often we are advised to diversify. Andrew Carnegie also advised: 'Put all your eggs in one basket, and then watch that basket.' Allen believes that wealth seekers at the beginning of their career should concentrate all their energy in the *right* investment so that they can avoid dissipating energy in different directions.
- **Wealth seekers are always on the offensive, not on the defensive**: many investors are concerned with security, and so, when faced with risk, they often choose low-yielding 'safe' investments. However, these do not produce wealth. Investors should therefore choose a balance between offensive and defensive assets, some designed to give security, while others for growth. Tim Hale, in *Smarter Investing* (2013) discusses the whisky-water approach to investment. Depending on attitude to risk, investors choose a mix between defensive stocks

(water) such as short-dated bonds and inflation-linked bonds, and growth-oriented assets (whisky) such as investments in global markets, smaller companies and emerging markets.

- **Choose investments that are both powerful and stable**: it is important to choose stable and powerful investments. According to Allen, only certain collectibles (such as high-quality rare coins) and real estate (property) qualify.
- **Control is essential**: to be successful, investors need to ensure they do not relinquish control over their investments. They must understand how investments, leverage and compound interest work and keep a close eye on their investments. (See Section 7.3 below for what is meant here by 'leverage'.)

Besides the importance of assets, it is also important to understand three other fundamental aspects of wealth building. First, it is necessary to have multiple streams of income from different and diversified sources to reduce dependence on one type of income. If one source of income goes dry, our lifestyle is not being affected. It is like driving on the motorway where there are several lanes. If one lane is closed, we can use other lanes. Likewise, it is important to have several lanes of wealth. Second, we need to understand the power of leverage. Third, we need to recognise the magnifying effect of compound interest.

ACTIVITY 7.3

Imagine that you have won £100,000 from the lottery. How much would you spend on the following items?

Jewellery	----------------
Holidays	----------------
Bank savings	----------------
Cars	----------------
Stock market	----------------
Property	----------------
Give to family	----------------
Give to charity	----------------
Pay off debts	----------------
Set up a business	---------------
Buy more lottery tickets	--------------

7.1.3 Risks

Acquiring assets involves taking risks, but many people are afraid to take risks. It is generally accepted that there is a close relationship between risk and reward but loss aversion bias prevents people from acting in a way conducive to wealth building. An individual, for example, holds money in cash because he is fearful of losing his money on the stock market. By holding money in cash rather than investing it in the stock market or property, the saver might destroy his wealth in the long term because inflation erodes the purchasing power of cash.

Risk means different things to different people and many may not be clear what the term means. There are two sources of risk: *systematic* (or *non-diversifiable, market risk*) and *unsystematic risk*. The first is attributable to the market movements and cannot be eliminated even with diversification. Unsystematic risk, by contrast, can be diversified because it relates to the risk of a specific firm. The sources of risk can be classified as follows (Laopodis, 2012, p.70):

- **Business risk**: risk of business failure is present when we invest in a business or run a business. BHS, for example, went into administration in April 2016 because of its financial losses.
- **Liquidity risk**: this refers to the ability to convert an asset into cash quickly. For example, a Treasury Bill is a highly liquid asset but property is illiquid. Property owners may not be able to sell when they want to, especially in periods when property values decline.
- **Inflation risk**: this is also called the purchasing power risk, because inflation erodes the purchasing power. This risk is invisible and many savers may not be able to see the effects of inflation on the value of their cash.
- **Interest rate risk**: this involves a possibility of loss because of changing interest rates. Investors who have mortgages will be affected with interest rate movements.
- **Credit or default risk**: involves a change in the creditworthiness of a borrower and investors may lose their investments. For example, local authorities in the UK lost £1.05 billion of savings when the Icelandic banks collapsed in 2008 (BBC, 2014).
- **Foreign exchange risk**: this affects investors who invest internationally. Investors who invest abroad are also faced with the risk of changes in the values of their investments when these are denominated in foreign currencies. Changes in exchange rate will thus affect the value of investments. For example, a UK investor buys a property in Florida (US) for $200,000 when the exchange rate was £1 to $1.6 (£125,000). When exchange rate changed to £1 to $1.5, the value of the investment increases to £133,300. However, if the exchange rate changes to £1 to $1.8, then the value of the US investment goes down to £111,100.
- **Capital risk**: when people talk about risk, they often mean capital risk – that is the risk of losing the money invested. The potential of losing your money is present in many investments. The value of shares, for example, can go down or be wiped out altogether as demonstrated by the technology bubble. In March 2000, the Nasdaq index of technology shares peaked before losing 80 per cent of its value in two years – about $5 trillion was lost, as the index fell from 5048 in March 2000 to 1114 in 2002 (Hudson, 2010, Reuters, 2015).

Investors face many risks and many fear the risk of capital loss but inflation risk may be more dangerous. Understanding risks enables investors to adopt the necessary strategies to mitigate them.

ACTIVITY 7.4

Let's imagine the following investors have asset holdings as follows:

Types	Investor 1	Investor 2	Investor 3
Cash in the bank	£75,000	£500	£100
Shares	£0	£75,000	£100
Houses	£0	£0	£75,000
Debts	£5,000	£7,000	£8,000
Gold	£0	£500	£0
Total	£80,000	£83,000	£83,200

Suggest the value of the assets in ten years' time. What are the risks of the portfolios? Would you recommend any changes? How would you invest your money?

7.2 Sources of residual income

Residual income can come from many sources but the most accessible sources for the general public are renting out investment properties, receiving dividends from shares, receiving interest from savings, and income from a traditional or internet business.

7.2.1 Property

Property as an investment has always attracted a lot of interest from investors because it is a tangible asset, providing investors with a potential source of income and capital growth. Figure 7.4 shows that the average price of property in the UK rose by 520 per cent between 1986 and 2014, from £48,000 to £250,000. London experienced 894 per cent growth, with prices rocketing from £55,000 to £492,000 over the same period. The North East, however, shows a lower growth, 312 per cent, increasing from £48,000 to £150,000.

❖ CASE STUDIES 7.2 AND 7.3

- A young accountant living in Camden was considering buying somewhere to live in 1996. He had been working as an accountant for ten years. He did not like the idea of taking on debt and so decided to save longer so that he could buy a property with cash. Property prices in London, especially Camden, rocketed. Unable to buy in London, he had to move to another city where property prices were cheaper.
- A young man was considering buying a property. Having been employed for many years, he did not like the idea of debt and would prefer to buy property with cash. His uncle also told him not to buy as property prices were going to fall. He was persuaded to go ahead and buy so that he and his wife could have somewhere to live. Prices went up and he was able to use some equity from his first home to buy a bigger property to live in.

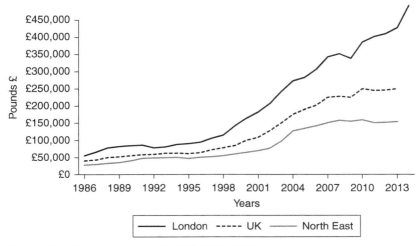

Figure 7.4 House prices in the UK, 1986–2013
Source: adapted from ITV (2014) (for illustrative purposes).

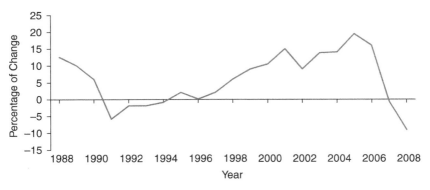

Figure 7.5 US house prices
Source: http://news.bbc.co.uk/1/hi/business/7373158.stm.

In the UK, the buy-to-let market has experienced a massive growth, thanks to pension changes, housing shortage and the availability of specialist mortgages for investors. *The Telegraph* reported that in October 2014 there were 2 million landlords in the UK owning 4.9 million properties worth nearly £1 trillion. It was estimated that buy-to-let properties would increase by another 1 million in five years (Dyson, 2014). The property boom was not unique to the UK. Other countries such as the USA (Figure 7.5) and Asia (Figure 7.6) also experienced phenomenal growth. In the USA, house prices started to increase from 1991 but collapsed in 2007. For China, Singapore and Hong Kong, prices rose and dipped slightly after 2009 before picking up again (Figure 7.7).

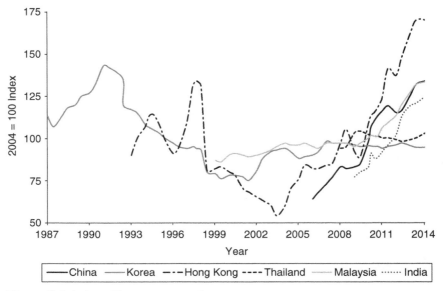

Figure 7.6 Index of house prices in Asia
Source: Scatigna *et al.* (2014, p.71).

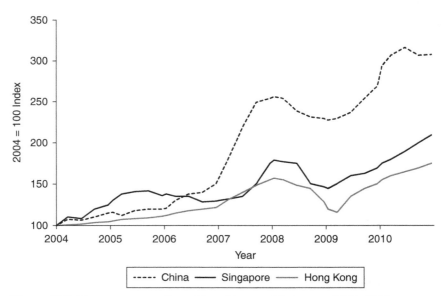

Figure 7.7 House prices in China, Hong Kong and Singapore, 2004–2010
Source: http://churchousepublishing.com/the-churchouse-letter/inflation-cost-push-demand-pull.

As Warren Buffett says, to be a successful investor we must either find or create value. With properties, it is possible to do both. It is possible to find properties below market value and add value by carrying out minor renovation such as painting and changing the floor, to a more substantial refurbishment project by fitting new windows, kitchen and bathroom.

For example, Sally buys a three-bedroom house in poor condition for £150,000. She spends a total of £10,000 on refurbishment by fitting new windows, a new kitchen, a new bathroom, new flooring and painting the walls. After several years, the house is worth more than £200,000 and she rents it out for £880 per month. Her mortgage is £380 per month, giving her a monthly profit of £500. Assuming that her monthly costs amount to £100, she still nets £400 per month of residual income.

Now imagine she has a portfolio of five properties. Let's look at the monthly residual income as shown in Table 7.2.

In this simple scenario, Sally receives £2,000 of residual income per month. Just imagine the rental income if she has 10, 20 or 30 properties.

Let's imagine another situation where she buys a house and rents out several rooms, known as a house in multiple occupation (HMO). Assume that she buys a three-bedroom house for £150,000 and again spends £10,000 on refurbishment. The house has three good bedrooms, one lounge and one big kitchen. Potentially she can rent out 3–4 rooms in this house (see Table 7.4).

In this scenario, renting out four rooms can generate as much as £1,500 per month of rental income. However, this way of renting can be more demanding due to higher turnover of tenants and a greater level of property management. Potentially, the profit is much higher, more than double the amount she would get if she rents out the whole house to one tenant. Imagine if she has a portfolio of five properties. She would earn enough to merit hiring someone to manage the properties for her.

Table 7.2 Investing in property

Property	Rental income	Mortgage	Running costs	Net profit per month
Property 1	£880	£380	£100	£400
Property 2	£880	£380	£100	£400
Property 3	£880	£380	£100	£400
Property 4	£880	£380	£100	£400
Property 5	£880	£380	£100	£400
Total	£4,400	£1,900	£500	£2,000

Table 7.3 Renting out rooms

Room	Rental income	Mortgage	Running costs	Net profit per month
Room 1	£400			
Room 2	£400			
Room 3	£400			
Room 4	£350			
Total income	£1,550	£370	£100–£300	£880–1,080

To create residual income from property requires capital investment. Money is needed for a deposit for a mortgage, costs of property purchase, and refurbishment. This is discussed in Chapter 8, but broadly the amount of money required for a deposit depends on the mortgage market. In the past, some lenders offered 90 per cent LTV for buy-to-let mortgages, meaning that individuals only needed to come up with 10 per cent deposit. However, after the financial crisis in 2009, many lenders required a 25 per cent deposit. To buy a property valued at £150,000 individuals would have needed at least £37,500 for a deposit. They also need to pay for acquisition and, in the UK, stamp duty costs. From April 2016, the government has substantially increased stamp duty for buy-to-let and second home property purchases. Individuals now need to pay 3 per cent extra stamp duty for these purchases. The stamp duty tax for a £150,000 property was £500, but now costs £5,000.

In the past, many people have bought buy-to-let properties using the equity in their home. They first buy a house to live in, and once this increases in value, they borrow more from the bank to enable them to raise a deposit for another property. The climate now is much more challenging for young people. House prices have risen a lot and many first time buyers struggle to buy even their first home. Research from L&G suggests that the help of the so-called 'Bank of Mum and Dad' is crucial for first time buyers to get onto the property ladder. Research by L&G shows that parents were set to lend (or give) £5 billion to their children in 2016, providing deposits for more than 300,000 mortgages, with an average financial contribution of £17,500 or 7 per cent of the purchase price (Wilson, 2016). The changes in the property market render it difficult for young people to exploit opportunities in the property market to create residual income in the future.

7.2.2 Business

Residual income can be generated from setting up successful businesses and these have created many wealthy people (such as Sir Richard Branson and Lord Alan Sugar). In the nineteenth century, people like Andrew Carnegie, Henry Ford, Thomas Edison, J. P. Morgan and others made their fortunes from business. In the twentieth century, successful businesses were created by the likes of Bill Gates, Steve Case, Larry Ellison, Ross Perot and Sam Walton. Each of these people started with nothing but turned into wealthy people by building a business from scratch. Business was the vehicle to wealth for 74 per cent of self-made millionaires in the USA (Tracy, 2016).

Table 7.5 shows examples of successful business-to-consumer (B to C) businesses (see Table 7.4 for definitions). Unlike common perception, some successful businesses began with very little capital – Lord Alan Sugar with £100 and Sir Richard Branson with £300.

Although financial rewards might be high, many do not like the idea of running a business because the risk of business failure is very high and a high capital outlay may be required. In the UK more than half of the business start-ups fail within five years (Anderson, 2014). However, the internet offers the possibility of running a business with low costs. It is now possible to have a business on eBay with very low investment (as little as £50), simply by buying under-valued items on eBay and then selling them back on eBay at a higher price (Minalto, 2016).

Table 7.4 Different types of business

Types of business	Nature	Examples
B to C Model	Businesses selling to individual customers	McDonald's, Burger King
B to B Model	Businesses selling to other businesses	Known as wholesalers
B to G Model	Businesses selling to governments	
B to P Model	Businesses selling to charities	Red Cross

Source: Hansen (2002, p.318).

Table 7.5 Examples of famous businessmen

Names	Initial business	Current business	Initial capital	Net worth
Sir Philip Green	Import jeans from Far East and sell to London retailers	Arcadia Group (Burton, Miss Selfridge, TopShop)	£10,000	£4.00 billion
Mike Ashley	1980s opened first Sport & Ski shop in Maidenhead	Sports Direct	£10,000	£3.75 billion
Sir Richard Branson	1970 opened mail order record company	Tourism, finance, media	£300	£3.60 billion
Peter Hargreaves	Hargreaves started business with partner Stephen Lansdown	Finance – investment broking business	£500	£2.39 billion
John Caudwell	1987 – built up Caudwell	Mobile phones	£25,000	£1.50 billion
Lord Alan Sugar	Computers	Property/business	£100	£1.40 billion
Jon Hunt	1981 founded Foxtons	Property/estate agency	£100	£1.07 billion

Source: www.thisismoney.co.uk/money/smallbusiness/article-2809685/Top-25-self-entrepreneurs-started-small-sums-money.html#ixzz3xDbd5OoV; www.telegraph.co.uk/finance/enterprise/11930889/How-wealthy-is-Lord-Sugar-A-billionaire-thanks-to-clever-property-investments.html.

❖ BOX 7.2 EXAMPLES OF TWO WEALTHY BUSINESSMEN

SIR RICHARD BRANSON

Sir Richard Branson was a school dropout and dyslexic. At 16, he left school and, with the help of a friend, founded a magazine for students. He made money by selling advertisements to local businesses and ran the operation out of the crypt inside a local church.

According to legend, the youngster was on his way to the Virgin Islands to meet a pretty girl, and was impatient to get there. But he was out of luck – on arrival at the airport he was told flights to the Virgin Islands had been cancelled. He decided to charter a private airplane, picked up a small blackboard, wrote 'Virgin Airlines: $29' on it, and sold the remaining seats to other people who had also meant to be on his flight. The idea for Virgin Atlantic was born.

JACK MA

Ma is a true rags-to-riches story. He grew up poor in communist China, failed his college entrance exam twice, and was rejected from dozens of jobs, including one at KFC, before finding success with his third internet company, Alibaba.

Ma had no experience with computers or coding, but was captivated by the internet when he used it for the first time during a trip to the USA in 1995. Ma's first online search was 'beer', but he was surprised to find that no Chinese beers turned up in the results. It was then that he decided to found an internet company for China. In 1999, he called 17 of his friends to his apartment and persuaded them to invest in his online marketplace called Alibaba. Soon the service began to attract business from all over the world. By October 1999, he had raised $5 million from Goldman Sachs and $20 million from SoftBank, a Japanese telecom company that also invests in technology companies. In the 2000s, the company founded Taobao, eBay's competitor. In 2005, Yahoo invested $1 billion in Alibaba in exchange for a 40 per cent share. In 2013, the company went public.

Source: www.thisismoney.co.uk/money/smallbusiness/
article-2514864/Five-best-British-start-ups-came-great-
ideas-hit-big-time.html; www.businessinsider.com/
the-inspiring-life-story-of-alibaba-founder-jack-ma-2014-10?IR=T#.

7.2.3 Investments

Investing is a popular method to create residual income. When you invest in shares, you receive two potential forms of return: capital growth and income in the form of dividend. Table 7.6 lists selected companies and the dividends they paid in 2015. Investing in one share might prove risky and so individuals invest in a portfolio to spread the risks.

Table 7.6 Yields from investing in selected companies

Name of company	Yield	Sector	Income from £1,000 investment p.a.
WM Morrison Supermarkets	7.52%	Consumer defensive	£75
BHP Billiton (BLT)	7.08%	Basic materials	£71
Anglo-American (AAL)	7.02%	Basic materials	£70
Royal Dutch Shell (RDSB)	6.89%	Energy	£69
BP	6.59%	Energy	£66
GlaxoSmithKline (GSK)	6.00%	Healthcare	£60
HSBC (HSBA)	5.74%	Banks-global	£57
Standard Chartered (STAN)	5.59%	Banks-global	£56
National Grid (NG)	5.13%	Utilities	£51
J Sainsbury (SBRY)	5.08%	Consumer defensive	£51
Aberdeen Asset Management (AND)	5.26%	Asset management	£53
Centrica (CAN)	4.93%	Utilities	£49
Vodafone	4.76%	Communication services	£48
Pearson (PSON)	4.39%	Publishing	£44

Source: Morningstar (2015).

In order to receive a sizeable amount of dividend income, it is necessary to have a substantial amount of capital invested. Regular monthly investing over a period of time will enable the accumulation of a capital lump sum.

7.2.4 Internet

The internet is the ultimate 24-hour money-making machine. While you eat, while you sleep and while you play, money can be pouring in from all over the world. In his book *The 4-Hour Work Week*, Ferriss (2011) emphasises another powerful factor: the internet gives you mobility, allowing you to live anywhere in the world and freeing you from a 9–5 job. The rise of the internet has produced many wealthy individuals. Mark Zuckerberg, the founder of Facebook, was worth $51.8 billion in May 2016, while Martin Lewis sold MoneySavingExpert.com for £87 million in 2012 (BBC, 2012). In China, Jack Ma, the founder of Alibaba (the Chinese version of Amazon), made his fortune of $25 billion from e-commerce. In September 2013, Alibaba went public and the IPO made both Yahoo and Ma extremely wealthy (Stone and D'Onfro, 2014).

While making these fortunes may be beyond some of us, there are other simple ways to make money from the internet. One popular method is affiliated marketing, an industry born in the late 1990s. An affiliate, or a third party, acts as part of a virtual sales team by placing ads and links on their website, which will direct visitors to the home page of an established retailer. Every time that visitor goes on to make a purchase, or another specified transaction, the third party receives a commission. The attraction of affiliated marketing is that it can be fitted around other commitments, such as work, studies and does not require a high capital outlay. One of the most successful affiliated marketers in the UK is Andrew Slack. A computer science graduate from Aberystwyth, he has built a £5 million affiliate marketing network (MoreNiche) for health and beauty firms. MoreNiche's highest earning affiliate is generating £3 million a year (Bennett, 2013).

In the USA, Pat Flynn, founder of Smarterpassiveincome.com, also made his fortunes from the internet. Forbes describes him as a passive income whiz, as he has earned $3 million in the first six years by creating authoritative and helpful websites in areas such as passing a green building exam, becoming a security guard, and establishing and growing a successful food truck business. Initially, Pat set up a website to help individuals pass architectural exams in the USA. The site attracted many visitors, and this allowed Pat to start building his digital empire. After losing his job during the financial crisis, he began to work full-time on his business (Shin, 2014).

Table 7.7 Examples of firms offering an affiliate marketing programme in the UK

Name of business	Sector
Amazon	E-commerce
eBay	E-commerce
Experian	Information services
Hargreaves Lansdown	Financial service company selling funds
Google Apps	Technology
Apple ITunes	Online digital media store

There are many ways in which individuals can take advantage of the internet to make money and the popular ones include selling e-books, writing a blog and setting up a YouTube channel. Many people sell e-books on Amazon and this can create a source of residual income because if an e-book sells, it will produce a source of income without much more work. Some people use ghost writers, as in the case of Saeed Rajan of *Escape Your Desk Job*, who is reported to make around $2,700 a month by publishing e-books on Amazon, and he hasn't written a word himself (Assadi, 2016). Elance and Freelancer provide access to writers who can take care of the writing while Fiverr.com can help with logos and design the front cover of the book. Creating a residual income now gets easier and easier. All you need is an idea.

Though blogging involves regular work, it also generates residual income from affiliate marketing fees. Bloggers need to focus on creating content on their site and generating traffic. Martin Lewis, the founder of MoneySavingExpert.com, is a prime example of blogging success. He started with a newsletter blog in 2003, sent it to friends and families, and in 2012 sold the resulting website to Moneysupermarket.com for £87 million. It is unlikely that anyone starting out today will make huge amounts – certainly not from a blog alone. In the USA, a blogger called Gala Darling (galadarling.com) made money by offering her own digital products. She sells 'radical self-love' – personal empowerment – courses via downloads from her site. She is very successful because she uses blogs as a springboard for her brand. It is reported that she earns a six-figure income from advertising, sponsorships and online courses. In Australia, bikini model Natasha Oakley, a 23 year old from Sydney, is a successful blogger. She has almost a million Instagram followers, and is building a business empire after co-founding A Bikini A Day, designing Monday Swimwear and launching a successful blog (Shorten, 2015).

Setting up a YouTube channel creates residual income for some. Felix Arvid Ulf Kjellberg, aka PewDiePie, has had the most subscribed channel since 2013. Almost 36 million have signed up for his narrated YouTube clips of himself playing video games (King, 2014).

7.3 Leverage

Leverage is an important concept in wealth creation because it can magnify returns. Leverage is the power to control a lot with just a little. There are five kinds of leverage (Hansen, 2002, p.124):

- **OPM – Other People's Money**: In property investment, we buy residential property with 5–10 per cent deposit and yet we control 100 per cent of the property (see also Lechter, 2005).
- **OPE – Other People's Experience**: It takes too long to learn it yourself, so borrow or learn from others. The easiest way to become rich is to apprentice personally with someone who is rich – learn all they know, meet all their contacts and do what they do. It is for this reason that *The Apprentice* in the UK is so popular. Young people have a chance to partner with one of the UK's leading businessmen (Lord Alan Sugar) and become part of his world.
- **OPI – Other People's Ideas**: The objective here is to associate with people who can share their powerful moneymaking ideas.

- **OPT – Other People's Time:** Individuals will sell you their time, talent, connections, resources and know-how relatively inexpensively. A mentor/coach is a good example of getting someone's time.
- **OPW – Other People's Work:** Most people want a job and they want security rather than taking risks. Therefore we can hire and delegate to them everything we do not want to do.

One reason why property investment is a powerful form of investment is due to the power of leverage. For example, you buy a house worth £200,000 and you need a 10 per cent deposit (£20,000). The mortgage therefore is £180,000. In one year, the property increases by 10 per cent and is now worth £220,000. You sell the property and, after paying off the mortgage, you are left with £40,000 profit. This is 100 per cent return on your investment. This is because although you have only put down £20,000, you get leverage on the total value of the property (£200,000). A 10 per cent increase produces 100 per cent return on your investments.

Imagine, however, you have £20,000 to invest and you decide to buy shares and stocks instead. It is difficult to borrow money from banks to buy more shares and so your total investment is £20,000. The next year the shares have risen by 10 per cent and so now your shares are worth £22,000, giving you a profit of £2,000 or 10 per cent of your initial investment. A 10 per cent increase in the value of the shares gives you a direct proportionate rise in the value of your investments in the absence of leverage.

Leverage, however, can work in the opposite direction – magnify losses. In the above example, a 10 per cent fall in the property value means that you lose 100 per cent of your deposit (£20,000), in comparison with a 10 per cent loss (£2,000) when the value of shares falls by 10 per cent.

Financial leverage increases risks as well as potential returns. Although, as Chapter 8 explains, the downside risk with UK housing has in the past been abnormally low, it is still important to use leverage with great prudence to avoid undesirable financial consequences.

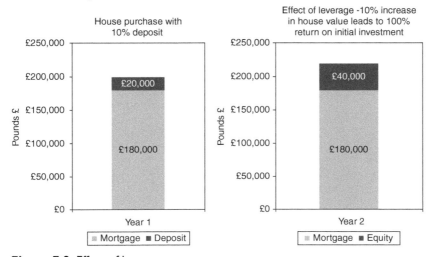

Figure 7.8 Effect of leverage on return

7.4 Conclusion

Despite popular perception, financial security does not come from paid employment but from residual income generated from assets. Acquiring assets involves taking risks and it is important to understand the risks involved and the ways to mitigate these. With willingness to take risks, investors are assisted by powerful forces of leverage and compound interest in their endeavour to build wealth.

End of chapter test

1. Explain different types of income.
2. Discuss three reasons why residual income is important.
3. Describe the different methods to create residual and passive income.
4. Discuss the advantages and disadvantages of each.
5. Discuss your ideas of creating passive and residual income.

References

Allen, R.G. (2006), *Creating Wealth: Retire in Ten Years Using Allen's Seven Principles of Wealth* (New York: Free Press).

Anderson, E. (2014), 'Half of UK start-ups fail within five years: Business owners blame the UK tax system and lack of bank lending for stifling growth', available at www.telegraph.co.uk/finance/businessclub/11174584/Half-of-UK-start-ups-fail-within-five-years.html (Accessed 19 October 2016).

Assadi, A. (2016), 'Passive income case study: $2700/month publishing Kindle eBooks with no writing', available at www.armanassadi.com/passive-income-publishing-ebooks (Accessed 11 June 2016).

BBC (2012), 'Martin Lewis sells MoneySavingExpert.com for £87m', available at www.bbc.co.uk/news/business-18295587 (Accessed 11 June 2016).

BBC (2014), 'Councils recoup most of deposits lost in Icelandic banks crash', available at www.bbc.co.uk/news/uk-politics-26052949 (Accessed 11 June 2016).

Bennett, A. (2013), 'Q&A: Andrew Slack, the 29-year old boss of the £5m MoreNiche marketing firm', available at www.londonlovesbusiness.com/entrepreneurs/young-entrepreneurs/qa-andrew-slack-the-29-year-old-boss-of-the-5m-moreniche-marketing-firm/5854.article (Accessed 11 June 2016).

Dyson, R. (2014), '1996: the birth of buy-to-let Britain – in numbers', available at www.telegraph.co.uk/finance/personalfinance/investing/buy-to-let/11176988/1996-the-birth-of-buy-to-let-Britain-in-numbers.html (Accessed 11 June 2016).

Ferriss, T. (2011), *The 4-Hour Work Week: Escape the 9-5: Live Anywhere and Join the New Rich* (London: Vermilion).

Hale, T. (2013), *Smarter Investing: Simpler Decisions for Better Results* (Harlow: Pearson, 3rd edition).

Hansen, M.V. (2002), *The One Minute Millionaire* (London: Vermilion).

Harv Eker, T. (2005), *Secrets of the Millionaire Mind: Think Rich to Get Rich* (London: Piatkus).

Hudson, A. (2010), 'What ever happened to the dotcom millionaires?', available at http://news.bbc.co.uk/1/hi/technology/8505260.stm (Accessed 11 June 2016).

ITV (2014), 'The rise and rise of London house prices: 1986 to 2014', available at www.itv.com/news/london/2014-07-15/the-rise-and-rise-of-london-house-prices-1986-to-2014/ (Accessed 11 June 2016).

King, B. (2014), 'PewDiePie is the world's most popular channel on YouTube!', available at www.salem-news.com/articles/january252014/pewdiepie-youtubebk.php (Accessed 11 June 2016).

Kiyosaki, R. (2000), *Rich Dad Poor Dad* (London: Timewarner).

Kiyosaki, R. (2002), *Rich Dad Poor Dad 2: The Cashflow Quadrant: Rich Dad's Guide to Financial Freedom* (London: Timewarner).

Laopodis, N.T. (2012), *Understanding Investments: Theories and Strategies* (London: Routledge).

Lechter, M. (2005), *OPM Other People's Money: How to Attract Other People's Money for your Investments – the Ultimate Leverage* (New York: Little, Brown & Company).

Morningstar (2015), 'Top 20 FTSE 100 dividend paying stocks', available at www.morningstar.co.uk/uk/news/132966/top-20-ftse-100-dividend-paying-stocks.aspx (Accessed 28 July 2015).

Minalto, A. (2016), 'How to start a profitable eBay business with £50!', available at http://andrewminalto.com/how-to-start-a-profitable-ebay-business/ (Accessed 11 June 2016).

Murray, R. (2010), 'Michael Jackson royalties up 70%: Massive increase in earnings', available at www.clashmusic.com/news/michael-jackson-royalties-up-70 (Accessed 11 June 2016).

Reuters (2015), 'US STOCKS-Nasdaq sets closing record', available at http://uk.reuters.com/article/markets-stocks-usa-idUKL1N0XK3QX20150423 (Accessed 11 June 2016).

O'Malley Greenburg, Z. (2013), 'How The Beatles earned $71 million this year, sort of', available at www.forbes.com/sites/zackomalleygreenburg/2013/10/23/how-the-beatles-earned-71-million-this-year-sort-of/#7ec7632b5326 (Accessed 17 January 2017).

Scatigna, M., Szemere, R. and Tsatsaronis, K. (2014), 'Residential property price statistics across the globe', *BIS Quarterly Review*, September, 61–76.

Shin, L. (2014), 'How Pat Flynn made his first $3 million in passive income', available at www.forbes.com/sites/laurashin/2014/09/12/how-pat-flynn-made-his-first-3-million-in-passive-income/#452641771af4 (Accessed 11 June 2016).

Shorten, K. (2015), 'Coolest online influencers share their secrets to six-figure success', available at www.news.com.au/technology/online/social/coolest-online-influencers-share-their-secrets-to-sixfigure-success/news-story/22d27de6f7d37055674186a50f287ff6 (Accessed 11 June 2016).

Stone, M., and D'Onfro, J. (2014), 'The inspiring life story of Alibaba founder Jack Ma, now the richest man in China', available at www.businessinsider.com/the-inspiring-life-story-of-alibaba-founder-jack-ma-2014-10?IR=T (Accessed 11 June 2016).

Telegraph (2008), 'Harry Potter author JK Rowling earns £3m a week', available at www.telegraph.co.uk/news/celebritynews/3121761/Harry-Potter-author-JK-Rowling-earns-3m-a-week.html (Accessed 17 January 2017).

Tracy, B. (2016), '5 ways self-made millionaires and wealthy people achieved financial freedom', available at www.briantracy.com/blog/financial-success/5-ways-self-made-millionaires-and-wealthy-people-achieve-financial-freedom/ (Accessed 11 June 2016).

Wilson, B. (2016), 'Bank of mum and dad lends £5bn a year in UK, says L&G', available at www.bbc.co.uk/news/business-36181318 (Accessed 11 June 2016).

Chapter 8

A place to live

Jonquil Lowe

❖ CONTENTS

A home is first and foremost a place to live but, if you own it, a home may also become your most important source of wealth. The normal way of buying a home – by taking out a loan – magnifies any profit you make, although, in theory, it should make buying a home more risky by magnifying any losses too. However, across many developed countries, a combination of economic and political factors have in the past tended to push house prices upwards. In some places, this upward pressure has been so great that new would-be homeowners are squeezed out of the market.

Learning outcomes

By the end of this chapter you will:

- be able to describe the advantages and disadvantages of different types of housing tenure;
- understand how homes can be a source of wealth, including the concept of leverage;
- be able to compare different ways of financing home purchase;
- be able to explain key economic and political factors that affect house prices.

8.1 Rent or buy?

Research (Diaz-Serrano, 2009) suggests that, across the countries that make up the Organisation of Economic Co-operation and Development (OECD), people are more satisfied with their homes if they own them rather than rent and more likely to downplay drawbacks, such as a lack of space or a bad neighbourhood, provided their home has basic amenities (such as an indoor toilet). Yet, home ownership does not suit everyone and the choice will also depend on the quality and quantity of the alternatives available.

8.1.1 Tenure around the world

Across Europe, home ownership is the dominant form of housing **tenure**. Figure 8.1 shows the proportion of the population in selected European Union (EU) countries who own and rent their homes. The average level of owner-occupancy is 70 per cent across the EU as a whole (the dashed horizontal line in Figure 8.1) and the picture is similar in, for example, the United States where 64 per cent of households are owner-occupiers (US Census Bureau, 2014) and Australia 67 per cent (ABS, 2012). Note that home ownership includes people who own their home outright and those who are buying with a **mortgage**.

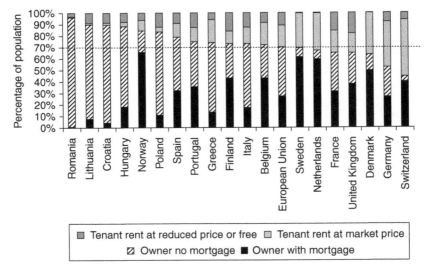

Figure 8.1 Housing tenure for selected European countries in 2014
Source: data from Eurostat (2016a).

ACTIVITY 8.1

Looking at Figure 8.1, do any countries stand out as having a different pattern of tenure from the average 70 per cent home ownership?

Figure 8.1 ranks the countries from highest levels of home ownership to lowest and, at either end, some countries stand out. Eastern European countries, such as Romania and Croatia, have very high levels of outright home ownership (with no mortgage) while, at the other end of the chart, Denmark, Germany and Switzerland have high levels of renting at the market price (private renting). You might also notice that the UK, France and Finland have relatively high levels of tenants renting at less than the market price, which typically indicates social renting (from local governments, housing associations and similar bodies) rather than from private landlords.

8.1.2 Pros and cons of renting or buying

It is common to think of home ownership as a superior form of tenure, but this is not necessarily true across all countries. For example, on average across the EU, around one-sixth of the population live in overcrowded housing conditions, but the proportion is over half in Romania and four out of ten in Hungary (Eurostat, 2016b), both, as you have seen, countries with very high levels of home ownership. However, in many other countries, citizens aspire to own their own home and the reasons are complex.

ACTIVITY 8.2

1. How many reasons can you think of for wanting to own a home rather than rent it?
2. Why might you prefer to rent rather than buy?

Your answers to these questions probably vary depending on where you live and what stage of life you are at, but some key reasons for wanting to own a home might include:

- **Quality of life**. Rental properties are sometimes poorly maintained, may have restrictions on how you use them (for example, no pets) and, even if you are allowed to decorate and make alterations, you might feel it's not worth spending money that ultimately benefits your landlord rather than you. By contrast, a home that you own gives you the freedom to live as you choose and create the environment within your home that you want.
- **Stability**. Rental contracts do not necessarily give you the right to stay in the same home for as long as you would like. Owning your own home generally means you can stay in the same place for as long as you choose, which avoids disrupting work, schooling, family ties and social life. Living in the same area for a long time helps you to build up a greater sense of belonging and to form better support networks – sometimes called **social capital**.
- **Psychological reasons**. Owning a home may be viewed as a sign of status or achievement.
- **Investment potential**. Sometimes, the monthly outlay to buy a home is little different from the amount paid in rent. Therefore, renting is sometimes described as 'dead money', whereas buying lets you build up a potentially valuable asset – see Section 8.2. This asset can increase your financial security and options, not just by selling your home at a profit, but also by borrowing against its value – for example, to provide yourself with additional income in retirement.

However, owning a home can have drawbacks too. For example, it is much more difficult and costly to move if you have to sell your home rather than just give notice to a landlord. This can make it harder to change jobs or move for family reasons and may be particularly important when you are at the early stages of your working life and need job mobility. If you rent, your landlord is responsible for keeping the building maintained and insuring it; if you own your own home, you bear these costs. This can mean large and unexpected bills, for example to repair a roof or keep woodwork painted and weatherproof.

Whether you rent or buy, you normally need to pay a deposit before you move in, but this is much bigger if you are buying. In addition, buying typically involves other significant costs, such as legal fees and taxes, so renting may be the more affordable choice. Renting might also let you live in a home that is nicer than you could afford to buy.

Whether renting or buying your own property with a mortgage, you may lose your home if you fail to keep up the regular payments. However, while paying rent goes on for as long as you are a tenant, eventually mortgage payments stop. When your mortgage has come to an end and you own your home outright, you in effect live in your home rent-free. The value to you of the rent you save is sometimes called **imputed rent**.

Table 8.1 Main advantages and disadvantages of renting and buying

	Renting	Buying
Advantages	Easier to move, for example for work. Relatively small deposit needed. Maintenance costs and buildings insurance borne by landlord. Rent may be subsidised (social renting). Might be able to rent nicer home than you could afford to buy.	Can stay as long as you choose. You control what you can do in your home. You benefit if you decorate and improve your home. May feel sense of achievement or status. You benefit if house prices rise. Ability to borrow against the value of your home. You live rent-free once the mortgage is paid off.
Disadvantages	May be asked to move out before you are ready. Might be restrictions on what you can do in your home. Not worth making home improvements if they benefit landlord but not you. No benefit from rising house prices. Cannot borrow against your home. You may lose your home if you do not keep up the rental payments.	Usually need a large deposit to buy. Fees and taxes when you buy may be substantial. May be hard to sell if you need to move, for example for work. Costs of selling and moving may be high. You pay the maintenance costs and buildings insurance. You may lose your home if you do not keep up the mortgage payments.

Table 8.1 summarises the main advantages and disadvantages of renting and buying a home, but you may have thought of some others.

❖ BOX 8.1 HOUSING TENURE IN GERMANY AND SWITZERLAND

The German and Swiss housing markets stand out for having low levels of home ownership (52.5 per cent and 44.5 per cent, respectively) compared with other developed economies. Both are countries with relatively high standards of living and sound economies, and they escaped the sharp rise in house prices experienced in many other countries both before and since the global financial crisis (see Section 8.2.2 below). What might explain these differences in tenure and house price movements? There is no simple answer, but there are some distinctive features in both countries' housing markets.

In both countries, the tax-and-subsidy system is fairly neutral between renting and owning a home. For example: in Germany, there is no tax relief on mortgage interest payments; in Switzerland, there is mortgage tax relief but this is offset by income tax on the 'imputed rent' from owning a home.

Both countries have some form of rent control. In Germany, most rents are set and increased with reference to the level of local rents. In Switzerland, rents may be linked to either mortgage interest rates, in which case both falls as well as rises must be reflected, or price inflation. In general, this has resulted in lower and more stable rents than in many other countries.

In Germany, rental contracts are generally for indefinite periods. They can be terminated by either side at any time with appropriate notice, but landlords can evict tenants only for specified reasons and not if this would cause hardship. In Switzerland, too, the law fosters long-term rentals and protection of tenants. In Germany, landlords are able to pass on to tenants part of the cost of property improvements (but not routine maintenance) through a rent increase, which provides an incentive to modernise and improve the quality of rental homes.

That's not to say that the Swiss and Germans would not like to own their own homes. In surveys, most Swiss people say they would like to be homeowners if the price of buying were not so high and it were easier to get a mortgage. In Germany, too, there is a preference for home ownership but this tends to be viewed as an eventual once-in-a-lifetime ambition to be fulfilled in later life, in contrast to the idea of getting onto the housing ladder early and working up that is prevalent in, say, the UK. The stability of house prices in Germany underpins this approach, because there is less pressure to buy now for fear that home ownership will become unaffordable later. In the meantime, both German and Swiss households seem content to rent because they have security of tenure in good quality homes.

Sources: Bourassa *et al.* (2010); Eurostat (2016a); Kofner (2014).

8.2 Home as an investment

There are several factors that may conspire to make a home – and, in fact, any residential property – particularly attractive as an investment. Some of these factors are economic and political (see Section 8.4), but a key factor is **leverage** (Section 8.2.1), though the return to investors will depend ultimately on growth in value (Section 8.2.2) and also on how property is taxed (Section 8.2.3).

8.2.1 Leverage

The most basic way to make money from an investment is to buy when the price is low and sell later after the price has risen. Any gain from this strategy is magnified if you can increase the amount you invest by borrowing, a process called 'leverage' (also known as 'gearing'). Since homes normally cost several times average annual earnings, most people have to borrow to buy and do this by taking out a mortgage (see Section

8.3.2 below). This means, even if you are not looking on your home as an investment, you are still using leverage and, as a result, could make a sizeable gain if house prices rise. The easiest way to see why leverage magnifies any gain is to start with a simplified example – see Case Study 8.1.

❖ CASE STUDY 8.1 LEVERAGE MAGNIFIES GAINS

Jan has enough money to buy a home outright without borrowing at all. He buys a cottage costing £100,000. Ten years later, he sells it for £200,000, making a profit of 100 per cent ((£200,000 – £100,000) / £100,000 × 100).

Linda buys a flat costing £100,000, but she has only £10,000 of her own money and has to borrow the remaining £90,000. Ten years later, she sells the flat for £200,000. Out of the proceeds, she must pay back the £90,000. This leaves her with £110,000, which is a profit of 1000 per cent ((£110,000 – £10,000) / £10,000 × 100) on her original investment of £10,000.

While Case Study 8.1 is very simplified – for example, ignoring interest on the loan and the fact that repayments might be made regularly during the ten years – you can see the general principle. This potential for making impressive profits even if you have only a relatively small sum to invest explains part of the popularity of property as an investment.

ACTIVITY 8.3
1. Looking at Case Study 8.1, work out the loss Jan would have made if, having bought his home for £100,000, ten years later he could sell it for only £50,000.
2. Looking at Case Study 8.1, what loss would Linda have made if she had to sell for £50,000?

If Jan had to sell for £50,000, he would have lost half his money – a 50 per cent loss ((£50,000 – £100,000) / £100,000 × 100). If Linda had sold at £50,000, she would have put all of that towards repaying the mortgage and still owed a further £40,000, so her loss would be 500 per cent ((–£40,000 – £10,000) / £10,000 × 100). You can see that, although leverage magnified the gains in Case Study 8.1, it has also magnified the losses in Activity 8.3.

8.2.2 Housing and the stock market compared
Since leverage increases losses as well as gains, it is an investment strategy that would normally be suitable only if you have a strong appetite for risk. However, many home-owners view housing as a safer investment than, say, investing in the stock market.

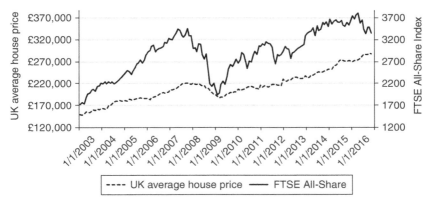

Figure 8.2 Share prices and house prices compared, 2003–2015
Sources: data from ONS (2016); London Stock Exchange Group cited in Yahoo! Finance (2016).

Using the UK as an example, Figure 8.2 compares the level of house prices with the level of the stock market each month during the period 2003 to 2015. This period includes the aftermath of the global financial crisis of 2008 when both property and share prices fell.

Figure 8.2 does support the suggestion that the housing market is less risky in the sense of being less volatile with fewer and much shallower swings up and down. However, over the total period, the increase in the level of share prices and house prices has been broadly similar, with share prices rising 77 per cent (4.5 per cent a year) and house prices 89 per cent (5.0 per cent a year). Bear in mind, though, that the rise in price is only part of the return on shares; once dividends (income from shares) are taken into account, the total return over the period is 181 per cent (8.3 per cent a year) (FT Business, 2006; *Financial Times*, 2016) – well in excess of the return on the average home. (With both investments, there are also costs and taxes to take into account.) Thus, without leverage, the returns from UK housing have historically been steady but not exceptional.

In addition, it would be wrong to assume that house prices must always be on an upward trend. Figure 8.3 shows how house prices have changed over the 20-year period 1996–2015 in selected countries. The solid grey line repeats the pattern for Britain, showing a fall in prices after the global financial crisis but a strong recovery since, taking house prices up to new highs. By contrast, Ireland (the solid black line) experienced a much greater slump in prices after 2007 and, despite some recovery, remained lower than before the crisis. The USA (whose housing slump triggered the global financial crisis) and Spain, which are not shown in Figure 8.3, have had a similar experience. Italy (the dashed black line in Figure 8.3) has had a gentler fall in house prices that was still continuing in 2015. Germany (grey dashed line) and Switzerland (black dotted line) have had relatively stable prices throughout the period shown on the chart, while house prices in Japan have been gently but steadily falling.

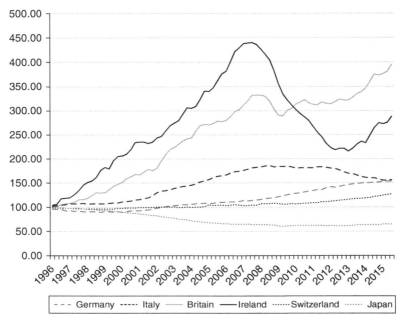

Figure 8.3 Index of house prices for selected countries
Source: data from BIS (2016).

8.2.3 Taxation of property

There are a variety of ways in which property can be taxed and this may reduce any profits from a property investment. Taxes may include:

- **Recurrent (for example, annual) taxes on the property** itself payable by owners or tenants. In the UK, this is Council Tax (England, Scotland and Wales) and Rates (Northern Ireland) on residential property. Businesses also pay Rates on their commercial premises. These are taxes charged by local councils and the amounts charged vary from one district to another and with the value of the property.
- **Recurrent taxes on wealth**. Property is a part of wealth, and tax is payable on total wealth less debts. The UK does not have an annual wealth tax, but some other countries, like France and Norway, do (Evans, 2013). Generally, the rate of tax is low and starts only once wealth reaches a certain threshold.
- **Tax on increases in wealth when it changes hands**. In the UK, you may have to pay Capital Gains Tax on any profit you make when you sell or give away an asset (see Appendix). However, there is an exemption for your only or main home, but not for any additional property, such as a second home, holiday

home or buy-to-let property (on which tax at 18 and/or 28 per cent is payable on gains above an annual exemption of £11,100 in 2016).

- **Taxes on estates, inheritances and gifts.** Where property is part of an estate or the asset being given, this can result in tax being payable as the property passes from one owner to the next. Inheritance Tax paid by the giver is the example in the UK, although there are substantial allowances that means your only or main home is often passed on tax-free and most lifetime gifts are also tax-free (see Chapter 11).
- **Transaction taxes on property when it is acquired.** Examples in the UK are Stamp Duty Land Tax (England, Wales, Northern Ireland) and Land and Buildings Transaction Tax (Scotland) which are paid by the purchaser of a property – see Section 8.3.1 below.

ACTIVITY 8.4

If your home country is not the UK, do you know what property taxes exist in your country? Can you match the different types to the list above?

Property taxes can be used by governments in different ways. The rationale may simply be to raise money to finance government spending, but the structure of taxes can also be used to promote or deter certain types of behaviour. For example, some countries encourage home ownership by taxing your main or only home more lightly than other properties or wealth.

8.3 Buying a home

Homes are expensive, so that most people must borrow by taking out a mortgage. However, you will usually be required to put up part of the purchase price yourself, called the 'deposit' and there will be other upfront costs to pay.

8.3.1 Costs of buying

In the period immediately before the global financial crisis of 2008, it was possible in some countries, such as the UK and USA, to get 100 per cent mortgages, meaning that you did not have to pay any deposit at all. However, lenders have become more cautious since then, and typically you will need to pay at least 10 per cent of the purchase price yourself in the UK and as much as 20 per cent in some other countries, such as Switzerland.

You may also have to pay tax on your purchase if you are in a country like the UK that has a transactions tax. Table 8.2 shows the rates of Stamp Duty Land Tax charged on the purchase of residential properties in 2016. The rate shown applies to each slice of the purchase price.

Table 8.2 Stamp Duty Land Tax* rates and thresholds, 2016

Purchase price on each slice:	Rate for first or only property	Rate for a second property**
Up to £125,000	0%	3%
£125,001 to £250,000	2%	5%
£250,001 to £925,000	5%	8%
£925,001 to £1,500,000	10%	13%
More than £1,500,000	12%	15%

* Applies to purchases of homes in England, Wales and Northern Ireland.

** Costing more than £40,000. No tax on a property costing less than that.

Source: data from GOV.UK (2016a).

ACTIVITY 8.5

1. If you were buying a home in England costing £200,000, how much Stamp Duty Land Tax would you have to pay?
2. If you already own your home and were buying a second property costing £400,000, how much Stamp Duty Land Tax would you pay?
3. Why might the seller of a property be concerned if Stamp Duty Land Tax were increased?

Using the rates shown in the second column of Table 8.2, tax on the purchase of a £200,000 home would be £1,500. This is worked out as no tax on the first £125,000 slice of the purchase and 2 per cent tax on the remaining £75,000. If you were buying a second property, you would need to look at the rates in the third column of Table 8.2. If the property cost £400,000, tax would be £22,000. This is (£125,000 × 3%) + (£125,000 × 5%) + (£150,000 × 8%). The UK government introduced the higher rates for second properties from 2016 to try to reduce the attractiveness of buying property as an investment which was seen to be squeezing ordinary homebuyers out of the market (HMT and Osborne, 2015). Although it is buyers, not sellers, who pay Stamp Duty Land Tax, buyers might try to pass on some or all of an increase in tax to sellers by reducing the amount they are willing to pay.

In addition to the deposit and any tax, you typically also have to pay: a solicitor to handle the legal side of transferring ownership of the property to you; a valuation fee paid to a surveyor who determines how much the property is worth (and you might want a full structural survey if the property is likely to need major repairs or renovation); mortgage fees (see below); and moving costs. Thus, the total upfront costs of buying a home can be substantial. However, some mortgage deals will cover or refund legal and/or valuation fees up to a limit.

There are also ongoing costs of owning a home, such as insurance, taxes and maintenance.

> ### ❖ CASE STUDY 8.2 BUYING A HOME
>
> Lucy is looking to buy her first home, a flat, which in her area is likely to cost about £200,000. She has saved up £25,000, which she expects will be enough to cover her deposit (say, £20,000), Stamp Duty Land Tax (£1,500), legal fees (say, £700), valuation fee (say, £250), mortgage fee (maybe £1,000) and moving costs (luckily nothing as her mates will help).

8.3.2 Mortgages

Having sorted out your deposit and other costs of buying, you still need to get a mortgage. There are two main types of mortgage: repayment (also called 'capital and interest') and interest-only.

With both types of mortgage you agree to make regular monthly payments to the lender. With a repayment mortgage, these payments are made up of both interest on the loan and partial repayments of the amount you have borrowed (called the 'capital'). A repayment mortgage is an example of a 'reducing-balance loan' where the interest is calculated each month on the amount of loan still outstanding and the amount you pay each month is set at a level that clears the whole loan by the end of the mortgage **term**. Table 8.3 shows a simplified example of how a reducing-balance loan works. It shows the process of borrowing £1,000 for five years at a fixed yearly interest rate of 5 per cent and paying it off in five equal annual repayments. The fixed repayments are shown in column C. In the last row of the table, you can see that the five payments add up to a total of £1,155, which is made up of £155 interest plus the original sum borrowed of £1,000. Column E shows how the amount of capital paid off each year increases; this is because the outstanding balance (column A) and the interest charged on it (column B) are both falling which leaves more of each fixed payment (column C) to pay off the capital. Repayment mortgages are typically taken out for terms of 25 years or more and have monthly rather than yearly payments, but the way they work is the same as outlined in Table 8.3.

Table 8.3 Example of a reducing-balance loan

Year	Loan outstanding at the start of each year	Interest on A	Repayment	Loan outstanding at end of year A + B – C	Capital paid off this year A – D
	A	**B**	**C**	**D**	**E**
1	£1,000	£50	£230.97	£819.03	£180.97
2	£819.03	£41	£230.97	£629.00	£190.02
3	£629.00	£31	£230.97	£429.48	£199.52
4	£429.48	£21	£230.97	£219.98	£209.50
5	£219.98	£11	£230.97	£0.00	£219.98
Total paid		£155	£1,155		£1,000

With an interest-only mortgage, the monthly payments cover only the interest on the loan. The amount you owe does not fall and you pay it off in one chunk at the end of the mortgage term. If you have this type of mortgage, you need to plan how you will pay it off – for example, you could pay into a savings plan to build up a lump sum by the end of the term or you might expect to sell the property. In the UK, interest-only mortgages were common in the past and often linked to an insurance-based savings plan, called an endowment policy, in which case they were called 'endowment mortgages'. These days, most homebuyers in the UK take out repayment mortgages.

So far, we have considered loans with a fixed rate of interest, but often mortgages have a variable rate or the interest rate is fixed just for a few years at a time. These are the main interest-rate variations:

- **Standard variable rate (SVR).** The interest rate tends to go up and down in line with interest rates in the economy as a whole. Often it changes faster going up than it does coming down! When the interest changes, so do your monthly payments.
- **Tracker rate.** A variable rate that automatically goes up and down in line with a particular interest rate, such as the Bank of England base rate.
- **Discounted rate.** A variable rate that is a set number of percentage points lower than the SVR. For example, if the lender's SVR is 5 per cent and the discount is 2 per cent, the rate you pay is 3 per cent (5 − 2). Usually the discounted rate lasts just a few years and is useful if your budget will be tight when you first move in.
- **Fixed rate.** For a set period of time (one to five years, say, but could be longer), you pay a set interest rate that does not change, regardless of what happens to interest rates in the economy as a whole. At the end of the fixed-rate period, the mortgage will usually revert to the lender's SVR but you can shop around and switch to a new fixed-rate mortgage. Fixed-rate deals can help you budget because you know exactly what you'll have to pay each month. However, you need to be prepared for a rise in your monthly payments if interest rates have gone up at the time you need to switch to a new deal.
- **Capped and/or collared mortgage.** The interest rate can vary but will go no higher than a specified rate (the cap) and/or no lower than a set rate (the collar).
- **Offset mortgage.** You hold a current account and/or savings accounts with the same firm that provides your mortgage. The positive balance in these accounts is deducted from your outstanding mortgage before the monthly interest is worked out. Although the interest rate on the mortgage tends to be a fairly high standard variable rate, the offsetting may mean you pay less each month and in total and/or you pay your mortgage off more quickly.

In addition to paying interest, you may have to pay a mortgage fee, typically called an arrangement fee or booking charge. It might vary from a couple of hundred pounds up to a couple of thousand. Usually, you can add it to the amount you are borrowing and so pay it gradually spread over the whole mortgage term, but that makes the fee expensive because you are paying interest on it as well. If you can, it's more efficient to pay it in one go at the time you start the mortgage.

There may also be a fee if your mortgage is large relative to the value of the property you are buying – see Section 8.3.4 below.

The mortgage lender will also insist that you take out building insurance. This pays out if your home is damaged, for example, by flood, fire or subsidence (see Chapter 6). However, you can shop around and choose where you buy your cover.

❖ BOX 8.2 COMPARING MORTGAGE COSTS

It may seem daunting trying to compare the cost of different mortgages if they charge different interest rates, have different fixed-rate or discounted-rate periods and/or different charges. However, across the EU (European Union, 2014), lenders are required to publish an 'Annual percentage rate of charge' (APRC), just called the APR in the UK. This expresses the interest and other compulsory charges in a standardised way that also takes into account when you have to pay them. While the underlying calculation is a little complicated, the APR is very easy to use: a loan with a high APR is more expensive than a loan with a low APR.

However, a loan can be expensive in terms of its APR, but still have monthly payments that are less than a cheaper loan. For example, you might borrow £100 and pay it off over two years at a rate of £2 a week. While the payments might seem very affordable, the total you would repay would be £208 and the APR for this loan would be 435 per cent. This is an extreme example, but highlights why you might choose a mortgage, even though its APR is higher, if the monthly payments are more manageable.

ACTIVITY 8.6

Francesco needs to borrow £200,000 to buy a flat and has the offer of two mortgages:

- Mortgage A: a 20-year loan with an APR of 3 per cent and monthly payments of £1,104.
- Mortgage B: a 30-year loan with an APR of 5 per cent and monthly payments of £1,058.

Explain how Francesco might choose between these two loans.

Mortgage A has higher monthly repayments (£1,104), so Francesco would need to be confident he can budget for these. Otherwise, based on the APR, Mortgage A is cheaper and, because it will be paid off over a shorter term (20 years), the total Francesco will pay is £264,960 (£1,104 × 12 × 20). Mortgage B costs £54 less each month, so might be a bit more affordable, but the APR shows it is more expensive and the total Francesco would pay back is much higher at £380,880 (£1,058 × 12 × 30) because of the longer term.

8.3.3 Housing affordability

Rising house prices tend to make it more difficult to buy a home. First, you are likely to need a higher deposit, so it may be difficult to save up enough unless your earnings are rising as fast as house prices. So one measure of affordability is to compare house prices to earnings. In the UK, the price-to-earnings ratio (average house price divided by average earnings) for first-time buyers was for decades fairly stable between about 2 and 3, but started to rise around the turn of the century and by early 2016 stood at 5.2 for the UK as a whole and as high as 10.1 for buyers in London (Nationwide, 2016).

When house prices rise, you are also likely to need a larger mortgage, which could mean a larger drain on your income each month. However, a bigger mortgage is not necessarily more expensive because it also depends on interest rates. Nearly ten years on from the global financial crisis, interest rates in many developed countries were still at historically low levels as governments continued to try to stimulate their sluggish economies. This was tending to damp down mortgage payments, but raises concerns about whether households would be able to afford their mortgages if interest rates were to rise.

Across developed countries, in 2015, on average households (owners and renters) spent 19 per cent of their disposable income on housing costs (OECD, 2016). The lowest proportions were for Korea (16 per cent) and Norway (17 per cent) and the highest at 26 per cent in the Czech Republic and Slovak Republic. UK households spent 23 per cent of their income on housing.

8.3.4 How much can you borrow?

The size of mortgage a lender will be prepared to offer you depends mainly on two elements: the property you are buying and how creditworthy you are deemed to be.

The lender will insist that the property is valued and will usually have a maximum mortgage that it is willing to offer relative to the value of the property – this is called the **loan-to-value ratio** or **LTV**. Before the global financial crisis, LTVs of 100 per cent or sometimes more were fairly easy to get. In the years following the crisis, the maximum has usually been around 90 per cent for your only or main home and lower for a second property.

If the LTV is higher than 90 per cent, you might have to pay a high-lending fee. This covers the cost of insurance to make sure that the lender (not you) does not make a loss if you fail to keep up the mortgage payments and the home has to be sold to pay off the loan.

Before the global financial crisis of 2008, in the UK, it was common for lenders to judge how much mortgage a borrower could afford by basing the amount on their income. Common mortgage limits were three times a single buyer's income or two-and-a-half times a couple's joint income, although higher multiples were sometimes offered especially as house prices reached a pre-crisis peak (Moneyfacts, 2006).

The regulation of mortgages changed after the crisis and, since 2014 (when the recommendations of a Mortgage Market Review, MMR, were implemented), lenders must check affordability by looking at a would-be borrower's income, already committed spending and any changes in these that might be expected during the mortgage term. In addition, for most mortgages, the lender must check whether the borrower would still be able to afford the mortgage if interest rates were to rise. In 2016, this so-called 'stress test' was based on a rise in the mortgage rate of 3 percentage points (FCA, 2014). European Union (2014) law makes similar requirements across the other countries of the EU.

In addition to checking your income and spending commitments, the lender will normally carry out a credit check often using a **credit reference agency** (see Chapter 5, Section 5.1.4).

8.4 The economics and politics of housing markets

The market for housing is complex and made even more complicated by government policies that either directly intervene in the market or are designed to influence the behaviour of developers, homebuyers and property investors.

8.4.1 The economics of the market

As in any market, basically price is set by the interaction of supply and demand: if demand for housing exceeds supply, this will tend to push prices up; if demand is less than supply, prices will tend to fall. However, neither supply nor demand are as straightforward as they would be in the market for a cheap consumption good, such as bread or butter.

One way to increase the supply of housing is to build new homes, but a large part of supply is also the sale of existing homes. Only a small proportion of the existing housing stock will be up for sale at any point in time and, as well as being a factor that determines price, supply of existing homes is also influenced by price. This is because existing homeowners may defer selling if prices are currently lower than they were hoping to achieve. Instead, they might put off moving home or consider renting – increasing the supply of rental homes – as an alternative. The supply of existing homes can also be complicated by owners who hang on to properties that are larger than they need or second properties as a store of wealth.

Demand is equally tangled. Since house purchase is expensive, demand depends not simply on the intention to buy but also the ability to get a mortgage, a separate but related market. Demand is also influenced by the alternatives available – you have already seen in Table 8.1 how the cost, security and quality of rental homes may be a factor reducing demand for owning a home of one's own.

8.4.2 The politics of the market

Close on the heels of food, shelter is a fundamental human need (see Chapter 2, Section 2.1.2). As such, a caring society will always be concerned that individuals are adequately housed. More cynically, in a democracy, housing is often a key issue that will win or lose votes and so is likely to be high on political parties' agendas. In addition, governments are often keen to promote home ownership because they perceive that owners are more likely to occupy a home long-term which is associated with building community, low crime and a well-maintained housing stock. However, as you saw in Table 8.1, rental housing markets can also have similar outcomes. Homes are also increasingly being viewed by governments as a store of wealth that can be tapped into in later life to provide retirement income or pay for care.

Governments can adopt policies that work on the supply and demand side of the housing market, and the aims and outcomes of such policies are not necessarily consistent. On the supply side, town and country planning, green-belt policies, and the like dictate how easily land can be made available for building new homes and where they are located. Governments can use public money to build homes or may offer incentives, such as grants and tax relief, to encourage private developers and social housing organisations to build. The new homes may be for sale, for rent or a mix of the two. Governments may impose conditions, for example, that a given proportion of homes on a new development are for social housing or must be 'affordable' (though even affordable homes may be out of reach of many who would like a home).

More subtly, governments could increase the supply of existing homes by encouraging more efficient use of the housing stock. Dorling (2014) has suggested that, in the UK, on the basis of bedrooms, there is sufficient housing for all, but too many owners carry on living in homes that are larger than they need. Dorling suggests that higher taxes on under-occupied homes could incentivise the owners to move to smaller properties enabling the existing housing stock to be reallocated on a more efficient basis.

Governments may introduce policies aimed at helping people, especially first-time buyers. This might include helping buyers to build up a deposit – for example, some countries (New Zealand and, from 2017, the UK) that encourage saving for retirement through tax-incentivised schemes allow these savings to be drawn out early if used for a deposit on buying a home. Other measures might help with obtaining a mortgage or accessing cheaper purchase deals. Box 8.3 outlines some of the schemes available to UK homebuyers in 2016. It's not just the government that may provide help for homebuyers – families can also be an important source of help and we will look at this in Chapter 11.

❖ BOX 8.3 HELP FOR HOMEBUYERS IN THE UK IN 2016

Help-to-Buy Individual Savings Account (ISA) Savings scheme where first-time buyers can build up tax-free savings and the government adds a bonus if you use the money as a deposit on a home (new-build or existing housing stock). You can kick off the ISA with a lump sum up to £1,000 and then add up to £200 a month. When you are ready to buy, the government adds a bonus equal to 25 per cent of your savings, up to a maximum bonus of £3,000.

Lifetime ISA Due to be available from 2017, a savings scheme for people aged between 18 and 40 where your savings – up to £4,000 a year – build up tax-free and the government adds 25 per cent to the amount you pay in. Savings can be drawn out tax-free from age 60 or earlier if used to pay for a deposit on your first home (new-build or existing housing stock).

Help-to-Buy equity loan The government provides a loan of up to 20 per cent of the purchase price (40 per cent in London) for the purchase of a newly built home. You must provide a deposit of at least 5 per cent and get a mortgage for the rest. The government loan is cost-free for the first five years and subject to an annual fee after that. It can be repaid out of the proceeds when you sell the home or paid off earlier if you prefer.

Help-to-Buy mortgage guarantee The government provides a guarantee to lenders to encourage them to offer 95 per cent loan-to-value (LTV) mortgages. This can help you get a mortgage if you have only a small deposit. The scheme applies to newly built and existing homes and is open to any buyer.

Shared ownership (co-ownership) These schemes are usually offered by social landlords. You buy part of your home (taking out a mortgage) and rent part. You are buying less than a whole property, so need less deposit. The rent is typically lower than the market rent and may be cheaper than mortgage payments would be, so the scheme reduces your total monthly housing expenses. You can usually buy additional shares of the home as and when you can afford to (a process called 'staircasing') until eventually you own the whole home. These schemes may be restricted to buyers on a low income.

Right-to-Buy Tenants living in social housing are given the right to buy their home at a discounted price. If you sell within five years, you must repay some or all of the discount.

Sources: GOV.UK (2016b, 2016c); HMT (2016).

ACTIVITY 8.7

Read Box 8.3 about different schemes to help homebuyers. Suggest what impact each scheme might have on the supply and/or demand for housing and house prices.

Schemes to help homebuyers are often criticised if, while helping some buyers, their overall impact is to increase demand relative to supply and so add to the upward pressure on house prices, since this can squeeze yet more would-be buyers out of the market. Of the schemes described in Box 8.3, only one (Help-to-Buy equity loan) is restricted to newly built homes. Arguably, this restriction may help to stimulate supply as well as demand, if it makes developers more confident that they will be able to sell the new homes they build. Three of the schemes (Help-to-Buy ISA, Lifetime ISA and Help-to-Buy mortgage guarantee) can be used to buy existing homes, not just newly built ones, and so risk increasing demand without any increase in supply. Right-to-Buy is unlikely to have an impact on house prices generally, since the tenant is buying their existing home. Shared-ownership schemes might increase supply if these are homes that would otherwise be part of the rental sector.

8.5 Conclusion

In this chapter, you have considered the different ways that people may occupy homes and the pros and cons of different types of tenure, including situations when renting may be the better option. You have gained an understanding of why there is a general preference for home ownership, particularly in those countries where rising house prices seem to be the norm and so make home ownership look an attractive form of investment, rather than simply a place to live. You have looked at the process of buying a home and seen how leverage enhances this investment potential and considered the way in which government intervention in housing markets can add to upward pressure on house prices. The result is that, in many countries, owning property does look like an attractive investment but may be increasingly out of reach for those who do not yet own a home.

In Chapter 11, we will return to the idea of property as an investment when we look at how family members can support each other both by acting collaboratively and through inheritance.

End of chapter test

1. Explain why both individuals and governments may prefer home ownership over renting.
2. Outline the main tax and subsidy schemes that governments may use to promote home ownership.
3. Discuss the problems faced by young people in the UK who would like to buy their first home.

References

Australian Bureau of Statistics (ABS) (2012) *Housing tenure data in the Census* [online] www.abs.gov.au/websitedbs/censushome.nsf/home/factsheetshtdc?opendocume nt&navpos=450 (Accessed 21 April 2016).

Bank for International Settlements (BIS) (2016) *Long series on international property prices* [online] www.bis.org/statistics/pp_long.htm (Accessed 6 May 2016).

Bourassa, S., Hoesli, M. and Scognamiglio, D. (2010) *Housing finance, prices and tenure in Switzerland* [online] https://mpra.ub.uni-muenchen.de/45990/ (Accessed 6 May 2016).

Diaz-Serrano, L. (2009) 'Disentangling the housing satisfaction puzzle: does homeownership really matter?' in *Journal of Economic Psychology* 30, pp.745–755. Available online at www.sciencedirect.com/science/article/pii/ S0167487009000622 (Accessed 1 May 2016).

Dorling, D. (2014) *All that is solid: the great housing disaster*, London, Penguin.

European Union (2014) *Directive 2014/17/EU of the European Parliament and of the Council of 4 February 2014 on credit agreements for consumers relating to residential immovable property and amending Directives 2008/48/EC and 2013/36/EU and Regulation (EU) No 1093/2010* [online] http://eur-lex.europa.eu/legal-content/EN/ TXT/PDF/?uri=CELEX:32014L0017&from=EN (Accessed 6 May 2016).

Eurostat (2016a) *Distribution of population by tenure status, type of household and income group* [online] http://ec.europa.eu/eurostat/data/database (Accessed 21 April 2016).

Eurostat (2016b) *Overcrowding rate by age, sex and poverty status* [online] http://ec.europa.eu/eurostat/data/database (Accessed 21 April 2016).

Evans, C. (2013) *Wealth taxes: problems and practices around the world* Briefing paper, Centre on Household Assets and Savings Management (CHASM) [online] www.birmingham.ac.uk/Documents/college-social-sciences/social-policy/CHASM/briefing-papers/2013/wealth-taxes-problems-and-practices-around-the-world.pdf (Accessed 6 May 2016).

Financial Conduct Authority (FCA) (2014) 'MCOB 11.4 Application' in *FCA Handbook* [online] https://www.handbook.fca.org.uk/handbook/MCOB/11/?view=chapter (Accessed 6 May 2016).

Financial Times (2016) 'Trust update – growth at a glance' in *Money Management*, January, London, *Financial Times*.

FT Business (2006) 'Trust update – growth at a glance' in *Money Management*, January, London, FT Business.

GOV.UK (2016a) *Stamp Duty Land Tax* [online] https://www.gov.uk/stamp-duty-land-tax/residential-property-rates (Accessed 7 May 2016).

GOV.UK (2016b) *Affordable home ownership schemes* [online] https://www.gov.uk/affordable-home-ownership-schemes/overview (Accessed 7 May 2016).

GOV.UK (2016c) *Right to buy* [online] https://www.gov.uk/affordable-home-ownership-schemes/overview (Accessed 7 May 2016).

HM Treasury (HMT) (2016) *Lifetime ISA* [online] https://www.gov.uk/government/uploads/system/uploads/attachment_data/file/508117/Lifetime_ISA_explained.pdf (Accessed 7 May 2016).

HM Treasury (HMT) and Osborne, G. (2015) *Chancellor George Osborne's Spending Review and Autumn Statement 2015 speech* [online] https://www.gov.uk/government/speeches/chancellor-george-osbornes-spending-review-and-autumn-statement-2015-speech (Accessed 6 May 2016).

Kofner, S. (2014) 'The German housing system: fundamentally resilient?' in *Journal of Housing and the Built Environment* 29, pp.255–275 DOI 10.1007/s10901-013-9383-0.

Moneyfacts (2006) 'Residential mortgages' in *Moneyfacts*, July, Issue 213, Norwich, Moneyfacts.

Nationwide (2016) *First-time buyer house price earnings ratio* [online] www.nationwide.co.uk/~/media/MainSite/documents/about/house-price-index/downloads/ftb-hper.xls (Accessed 6 May 2016).

Office for National Statistics (ONS) (2016) *House price index. Monthly and quarterly tables* [online] www.ons.gov.uk/economy/inflationandpriceindices/datasets/housepriceindexmonthlyquarterlytables1to19 (Accessed 2 May 2016).

Organisation for Economic Co-operation and Development (OECD) (2016) 'Housing' in *OECD Better Life Index* [online] www.oecdbetterlifeindex.org/topics/housing/ (Accessed 7 May 2016).

US Census Bureau (2014) *Selected housing characteristics 2014* [online] http://factfinder.census.gov/faces/tableservices/jsf/pages/productview.xhtml?src=CF (Accessed 21 April 2016).

Yahoo! Finance (2016) *FTSE All-Share. Historical prices* [online] https://uk.finance.yahoo.com/q/hp?s=%5EFTAS (Accessed 2 May 2016).

Chapter 9

Make wise investments

Tony Byrne and Jonquil Lowe

In Chapter 5, you looked at the first two pillars of wealth: budgeting and saving. Here, we are going to show you why the third pillar, investments, is often seen as the engine of financial growth and how you can harness that power.

Common issues that undermine long-term financial security are investing too little and investing unwisely. For example, in 2015, a fifth of Britons were not saving anything for retirement and a further 12 per cent were seriously under-saving (Scottish Widows, 2015). You also saw in Chapter 2 how the 'behaviour gap' means that the average investor loses out on returns of 2 per cent a year through bad market timing (Barclays, 2013). In this chapter, you will learn why individuals tend to make these types of mistake and how you can avoid these pitfalls.

Learning outcomes

By the end of this chapter you will:

- appreciate the importance of risk and the psychology of investing;
- understand the main types of investment, including their varying levels and types of risk;
- be able to discuss a range of investment strategies and the theories behind them;
- understand the impact of tax and charges on investment returns;
- be aware of the reasons for seeking investment advice.

9.1 Goals: the long and the short of it

In Chapter 5, Section 5.3, you considered eight motives for saving. Some of these, for example accumulating deposits to buy a house or car, are usually short-term goals that you hope to achieve over one or two years. Similarly, money that you set aside 'to build up a reserve against unforeseen contingencies' (Keynes, 1936/1961, p.107) must be available on demand, exactly when you need it (in other words, you need **liquidity**), and so can also be thought of as short term. However, other goals, such as 'the lifecycle motive' – for example, saving today so that you will be able to spend in retirement – are decidedly long term.

The time horizon of your goals is one of the key factors determining whether you should consider putting your money into savings (cash products, like bank and building society accounts) or investments.

9.1.1 Save or invest?

Throughout, this chapter uses the terms 'saving', 'investing', 'savings' and 'investments'. Typically, **investments** are those assets whose value can go up and down and which you usually buy, at least in part, because you hope that their value will rise. It follows that 'investing' is the act of buying investments.

There is no similar consensus on the meaning of 'saving' and 'savings'. For example, 'saving' (a verb) means the act of setting aside money today to use at some time in future. Only the context will tell you whether this is saving into a cash product or buying investments. Sometimes, 'saving' is used to mean saving regularly as opposed to setting aside a single lump sum of money. Similarly, 'savings' often means the stock of cash products that you have built up, but it can mean a stock of investments (or a mix of cash products and investments) as when people talk about their 'retirement savings'.

Unless the context indicates otherwise, we will usually use 'savings' to mean cash products and 'investments' to mean assets whose value can go up and down. Thinking about the time horizon for your goals, typically, it makes sense to choose savings for short-term goals (say, up to five years) or where you might need to withdraw your money at short notice, since, if you use investments, there is a risk that their price might be low at the time you need your money back.

Table 9.1 compares the returns on cash products and investing in equities in the UK for each decade between 1905 and 2015. The returns shown are the average annual return over and above the amount you would need simply to grow your money in line with inflation. You may wish to refer back to Chapter 4 to review how inflation reduces the buying power of money over time. You learned there about 'nominal' returns (the return without any adjustment for inflation) and 'real' returns (which are adjusted for the effect of inflation). Table 9.1 shows real returns.

ACTIVITY 9.1

Looking at Table 9.1, answer the following questions:

1. In how many of the decades shown did the real return on cash beat the real return on equities?
2. What comments can you make about the negative returns in the table?

Table 9.1 Real return on cash and investments in the UK, 1905–2015

Decade	Cash% pa	Equities% pa
1905–1915	−0.5	−0.2
1915–1925	0.8	3.9
1925–1935	4.7	8.7
1935–1945	−2.3	2.4
1945–1955	−3.0	5.3
1955–1965	1.8	7.3
1965–1975	−1.4	0.1
1975–1985	1.5	11.0
1985–1995	5.2	9.9
1995–2005	2.9	5.0
2005–2015	−1.1	2.3

Source: *Barclays Equity Gilt Study 2016* (Barclays, 2016, p.59).

Table 9.1 shows that equities beat cash in every decade between 1905 and 2015. A negative return in the table indicates a decade when cash or equities did not even grow enough to keep pace with inflation – so the buying power of your money would have fallen. For cash, this happened in five decades. By contrast, equities beat inflation in every decade except one (1905–1915).

The patterns you can see in Table 9.1 suggest that you are more likely to beat inflation and to get a higher return if you invest in equities rather than cash. This is true not just for the UK: Siegel (1998), in his book *Stocks for the Long Run*, produced data for 200 years showing that US equities produced average returns of 6.7 per cent a year that dwarfed the return from cash. Therefore, thinking about time horizon, if you are investing for the longer term (say, ten years or more) and you will not need your money back at short notice, it usually makes sense to choose investments rather than savings. Otherwise, there is a strong likelihood that your money will grow too slowly to allow you to meet your goals – or alternatively the amount you would need to save would be so high as to be unaffordable.

However, time horizon is not the only factor to consider. We now need to take a closer look at risk.

9.2 Risk and return

When investors think about 'risk', they usually mean **capital risk**: the risk that they might lose some of the money they originally invested or gains they have not yet cashed in because of the way that the value of investments can go down as well as up. You have already considered two other types of risk: **inflation risk** (losing buying power because of rising prices) and what is often called **shortfall risk** (the risk that you might fail to reach your goal because the return you are getting is too low). Figure 9.1 shows the trade-off between these risks.

To reduce inflation and shortfall risk, the investor needs a higher return. However, taking on a higher return increases capital risk. It is easy to see why: the return on assets that have little or no capital risk, such as cash, is typically low. A rational investor will need the prospect of some extra return if he or she is to be persuaded to give up the safety of the cash products. Sometimes this extra return is called the **risk premium**. So, there is a trade-off: if you want low capital risk, you must accept a low

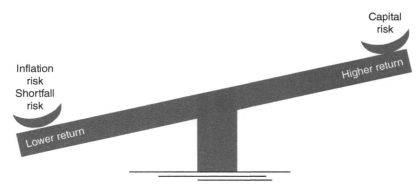

Figure 9.1 Risk and return trade-off

return; if you want a higher return, you must accept higher capital risk. How much risk depends on your personal attitude and your financial capacity to bear any losses.

9.2.1 Attitude towards risk

Before investing any money an investor should always find out their **attitude to risk**. This is not an exact science. However, it is generally accepted that psychometric risk profiling assessments are a useful tool. Psychometric tests are based on psychological theory and statistical research and are designed to measure a person's behavioural or attitudinal traits. When applied to investors, the aim is to assess how much risk they might take given their goals and how comfortable they feel about capital risk.

Risk profiling tools typically produce a report which includes a risk score. The higher the score, the more risk the investor is likely to be comfortable with and so the more of their money they might invest in higher-risk assets, such as equities. However, the report is not intended to provide detailed investment solutions. The aim is to help investors think through the risk level that might be suitable for them and how compatible that is with their goals.

ACTIVITY 9.2

A market leader in risk profiling is the firm, Finametrica. Visit its site www.riskprofiling.com/students where you can take a risk-profiling test yourself (without charge). Complete the questionnaire and review the report. Do you think the report accurately describes you? What questions might it prompt you to ask about your finances?

9.2.2 Capacity for loss

Attitude towards risk is one aspect of the amount of risk you might take with your investments, but just as important is your **capacity for loss**. For example, suppose you are living purely on your savings and investments and you face the following choice:

- Put all your savings in cash products where you can be reasonably sure of a regular income of £150 a week.
- Put your money into investments where the income you can draw off will fluctuate between £100 and £200 a week.

If the rock-bottom income that you could get by on is £125 a week, then you do not have the capacity to cope with investments that may deliver only £100 a week. Your capacity for loss is constrained by the need to clear at least £125 a week. In practice, then, you might consider splitting your money with enough in savings to ensure the £125 a week you need and the remainder in investments to give you the chance of a higher return.

Similarly, if your need is for a future lump sum rather than income, there may be an absolute minimum amount that you must have in order to meet your goal and that will define your capacity for loss.

9.3 Asset classes

So far we have thought about two ways of saving and investing: cash and equities. In practice, there is a whole spectrum of different investments to choose from, but many can be thought of as belonging to four broad **asset class**es. These are:

- cash
- fixed-interest (bonds)
- property
- equities.

9.3.1 Cash

Cash includes the sort of cash products used for savings that you looked at in Chapter 5. It also includes money-market products where, for example, banks lend each other cash overnight or for short periods. Private investors cannot invest direct in the money markets but can indirectly through investment funds (see Section 9.4 below).

As you have already seen above, cash is generally low risk in terms of capital risk, but vulnerable to inflation and shortfall risk.

9.3.2 Fixed-interest (bonds)

Fixed-interest mainly means government stocks (which, in the case of the UK, are known as gilt-edged securities or gilts – after the gilded edging to the original paper certificates) and corporate bonds. Collectively, these are sometimes referred to as 'bonds' (although 'bond' is a common term also used to describe various types of savings and investments).

Fixed-interest investments actually represent loans from investors to either the government or companies. As with any loan, the basic principle is that the lender (in this case the investor) eventually gets their money back and in the meantime receives interest. However, gilts and corporate bonds do not have to be held until the loan is paid back because they can be bought and sold on the stock market.

Box 9.1 describes the main features of fixed-interest securities. If investors buy fixed-interest stock on its issue date, or on the stock market, and hold it until redemption then they will get a return that is fixed at the time they invest. If, however, they sell before the redemption date, they cannot be sure in advance of the return they will get. In either case, they may make a gain or a loss on the amount invested.

UK government stocks are considered to have low capital risk because they are issued by the UK government which is very unlikely to default on paying the interest on gilts or the final payment on redemption. This is not true of all government-issued stocks – in particular, the return from government bonds issued by Greece has been cut back in the aftermath of the global financial crisis of 2008. Corporate bonds are considered to be at higher risk of default than gilts and so typically offer a higher interest rate.

❖ BOX 9.1 THE FEATURES OF FIXED-INTEREST SECURITIES

These bonds are issued in units that have a face-value, called the 'nominal value' or 'par value' (in the UK, this is typically £100), although investors can buy and sell in smaller or larger amounts.

Most bonds pay interest, called the 'coupon' which is fixed as a percentage of the nominal value – this is why these investments are called 'fixed-interest'. For example, a UK bond with a coupon of 6 per cent would pay out £6 a year for each £100 nominal unit held.

The actual interest rate that investors receive depends on the price they pay for the bond. In the example above, if the investor paid, say, £90 for a £100 nominal unit, then the £6 a year interest would be an interest rate of 6/90 × 100 = 6.67 per cent. On the other hand, if the investor paid £110 for each £100 nominal unit, the interest rate would be 6/110 × 100 = 5.45 per cent. Expressing the interest as a percentage of the market price in this way is called the 'running yield' or 'interest yield'.

The return the investor gets is made up of the interest plus any gain or loss when the bond reaches maturity (called 'redemption') or is sold before then on the stock market. When the interest plus any gain or loss are combined and expressed as a percentage of the market price, this is called the 'redemption yield'.

The market price of fixed-interest securities goes up and down in response to economic conditions. This means that the yield also fluctuates and so stays broadly in line with the return from competing investments. Therefore, as a general rule, when interest rates in the economy as a whole fall, the market price of fixed-interest stocks rises. Conversely, when interest rates generally rise, the price of such stocks falls.

Unless they are held to redemption, fixed-interest securities also involve capital risk due to fluctuations in their stock-market price (see Box 9.1). Overall, fixed-interest securities are considered to be lower risk than equities. However, their values can still fluctuate considerably especially during periods of interest-rate volatility and inflationary changes. Fixed-interest stocks with very short terms to maturity are much less volatile than longer-dated stocks.

The graph below gives a simplistic scenario of the relationship between interest rates and bond prices when interest rates are falling. It is not to scale but it wouldn't be misplaced as an example of what happened to UK bond prices in the years following the global financial crisis of 2008 when the Bank of England base rate was rapidly cut from just under 6 per cent to 0.5 per cent (Bank of England, 2016). If and when UK interest rates start to rise again then bond prices would be highly likely to fall because the directions of both arrows will then be reversed.

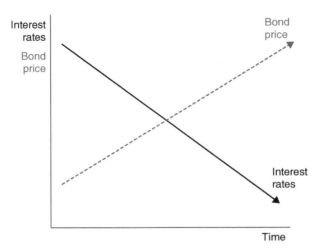

Figure 9.2 Inverse relationship between bond price and interest rates

9.3.3 Property

As an asset class, 'property' normally means commercial property, in other words office, retail including shops and retail parks and industrial property such as factories and warehouses. An advantage of commercial property in the UK is that it gives a relatively stable return from the rental income. There is also the possibility of a gain or loss when properties are sold.

Private investors do not usually invest directly in commercial property. They typically invest by buying the shares of property companies or through investment funds (see Box 9.2 below).

The main drawback with property is that, if it needs to be sold, it can be illiquid, so investors may have to wait to get their money back.

9.3.4 Equities

Equities are shares in companies. By buying its shares, you in effect become a part-owner of the company along with all the other shareholders. You invest either by buying new shares when they are first issued or existing shares through the stock market.

Unlike corporate bonds, you are not lending money to the company, but providing your money indefinitely. However, you can sell your shares on the stock market, in which case you might get back more or less than the amount you originally paid. Investors hope that the stock-market price will rise so that they make a profit.

Larger companies usually pay an income to shareholders (called 'dividends'). This is a distribution of part of the profits that the company has made. There is no guarantee that dividends will be paid and the amount can go up and down. Newer and smaller companies often do not pay dividends at all.

Because companies drive economic growth, over the long term the return from equities can be expected to rise with a country's **Gross Domestic Product**. This is the reason why equities are considered the most suitable investment for the long term and most likely to beat inflation. However, the shares of any one company will not necessarily perform well. In the worst case, a company might go bust and then the shareholders are likely to lose the whole of their investment (but usually no more than that).

Equities tend to be categorised as either medium risk or high risk. Medium-risk equities are generally those that consist of large companies, sometimes called 'blue chips' (after the high-value tokens in the game of poker), which are traded on large stock markets in developed economies. High-risk equities consist of smaller companies in any country as well as equities traded in emerging economies, for example, the so called 'BRIC economies' (Brazil, Russia, India and China).

9.3.5 The risk-return spectrum

The diagram in Figure 9.3 shows how the four asset classes relate to each other if they were to be plotted on a chart with capital risk along the horizontal axis and the expected return along the vertical axis. It demonstrates the key relationship that risk and return go hand in hand.

When considering the risk-return diagram, it is important to note two points. First, 'return' is in reality the *expected* return, not the return the investor will necessarily end up getting. A completely risk-free asset would offer a guaranteed return. However, by definition, capital risk means the return from any other asset cannot be known in advance, only estimated.

Second, it is important that the expected return includes estimated income as well as any estimated gain or loss when the investment is sold. The *Barclays Equity Gilts Study 2016* mentioned in Section 9.1.1 above, emphasises how reinvesting dividends can make a huge difference to overall returns in the long term. For example, an investment of £100 in shares in 1899 would only be worth £184 in real terms (after adjusting for inflation) by the end of 2015. If, on the other hand, all of the dividends

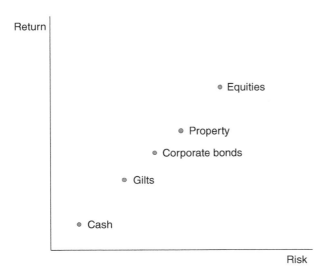

Figure 9.3 Risk-return diagram

arising from the initial investment had been reinvested, the total value of the portfolio would have risen to £28,232 over the same period.

ACTIVITY 9.3

Drawing on what you learned in Chapter 5, explain how compounding might contribute to the difference of over £28,000 in the return from investing £100 in UK equities in 1899.

When income is reinvested, it is added to your original investment and the income itself earns further income. Recall the quote in Chapter 4 attributed to Albert Einstein: *'Compound interest is the eighth wonder of the world'*. Whether or not he really said this, there is no doubt that compounding is a powerful reason for investments being a pillar of wealth. It is critically important to note just how fundamental is the role of reinvested income for both property and equity funds. The very fact that both asset classes produce a combination of both income and potential capital growth is what gives them the edge over fixed interest and cash over the long term.

9.4 Building a portfolio

You have seen that a crucial factor driving your investment decisions is the amount of risk you are willing and able to take. Looking at Figure 9.3, you could simply put all your money into the asset class that seems closest to that level of risk, but you will then be exposed to the ups-and-downs of that asset as economic and financial conditions change and, in any case, that asset may only approximate to the balance of risk and return that you really want.

You can manage risk and return more effectively if you build a **portfolio** that combines the different asset classes – this is called **asset allocation**. To do this, the role of cash and fixed-interest investments is crucial because these lower-risk investments provide a defensive cocoon that offsets downturns in the higher-risk asset classes, such as equities and property, giving you a more stable return over time. Most investors do not build their own portfolios, but instead use investment funds (see Box 9.2) which are ready-made portfolios.

The key questions are: in what proportions should you hold the assets; and should you aim for the same allocation (static asset allocation) or vary it according to changes in economic and financial conditions (dynamic asset allocation)? The answers to these questions may depend on how persuaded you are by a range of different financial theories.

9.4.1 Theory 1: Markowitz-efficient diversification

Diversification is a term that, at its simplest, captures the adage: 'don't put all your eggs in one basket'. The principle behind it is that different investments or asset classes react differently to changes in economic and financial conditions – or, to use a more technical term, the **correlation** between the different investments or assets is not perfect.

❖ BOX 9.2 INVESTMENT FUNDS

Investment funds (called mutual funds in the USA) are ready-made portfolios run by professional investment experts, called fund managers. Private investors invest by buying shares or units in a fund. There are many thousands of different funds to choose from, some aim to produce investment growth, others aim to provide income, yet others a combination of growth and income.

Different funds specialise in different assets and different types of investment, for example UK equities, global equities, Asian equities, smaller companies, property, cash, and so on. Some funds are designed to hold a mix of assets to produce asset allocations tailored to cautious or more adventurous investors. Alternatively, investors may create their own asset allocation by combining several different funds that each focus on one asset class.

Traditionally, funds have been based on a strategy of buying investments, holding them and selling later at a higher price (called 'long' investing), but some funds use other strategies. For example, some funds may borrow investments (for a fee) so that they can sell them now with a view to buying them back later at a lower price (called 'short selling'). Some funds borrow to invest – the process of leverage (also called 'gearing') that you looked at in Chapter 7, Section 7.3 – which increases potential returns but also risk.

It's important to distinguish between two types of fund: 'close-ended' and 'open-ended'.

A close-ended fund has a set number of shares; the value of the shares reflects the value of the investments in the fund but also the demand for those shares. If demand is high, the shares may trade at a premium, so that investors are paying more than the investments in the fund are actually worth. Conversely, if demand is low, the shares may trade at a discount, looking cheap compared with the value of the investments in the fund. Examples of close-ended funds in the UK are investment trusts.

With an open-ended fund, the number of shares or units is increased when there is heavy demand, and the extra money coming in is used to buy more investments, or cancelled if there are more sellers than buyers and so the investment fund contracts. This ensures that the price of the shares or units is always closely aligned with the value of the investments in the fund. Examples of open-ended funds available in the UK are unit trusts, open-ended investment companies and exchange-traded funds.

Professor Harry Markowitz, a US maths professor and economics Nobel laureate, published a seminal paper in 1952, setting out a theory of how portfolios could be selected based on the correlation between investments. This, together with the next theory described in Section 9.4.2, below, are often called **Modern Portfolio Theory (MPT)** and they are still the basis of much portfolio construction today.

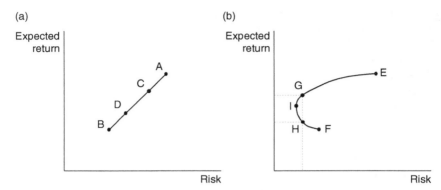

Figure 9.4 Constructing a two-investment portfolio using Markowitz theory

To explain the basics of Markowitz-efficient diversification, consider a simple two-investment world as shown in Figure 9.4.

In Figure 9.4(a), the straight line in the chart labelled A joins up all the possible portfolios made up of these two investments if the correlation between them is perfect. Perfect correlation does not mean that these investments are identical (so they can have different levels of risk and expected return), but it does mean that the return on them moves up and down in an identical way. Point A represents a portfolio invested entirely in Investment A, which is a high-risk-high-expected-return investment, while B is invested only in Investment B which has lower risk and expected return. Point C combines Investments A and B, with more in A than B. Point D shows another combined portfolio but, this time with more of Investment B than A. As an investor, you can choose any portfolio on the straight line by mixing the two investments in different proportions and there is a clear trade-off: if you are willing to accept more risk, you can achieve a higher return.

In Figure 9.4(b), the line represents all the possible portfolios combining two investments E and F where the correlation between them is not perfect. This time, the line joining all the possible combinations of the two investments is curved, not straight. The mathematical reasons for this are beyond the scope of this book, but you should aim to understand the consequences.

ACTIVITY 9.4

Looking at Figure 9.4(b), compare the risk and expected return of the portfolios represented by points G and H. If you are an investor, which of these two portfolios would you choose and why?

Portfolios G and H have the same level of risk, but G has a higher return, so, if you were an investor, you would probably prefer Portfolio G. In fact, all of the portfolios on the part of the curved line between I and F can be beaten by portfolios between I and E that offer a higher return for the same level of risk. Therefore, the part of the curved line between I and E is called the **efficient frontier**. It traces the portfolios that offer the highest return for any given level of risk or, conversely, the lowest risk for any given level of return. These portfolios are said to be Markowitz efficient.

Rational, risk-averse investors will choose a portfolio that lies on the efficient frontier, confident that there is no other portfolio with a better combination of risk and expected return. Which particular **Markowitz-efficient portfolio** they choose will depend on how much risk they are willing and able to take. For example, a very risk-averse investor would choose Portfolio I in Figure 9.4(b) because that is the portfolio with the least possible risk. A more adventurous investor might choose, say, Portfolio G.

Figure 9.4 only considers two investments, but the theory holds however many investments there are and can be applied to whole markets. Moreover, the investments do not need to be, say, shares in single companies, but could be investment funds or asset classes.

Now, here is an important point: the less perfect the correlation between the investments, the more the curve in Figure 9.4(b) bows towards the left and so, for a given expected return, the greater the reduction in risk that can be achieved by combining the investments in a portfolio. This explains why investors are so keen to find asset classes that move in different ways in response to changes in economic and financial conditions.

ACTIVITY 9.5

If you wanted to combine just two of the following asset classes into a portfolio, which combination would enable the biggest reduction in risk for a specified level of return?

a) Equities and cash: correlation low.
b) Equities and gilts: correlation very low.
c) Cash and gilts: correlation middling.

[The answer to this Activity is at the end of the chapter.]

9.4.2 Theory 2: Capital Asset Pricing Model

In the 1950s, when Markowitz published his portfolio theory, computers were still very primitive. This meant that crunching all the numbers – testing the correlations between every possible combination of investments that could be combined to make a portfolio – was a job that would take days. The Capital Asset Pricing Model (CAPM), developed simultaneously by several theorists (such as Sharpe, 1964), suggested a simpler way to construct portfolios that could deliver the investor's desired combination of risk and expected return. Figure 9.5 shows the main features of the CAPM.

The CAPM relies on some assumptions, in particular:

● There is a risk-free asset that all investors can either buy (in order to invest in it) or sell (in order to borrow).
● All investors have exactly the same information about every investment in the market and the same preferences, so they will all want to hold identical portfolios.

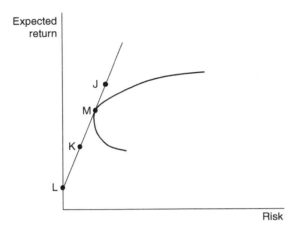

Figure 9.5 Constructing a portfolio using the Capital Asset Pricing Model

Now, suppose investors have chosen to hold all the investments on the market except one. That one investment will fall in price because there is no demand for it at all. However, at some point, its price will become so low that investors will see it as a bargain and buy it after all. Using this logic, the CAPM concludes that all investors will want to hold all the investments on the market and, since all investors have the same preferences, they will all hold the investments in the same proportions. In other words, everyone will hold the market portfolio, shown as M in Figure 9.5.

The market portfolio, M, corresponds to a specific combination of risk and return, but by buying and selling the risk-free asset, investors can adjust the combination of risk and return that they are willing to take. In Figure 9.5, the risk-free asset is shown by the point L, which lies on the vertical axis because that is where risk is equal to zero. It is possible to draw a straight line that passes through point L and point M and beyond – this is called the capital market line and it describes all possible portfolios that combine the risk-free asset, L, and the market portfolio, M:

● At point L, the portfolio is 100 per cent invested in the risk-free asset.
● Between L and M, the portfolio holds both the risk-free asset and the market portfolio.
● At point M, the portfolio is 100 per cent invested in the market portfolio.
● Above point M, the investor is borrowing (by selling the risk-free asset) in order to increase his or her holding of the market portfolio beyond 100 per cent. This is the same principle of leverage that you looked at in Chapter 7, Section 7.3. You may wish to review that section now to remind yourself how leverage increases risk.

9.4.3 Theory 3: Efficient Markets Hypothesis
The two theories above offer a way to combine asset classes (or investments) in order to produce a portfolio with the level of risk and expected return that the

investor wants. Traditionally, this has been used as a way to manage risk and produce more stable returns over time. This rests on the notion that you would stick with the same asset allocation, so can be called 'static diversification'.

However, some experts advocate 'dynamic diversification' where the person creating the portfolio — a fund manager, say — shifts the asset allocation in response to changing economic and financial conditions. This seems at odds with the very aim of diversification to smooth out risks when conditions change and relies on the belief that investment experts, such as fund managers, can use their skills to predict how assets and investments will perform. That same belief underpins other strategies, such as 'stock picking', in other words selecting those investments that are expected to do better in future than others. Whether or not investment experts can consistently exercise such skills is a hotly debated topic and underpinned by our third theory: the Efficient Markets Hypothesis (EMH).

Eugene Fama, another American economist and economics Nobel laureate, is the father of this theory. He (Fama, 1970) proposed that the markets for investments are very efficient, adjusting instantly to new developments, so that the price at any point in time already reflects all known information. This makes it impossible to predict future price movements. He described three possible forms of the EMH:

- **Weak form.** The price today reflects everything that is known about past price and return histories. This means there is no way to predict future price movements based on the past.
- **Semi-strong form.** In addition to price and return history, today's price already reflects all publicly available information. This rules out trying to predict future prices on the basis of, say, economic forecasts, since investors will already have evaluated these and their resulting actions will already have been captured in investment prices.
- **Strong form.** Today's prices reflect all information, including that not publicly available, so even if you have 'insider information' that will already have caused prices to adjust so does not help you to know what will happen next.

Fama (1970) tested these forms of the EMH and reviewed evidence from other researchers' tests, using data for the US stock market. He concluded that some investment professionals might be able to exploit insider information but, for ordinary investors, the strong form of the EMH held.

9.4.4 Theory 4: Behavioural finance

The three theories above all assume that investors are rational, so will make the best, well-reasoned decisions based on the information available, weighing up trade-offs in a logical way. However, there is a growing body of evidence that real people do not necessarily make rational decisions, but are driven by their emotions and frequently rely on short-cuts and rules of thumb (heuristics). This produces the sort of behavioural biases that you looked at in Chapter 2, Section 2.3.2.

Behavioural biases do not just affect individual financial decisions. They can affect whole markets, potentially making these markets less efficient and suggesting that maybe the prices of investments can therefore be predicted at least in the short run. The types of bias that are particularly relevant to investment markets are:

- **Herd behaviour.** Following what others are doing rather than making an individual decision. This tends to give markets momentum, so that a rising market carries on rising or a falling market carries on falling.
- **Hot-hand fallacy.** The assumption that the winners of the past will carry on being winners in the future. This can account for investors favouring star fund managers, believing they have the golden touch and will carry on making good returns indefinitely.

9.5 Investment strategies

The theories outlined in Section 9.4 above underpin many of the investment strategies that are popular with investors and their advisers, but do not necessarily point towards the same investment decisions.

9.5.1 Rules of thumb

It is not just investors who use rules of thumb rather than rationally processing data; financial advisers also have some heuristics based on experience that they may use as a starting point. This is not surprising because, first, there is no automatic way of bridging the gap between an investor's attitude towards risk (which measures risk in a subjective way) and an asset allocation based on the statistical measures of risk used in the theories above. Thus, as a rule of thumb, many professional advisers would suggest portfolios with allocations along the lines of those shown in Figure 9.6. This is not an exact science and other factors, such as time horizon and capacity for loss will also be crucial. However, the broad principle is that the higher the attitude to investment

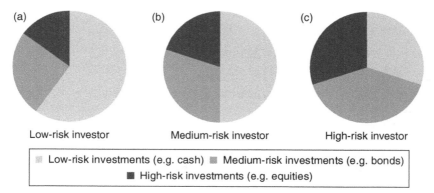

Low-risk investor   Medium-risk investor   High-risk investor

Low-risk investments (e.g. cash) ■ Medium-risk investments (e.g. bonds)
■ High-risk investments (e.g. equities)

Figure 9.6 Possible portfolios depending on attitude to risk

risk of the investor the more money may be invested into higher-risk investments and less into lower-risk ones.

9.5.2 Rebalancing

An investor who follows a traditional approach to asset allocation will want to maintain the same allocation over time. However, without regular adjustment, the make-up of the portfolio will change – in particular, it is likely to become more risky. This is because the higher-risk-higher-expected-return investments, such as equities, will tend to grow more strongly over the long term than the assets such as cash and fixed-interest, and so take over an increasingly larger share of the portfolio.

To revert back to the original asset allocation and level of risk, the investor will need periodically to sell some of their high-performing assets and buy more of the low performers (or adjust the proportion of each asset class bought with any new investment).

An advantage of rebalancing is that it enforces a 'buy-low-sell-high' discipline, which is the classic way to make a profit. However, some critics suggest that selling winners and buying the under-performers amounts to picking the flowers and saving the weeds! You may want to reflect on the contrast between the advice to rebalance periodically and the claimed drawbacks of the disposition bias discussed in Chapter 2. This underlines how practical investment is as much art as science and different theories may conflict.

A disadvantage of frequent rebalancing is cost – see Section 9.6 below.

ACTIVITY 9.6

Which one of the theories described in Section 9.4 above is relevant to the practice of rebalancing?

[The answer to this Activity is at the end of the chapter.]

9.5.3 Active versus passive investing

Managers who believe they can deliver superior returns by **market timing** and **stock picking** are known as active managers. The funds they manage are known as actively managed funds. Investors who put faith in this type of approach are using **active investing**.

The ability of active managers to consistently beat the market is hotly disputed and those who believe it is not possible tend towards a different approach called **passive investing**. This involves investing in a particular market or sector as a whole rather than trying to pick individual stocks. Typically this is done by buying investment funds that simply aim to track the performance of the market or sector as measured by an index – for example, investors wanting to invest in the whole UK equities market might choose a fund that tracks the FTSE All-Share Index. These types of fund are called index funds or tracker funds and investors who favour them are called passive investors or index investors.

A large body of research (for example, Blanchett and Israelsen, 2007; Rhodes, 2000) suggests that active investors do not consistently outperform. As John Bogle, the founder of Vanguard, one of the USA's largest fund management firms and a specialist in tracker funds, puts it:

> A lifetime of experience in this business makes me profoundly sceptical of market timing. I don't know anyone who can do it successfully, nor anyone who has done so in the past. Heck, I don't even know anyone who knows anyone who has timed the market with consistent, successful, replicable results.
>
> (Bogle, 2003)

Moreover, passive investors will beat the majority of active investors because of costs. An active investment fund spends more on research and buys and sells investments more frequently. This makes the cost of active investment higher than the passive approach.

In spite of the overwhelming evidence in favour of passive investing, there seem to be exceptions – star fund managers or investors who do have consistent success, such as Anthony Bolton who managed a highly successful fund for Fidelity, and Warren Buffett, the legendary sage of Omaha and proponent of 'value-investing'. In addition, a relatively recent branch of research (Cremers and Petajisto, 2009) claims some predictive powers. It focuses on a measure called Active Share, which assesses the percentage of stock holdings in a fund manager's portfolio that differ from its 'benchmark index'. The researchers conclude that managers with high Active Share outperform their benchmark indices.

Active Share is also useful in identifying **closet trackers** which purport to be active funds, charging high fees, yet are in reality effectively tracker funds.

ACTIVITY 9.7

What is your preferred investment strategy and why? Use the theories in Section 9.4 above to provide arguments in favour of your preference.

[The answer to this Activity is at the end of the chapter.]

9.5.4 Pound-cost averaging

Investors would ideally like to buy investments when their price is low and sell when prices are at their peak, but, as you have already seen, it is unlikely that investors are able to correctly predict the timing of peaks and troughs in the market – and private investors are notoriously bad at timing, often buying when the market is near its peak. **Pound-cost averaging** is a way of dealing with this uncertainty and can be thought of as diversifying your investing over time.

It simply involves regularly investing a fixed sum of money to smooth out the impact of the highs and lows in the price of an investment. As a result, pound-cost averaging reduces the risk of investing at the worst time, though equally it reduces the chance (the upside risk) of investing at the best time.

❖ **CASE STUDY 9.1**

Rasheed has £12,000 to invest in the shares of an investment fund. He has the choice of investing £1,000 per month for 12 months or investing the full £12,000 upfront. Column 2 in Table 9.2 shows how the price of the shares changes throughout the 12-month period. Consider the possible scenarios:

- **Lump sum invested at the start** If Rasheed invests his full £12,000 as a single lump sum in January, he is able to buy 6,000 shares. In December, despite fluctuations throughout the year, the price is the same as it was in January, so Rasheed's investment is still worth £12,000 (6000 × £2).
- **Regular monthly investing (pound-cost averaging approach)** Table 9.2 shows the effect of drip-feeding his investment by investing £1,000 each month. In months where the price has fallen, Rasheed is able to buy more shares with his £1,000 than in the months where the price is high. Because the price has dipped in a majority of the months, over the whole 12-month period, Rasheed accumulates 6,517 shares which in December are worth £13,033 (6,517 × £2).
- **Investing at the best time** If Rasheed had perfect foresight, he would have invested his whole lump sum in July when the price was at its lowest (£1.50 per share). Then he would have been able to buy 8,000 shares (£12,000 / £1.50) which by December would have been worth £16,000 (8,000 × £2).
- **Investing at the worst time** However, Rasheed has no way of accurately timing the market. If he had delayed, he might just as easily have invested in March, which would have been the worst time because the price was at a peak of £2.20. In that case, he would have bought only 5,455 shares (£12,000 / £2.20) which by December would have been worth £10,910 (5,455 × £2).

Table 9.2 Rasheed invests £1,000 a month

Month	Price per share	Number of shares purchased	Cumulative number of shares held	Cumulative value of holding
Jan	£2.00	500	500	£1,000
Feb	£1.90	526	1,026	£1,950
Mar	£2.20	455	1,481	£3,258
Apr	£2.10	476	1,957	£4,110
May	£1.90	526	2,483	£4,718
Jun	£1.75	571	3,055	£5,346
Jul	£1.50	667	3,721	£5,582
Aug	£1.60	625	4,346	£6,954
Sep	£1.70	588	4,935	£8,389
Oct	£1.80	556	5,490	£9,882
Nov	£1.90	526	6,017	£11,431
Dec	£2.00	500	6,517	£13,033

9.6 Tax and charges

So far, we have assumed that you, the investor, will receive the full benefit of the return from your investments. There are two reasons why this is not in fact the case: tax and charges.

9.6.1 Tax

In most countries, there are taxes to pay on income and gains, including those from your savings and investments. There are also wealth taxes, which in some countries are levied annually, and in others just when wealth is given away or passed on as an inheritance.

However, governments often encourage particular types of saving or investing by giving tax incentives. For example, the incentives may be designed to encourage saving for retirement, help home-buyers or promote investing in new and growing businesses. The incentives vary but may include:

- Tax relief or a bonus when you invest.
- Tax-free build-up of income and gains.
- No tax to pay when you cash in your savings or investments.

Sometimes the incentives are accessed by investing in a particular way – for example through **tax wrappers** (see below). In the Appendix, *UK tax and tax planning*, you will find more details of the tax incentives available to savers and investors in the UK.

There is a wise old saying in respect of investments: 'don't let the tax tail wag the investment dog'. What this means in essence is don't make investment decisions solely based on tax considerations. Before a tax efficient strategy is developed it is important to work out the correct investment strategy to suit your goals, timescale, attitude to risk and capacity for loss, as discussed earlier in this chapter. It is only once the investment strategy is agreed that a suitable tax-planning strategy can be developed.

Tax wrappers

In many countries, instead of investing directly in investments or investment funds, you may invest through a 'tax wrapper'. The most common type of tax wrapper is a pension scheme (see Chapter 10) and typically it ensures that the investments inside are treated in a special way for tax purposes. In the UK, other examples of tax wrappers are Individual Savings Accounts (ISAs) – see Box 9.3.

The reason governments create tax wrappers is usually to encourage certain types of behaviour (such as saving for retirement or building up a deposit for home-buying).

9.6.2 Charges

There is a myriad of charges on investments, not all of which are openly disclosed despite regulations designed to improve the transparency of charging. It's important for investors to be aware of the full effect of charges on investments, which can be large especially over the longer term. The higher the charges, the harder your investments will have to work to leave you with a good return.

> ❖ **BOX 9.3 A POPULAR UK TAX WRAPPER: INDIVIDUAL SAVINGS ACCOUNTS (ISAs)**
>
> An ISA is a tax wrapper that enables tax-free investing in a wide range of savings and investments. Each UK adult has an annual ISA allowance (£15,240 in 2016–17, increasing to £20,000 in 2017–18). This can be used to pay into any of the following types of ISA:
>
> - **Cash ISA**. Savings accounts offered by banks, building societies and the government saving agency, National Savings & Investments. There is also a special type of Cash ISA, called a Help-to-Buy ISA aimed at helping first-time buyers save for a deposit (see Chapter 8, Box 8.3).
> - **Stocks and Shares ISA**. Can be used to invest in stock-market investments such as equities and fixed-interest.
> - **Innovative Finance ISA**. Can be used to invest in, for example, peer-to-peer loans (loans to individuals and companies made direct to borrowers through an online platform).
> - **Lifetime ISA** (available from April 2017). Open to people aged 18 to 39, this can be invested in cash or investments and is designed mainly as a way to save for retirement but can also be used by first-time buyers towards house purchase (see Chapter 10, Box 10.5).
>
> Each year, you can open just one type of each of the ISAs and any allowance that is unused is lost. Savings and investments inside ISAs grow tax-free and (except for the Lifetime ISA) money can be withdrawn at any time tax-free.
>
> There is also a version of the ISA for children, called the Junior ISA (see Chapter 11, Section 11.2.2).

If, in common with most investors, you invest through investment funds, you can expect to pay the following fund charges, which are collectively called the **ongoing charges**:

- **Annual management charge (AMC)**. This pays for the investment management and is typically higher (say, around I per cent a year) for active funds than for passive funds (say, 0.3 per cent a year or less).
- **Fund administration costs**, including the costs of holding the investments safely (custodian fee), paying for regulation, regularly valuing the fund's investments, and so on.

Ongoing charges do not include some other costs that are deducted direct from the investment fund, in particular the dealing costs incurred when investments in the fund are bought and sold. The more active your fund, the higher the dealing costs will be.

Separately, you will normally have to pay:

- **Platform fees.** You normally hold your investments electronically and, increasingly, manage them through a website. This arrangement is called a **platform** and you may have to pay a regular fee (say, quarterly) and/or charges each time you buy and sell a holding.

If you choose to get help from a professional adviser, you will also pay fees separately for that advice.

9.7 To be advised or not advised

Whether to make your own investment decisions or seek the help of an adviser is a personal choice. Advice may help you to invest more wisely and can provide additional protection if things go wrong.

At the time of writing, the UK is recognised as having an advice gap, with investors of modest means unable to find investment advice at a price they are willing to pay and many advisers are turning such clients away because it is uneconomic to provide them with advice (HMT/FCA, 2016). The problem is not necessarily that advisers charge too much, but that investors may be unclear about the value of advice.

The fund management company Vanguard (2014) has conducted research in order to quantify the added value of using an adviser. In 2014, this was estimated as adding around 3 per cent a year to the return for the average client. You may also want to look back now to Table 2.2 in Chapter 2 which considers the 'behaviour gap' – the amount of annual return that the average investor loses as a result of their inability to make rational investment decisions. Financial advisers may help to close that gap.

Investing, by definition, means taking some risks with your money in order to increase your expected returns. It is essential to match the risks to your circumstances and personal characteristics, so that the investment strategy you choose is suitable for you. If you make those decisions yourself, but get it wrong, you have no-one else to blame. If you go to an adviser, the responsibility for recommending a suitable investment strategy rests with the adviser and, typically, you would have formal channels for complaint and compensation if the advice turned out to be unsuitable. However, this does not mean you are protected from investment risk – even a suitable investment strategy can result in a loss; that is in the nature of investing.

9.8 Conclusion

What constitutes the making of wise investments is debatable and some might say subjective. Investments have different levels of risk and this can be managed through constructing a portfolio with an appropriate asset allocation. What is appropriate will depend on the investor's goals, timescale, risk tolerance and capacity for loss.

In order to make wise investments it is important for investors to develop their own investment strategies, to become knowledgeable about investments and the theories that underpin them, but without having to be experts or fully understand investment risk. Modern Portfolio Theory suggests that a diversified approach using asset allocation is likely to produce consistently better returns for a given level of risk or, alternatively, lower risk given the desired return. The Efficient Markets Hypothesis and a large body of research suggest that the majority of investors would achieve better investment returns if they invested in low-cost tracker funds using a passive rather than an active investment strategy. Using a professional adviser could lead to better outcomes than self-investing.

Answers to Activity 9.5

If you wanted to combine just two of the following asset classes into a portfolio, which combination would enable the biggest reduction in risk for a specified level of return?

a)   Equities and cash: correlation low.
b)   Equities and gilts: correlation very low.
c)   Cash and gilts: correlation middling.
The answer is (b). Equities and gilts is the correct answer. The lower (less perfect) the correlation, the greater the reduction in risk associated with a given level of return.

Answers to Activity 9.6

Which one of the theories described in Section 9.4 above is relevant to the practice of rebalancing?

Rebalancing is consistent with the theory of a Markowitz-efficient portfolio. It suggests that it is possible to select an optimal combination of risk and return. Therefore, over time, it makes sense to maintain that combination through rebalancing.

Answers to Activity 9.7

What is your preferred investment strategy and why? Use the theories in Section 9.4 above to provide arguments in favour of your preference.

If you believe it is possible to 'beat the market' and so incline towards active investing, you are implicitly rejecting the Efficient Markets Hypothesis (EMH), since you think you have some system that can predict what will happen to the return from the investments you choose. Your system might rely on behavioural theories, for example herd behaviour may suggest a rising market will keep on rising for a while.

If you are a passive investor, it is likely that you are convinced by the EMH, subscribing to the view that there is no way to know what will happen to returns next. Alternatively, you might think that there is some scope to beat the market but that the superior gains are small and more than swallowed up by the higher costs of active investing. Another possibility is that you follow the Capital Asset Pricing Model and so passively choose a fund that tracks the whole market, combining that with a risk-free asset (or something close to it – say, cash or gilts) to achieve the combination of risk and return that you want.

End of chapter test

1. Discuss the risk and return characteristics of the four main asset classes.
2. Describe how pound-cost averaging may affect investment outcomes.
3. Explain how Modern Portfolio Theory and the Efficient Markets Hypothesis still influence the investment funds on offer today.

References

Bank of England (2016) *Statistical Interactive Database – official Bank Rate history* [online] www.bankofengland.co.uk/boeapps/iadb/Repo.asp (Accessed 31 May 2016).

Barclays (2013) *Overcoming the cost of being human (or the pursuit of anxiety-adjusted returns)* [online] https://www.investmentphilosophy.com/uploads/cms/overcoming-the-cost-of-being-human2.pdf (Accessed 9 June 2016).

Barclays (2016) *Barclays Equity Gilts Study 2016* [online] http://hungrydummy.com/media/pdf/EquityGiltStudy2016.pdf (Accessed 30 May 2016).

Blanchett, D.M. and Israelsen, C.L. (2007) 'Spotlighting common methodological biases in active-v.-passive studies' *Journal of Financial Planning*, November, Vol. 20(11), pp.64–66,68,70,72,74.

Bogle, J.C. (2003) *The policy portfolio in an era of subdued returns* [online] https://www.vanguard.com/bogle_site/sp20030605.html (Accessed 1 June 2016).

Cremers, K.J.M. and Petajisto, A. (2009) 'How active is your fund manager? A new measure that predicts performance' *The Review of Financial Studies*, September, Vol. 22(9), pp.3329–3365.

Fama, E. (1970) 'Efficient capital markets: a review of theory and empirical works' in Francis, J.C., Lee, C. and Farrar, D.E. (1980) *Readings in Investments*, New York, McGraw-Hill.

HM Treasury (HMT)/Financial Conduct Authority (FCA) (2016) *Financial Advice market review. Final Report* [online] https://www.fca.org.uk/publication/corporate/famr-final-report.pdf (Accessed 12 April 2016).

Keynes, J.M. (1936|1961) *The General Theory of Employment, Interest and Money*, London, Macmillan. (Also available online at, for example, http://cas.umkc.edu/economics/people/facultypages/kregel/courses/econ645/winter2011/generaltheory.pdf).

Markowitz, H. (1952) 'Portfolio selection' in Francis, J.C., Lee, C. and Farrar, D.E. (1980) *Readings in Investments*, New York, McGraw-Hill.

Rhodes, M. (2000) *Past imperfect? The performance of UK equity managed funds* [online] www.betterregulation.com/external/OP9%20Past%20Imperfect%20The%20performance%20of%20UK%20equity%20managed%20funds.pdf (Accessed 1 June 2016).

Scottish Widows (2015) *Retirement Report 2015* [online] http://reference.scottishwidows.co.uk/docs/46273-2015.pdf (Accessed 30 May 2016).

Sharpe, W. (1964) 'Capital Asset Prices: a theory of asset equilibrium under conditions of risk' in Francis, J.C., Lee, C. and Farrar, D.E. (1980) *Readings in Investments*, New York, McGraw-Hill.

Siegel, J.J. (1998) *Stocks for the long run: the definitive guide to financial market returns & long term investment strategies* [online] www.riosmauricio.com/wp-content/uploads/2013/05/Siegel_Stocks-For-The-Long-Run.pdf (Accessed 30 May 2016).

Vanguard (2014) *Putting a value on your value: Quantifying Vanguard Advisor's Alpha* [online] www.vanguard.com/pdf/ISGQVAA.pdf (Accessed 1 June 2016).

Chapter 10

Saving for later life

Jonquil Lowe

❖ CONTENTS

Even in your 20s, there is pressure on you to start saving for retirement and, if you have a job, you may find you are automatically put into a pension scheme. If thinking about retirement so early in life feels irrelevant, then you are not alone; you are sharing some common behavioural traits with millions of other people. In this chapter, you'll explore the challenges of financing retirement and why it may be worth overriding your behavioural traits if you do not want to work until you drop!

Learning outcomes

By the end of this chapter you will:

● understand why financing retirement is expensive for countries and individuals;
● be able to describe different systems for financing retirement and the risks involved;
● be able to explain the concept of compounding;
● be aware of the behavioural traits that can hinder or support saving for later life.

10.1 Live long and prosper

Economies across the world are facing a curious dilemma: their citizens are living ever longer as a result of medical advances, better diet and improved lifestyles, but the cost of supporting older age groups looks increasingly unaffordable. This tension is coming to a head in many developed countries as a large generation born between the 1940s and 1960s reaches retirement. As a result, most developed countries are experiencing an **ageing population**.

10.1.1 Increasing life expectancy

Across the globe, the more recently you were born, the longer you are likely to live. Figure 10.1 compares the average **life expectancy** at birth for the cohort of people born in 1970 with that of the cohort born in 2013 for a selection of countries around the world. The bars in the chart (whose values are shown on the left-hand axis) show how long someone born in 2013 can expect to live on average and you can see for most countries this is around age 80. The triangles (right-hand scale) show how many years longer the 2013 cohort can expect to live than the people born in 1970.

> **ACTIVITY 10.1**
> 1. Across all the countries of the OECD, by how many years has average life expectancy increased between 1970 and 2013?
> 2. Is your country shown in the chart? By how much has life expectancy increased there?

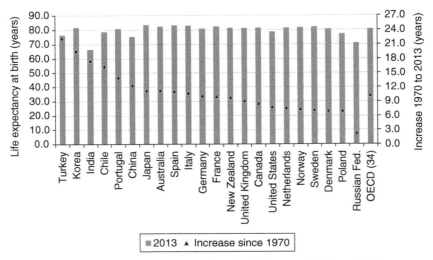

Figure 10.1 Increase in life expectancy at birth between 1970 and 2013
Source: data from OECD (2015a).

Looking at the average for all the countries in the OECD (the last bar on the right), average life expectancy has increased by around ten years between 1970 and 2013 to just over age 80. That's an increase of about three months every year.

Over the 43-year period, average life expectancy has increased by over 22 years for people in Turkey and there have also been big increases in Korea (20 years), India (18), Portugal (14) and China (13). In most other countries, the increase has been more modest (between 11 and 6 years) – for example, in the UK, average life expectancy has increased by 9 years to age 81. The Russian Federation has seen the lowest increase of just over 2 years and average life expectancy is still low for those born in 2013 at 71 years.

10.1.2 Life expectancy on reaching retirement

Average life expectancy at birth includes the minority of people who unfortunately die as children or during their working lives. Stripping these early deaths out of the data reveals that the people who reach retirement can expect to live to an even later age than the 80 or so predicted at birth.

Looking at averages is helpful when you want to consider the population as a whole, but says nothing about the experience of each individual – some will live for a shorter period and others for a longer period than average. Figure 10.2 shows the proportion of UK men and women aged 65 in 2015 who are likely still to be alive at different ages. The chart starts with 100 per cent (vertical axis) of the group alive at age 65 (horizontal axis). As age increases, some die and so the group who are still alive gets smaller. For example, by looking at age 85, you can see that roughly 54 per cent of men are expected to still be alive (follow the dotted lines from age 85 on the horizontal axis across to the percentage still alive as shown by the vertical axis).

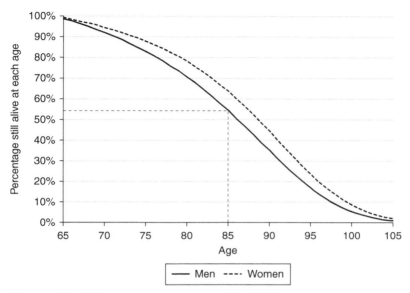

Figure 10.2 UK men and women aged 65 in 2015 expected still to be alive at different ages
Source: author's calculations using data from ONS (2015).

ACTIVITY 10.2

1.   Do women in the UK tend to live for a longer or shorter period than men?
2.   Roughly what proportions of UK men and women live to age 100 or older?

In Figure 10.2, the line showing the proportion of women surviving to each age sits above the line for men. This shows that, at every age, more women are still alive than men – in other words, UK women tend to live longer than men. By age 100, around 9 per cent of UK women are expected still to be alive compared with 5 per cent of men. The proportion of people living to these very old ages is increasing. For UK citizens aged 20 in 2016, one-fifth of males and over a quarter of females are expected to live until at least 100 (DWP, 2011) – if the custom survives, the monarch will be sending out a lot of birthday cards!

10.1.3 'Baby Boomers' and the support ratio

Living longer is one reason why populations across developed economies are ageing. Another is a bulge in births during the period 1945 to 1965. Economists are divided about what impact this so-called 'Baby Boom' generation may have on the economy as it reaches retirement, but governments across the OECD think it will put strain on their pension systems. Their concerns focus on the falling **support ratio**, which can be measured in various ways but is often defined as the number of people of working age for each person over pension age.

Table 10.1 Actual and projected old-age support ratios

Country	1976	1996	2016	2036
Australia	6.17	4.96	3.88	2.72
Canada	6.46	5.05	3.75	2.27
Denmark	4.16	4.04	3.04	2.30
France	4.02	3.83	2.97	2.12
Germany	3.75	4.06	2.79	1.64
Italy	4.49	3.66	2.70	1.74
Japan	7.49	4.20	2.06	1.56
Korea	13.33	10.21	4.94	1.96
Netherlands	5.09	4.71	3.18	1.93
New Zealand	5.86	5.02	3.91	2.50
Norway	3.96	3.70	3.52	2.51
Poland	5.82	5.10	4.04	2.50
Portugal	4.99	3.92	3.10	1.99
Spain	5.14	3.84	3.32	1.99
Sweden	3.74	3.33	2.83	2.33
Turkey	9.71	9.71	7.47	4.06
United Kingdom	3.88	3.72	3.20	2.30
United States	5.19	4.67	3.93	2.58
China	10.13	9.17	6.73	2.96
India	13.05	12.10	10.21	6.49
Russian Federation	6.32	4.86	4.86	3.36
OECD average	**5.57**	**4.98**	**3.82**	**2.45**

Source: United Nations, 2012, cited in OECD (2014).

The argument goes that those currently in work are creating the wealth of a country today (its **Gross Domestic Product**), part of which has to be redistributed to those who no longer work. If the number of workers supporting each pensioner falls, then workers must either give up more GDP or pensioners must receive less. If this argument is accepted, then Table 10.1 shows that most OECD countries are in trouble. Across the whole OECD, the support ratio averaged 5.57 (in other words, over five-and-a-half workers for every pensioner) in 1976, but had fallen to 3.82 by 2016 and is predicted to fall further to 2.45 by 2036. This is despite many countries implementing a variety of pension reforms. Even relatively young countries, like China and India, are expected to see a big fall in their support ratio by 2036.

The argument can be challenged: for example, not all pensioners completely stop work – some carry on working part-time; if the proportion of workers falls, their productivity may increase, especially if employers invest in increased information technology and machinery. In addition support ratios are hard to predict, since they rely not just on births and deaths, but also migration into and out of a country; and more correctly a support ratio would take into account all non-workers, including children and the unemployed, not just the retired.

ACTIVITY 10.3

Explain how increasing the age at which pensions start to be paid would affect the support ratio.

Among the reforms that OECD countries have been implementing are increasing the age at which pensions can start and making it illegal to discriminate against older workers. This should improve the support ratio because older people who stay on shift from being part of the pensioner population and remain part of the working population instead. Therefore, the number of workers increases and the number of pensioners falls.

10.2 Systems of retirement provision

The World Bank identifies five 'pillars' of retirement support as shown in Figure 10.3. The first pillar is state help, usually **means-tested**, for those who are already retired and in poverty. Typically, this will top up their income to a minimum level and might include non-cash benefits as well, such as subsidised travel and help with heating bills.

The next three pillars make up a country's pension system. They are about getting citizens to plan ahead so that they will have sufficient income to live on when they eventually reach retirement. There is usually a mandatory (in other words, compulsory to join) state pension and the State may require further saving through mandatory private pension schemes or encourage this by providing incentives.

The final pillar is a catch-all which may include, for example, using property as a pool of wealth (see Chapter 8) to fund retirement or receiving help from family, such as a place to live and long-term care.

10.2.1 Mandatory state pensions

State pensions are distinctive in two respects: the way they are financed; and their political context.

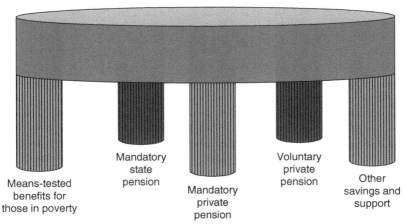

Figure 10.3 Five pillars of support for retirement
Source: author's representation based on World Bank (2008).

State pensions are normally financed on a **pay-as-you-go** basis. This means that the money paid out to today's pensioners comes from the taxes levied on today's workers, so there is a direct transfer of GDP from workers to pensioners through the tax-and-benefits system. Usually, the taxes used to finance pensions carry some rights to claim a state pension in future – for example, in the UK, entitlement to state pension (and some other benefits) depends on paying a tax called National Insurance contributions (see Box 10.1). Workers generally consent to pay these taxes on the basis that, when they themselves have retired, their own state pensions will be paid by the workers of the future, so this arrangement is sometimes called a 'contract between the generations'.

❖ BOX 10.1 STATE PENSION IN THE UK

UK citizens qualify for a state pension by paying National Insurance contributions set as a proportion of their earnings from a job or self-employment. They get credits in some situations when they are not working, for example because of unemployment, illness or caring for young children or disabled adults. Employers also pay National Insurance.

Citizens who reached state pension age before 6 April 2016 may get a **flat-rate pension**, equal to about three-quarters of the minimum income pensioners are deemed to need plus an **earnings-related pension**. Some or all of the earnings-related pension may be replaced by a private pension, through a system called 'contracting out', in return for a reduction in National Insurance.

Citizens reaching state pension age on or after 6 April 2016 are offered just a flat-rate pension, but it is set broadly equal to the minimum income that a single pensioner is deemed to need (just over £8,000 a year in 2016). People who have already built up more than this through the pre-2016 system have the excess protected. To qualify for the full flat-rate pension, citizens need 35 years' worth of contributions and/or credits; the pension is reduced pro-rata for fewer years. A minimum of 10 years' contributions/credits is required to qualify for any state pension at all. Once the pension is being paid, the amount increases each year at least in line with prices and, until 2020, by the greater of prices, average earnings or 2.5 per cent a year.

State pension age used to be 65 for men and 60 for women. Women's state pension age is being gradually increased to 65 by 2018. After that the equalised age for both men and women rises to 66 by 2020, 67 by 2028, and may rise in line with life expectancy after that. The pension cannot be drawn earlier than state pension age, but can start later in which case it is increased.

In 2016–17, government spending on state pensions was forecast to be 4.7 per cent of GDP (OBR, 2016a, 2016b).

The design of state pensions varies across different countries and has tended to be influenced by their political background. A seminal work by Esping-Andersen

(1990 cited in Pierson *et al.*, 2014) suggested three broad types of system, though subsequent reforms have tended to reduce the differences:

- **Anglo-Saxon (liberal) model**. Individuals are expected to look after their own financial security by saving through private pensions. Thus the State mainly provides just a safety net by focusing on means-tested benefits and modest state pensions that cover only basic needs. Examples include the USA, Canada, Australia and the UK.
- **Continental model**. State pensions are more generous, tend to be earnings-related and, in the past, provided different levels of pension for different types of workers (though these differences are declining). There is less reliance on private pensions. Examples include Austria, France, Germany and Italy.
- **Scandinavian model**. Again, state pensions are more generous and earnings-related but tend to be more inclusive, with the same or similar systems applying to all types of worker. This model is typically found in countries like Sweden, Finland and Denmark.

You have seen an example of the Anglo-Saxon model in Box 10.1 which looked at the UK. Boxes 10.2 and 10.3 outline the state pension systems in a European and a Scandinavian country. Box 10.4 considers the state pension system in China. In all countries, state pensions are typically increased throughout retirement at least in line with prices and sometimes in line with earnings (which tend to rise faster than prices).

❖ BOX 10.2 STATE PENSION IN GERMANY

Employees qualify by paying Rentenversicherung (pension insurance) contributions set as a proportion of their earnings from a job, but get credits in some situations when they are not working, for example because of unemployment, or caring for young children. Employers also pay National Insurance. The system is compulsory for most employees, but civil servants have different pension arrangements. Self-employed people can opt to join, but most take out private pensions instead. Civil servants are covered by a different arrangement.

Contributions must be paid/credited for at least five years to qualify for any pension. The pension is earnings-related. The contributions build up 'pension points' (more for higher earnings, fewer for lower earnings) which are multiplied by a 'pension point value' to work out the pension both at the point of retirement and during retirement. The pension point value usually increases each year in line with earnings but can be varied to take into account changes in the contribution rate and changes in the support ratio.

State pension age for men and women was just over 65 in 2016 and will reach 66 by 2023 and 67 by 2029. It is possible to start the pension up to two years early but at a permanently reduced rate. The pension can be started later, in which case it is increased.

In 2014, government spending on state pensions was 10.6 per cent of GDP.

Source: based on OECD (2015b).

❖ BOX 10.3 STATE PENSION IN SWEDEN

The Swedish state scheme has three parts. The main section is an earnings-related pension: contributions equal to 16 per cent of pay (in 2016) go into a notional pension pot where they are increased in line with average earnings but can also be adjusted up and down to take into account changes in life expectancy for people in the same age cohort. A smaller contribution (2.5 per cent of pay) is invested in the same way as a private pension to create an individual pension fund that is used at retirement to buy a pension, called the premium pension. This **funded** rather than pay-as-you-go section makes the Swedish state pension scheme very unusual. The third element is a means-tested pension that ensures pensioners receive at least a minimum income.

The earnings-related and premium pensions can be drawn at any age from 61 onwards, with the monthly income being lower the earlier the pension starts. The means-tested pension is payable from age 65.

In 2014, government spending on state pensions was 7.4 per cent of GDP.

Source: based on OECD (2015b).

❖ BOX 10.4 STATE PENSION IN CHINA

This is a relatively new scheme introduced in 1998. It covers urban workers and is made up of two parts. First there is a basic pension equal to 1 per cent of earnings for each year in the scheme, subject to a minimum of 15 years' contributions. The earnings used for the calculation are an average of the individual's own earnings and those for their province. Employees must also put 8 per cent of their pay into either an actual fund where the contributions are invested or a notional fund where notional interest is added. The fund is converted into pension at retirement at rates set by the government.

Normal pension age is 60 for men. For women in manual jobs it is 50 and office-based/professional jobs 55.

In 2014, government spending on state pensions was 3.4 per cent of GDP.

Source: based on OECD (2015b).

ACTIVITY 10.4
1. Who might benefit most from a flat-rate state pension? Who might benefit more from an earnings-related state pension?
2. Why might increasing state pension age in line with average life expectancy be considered less fair to some citizens than others? Which citizens are likely to be disadvantaged?

There is no simple way to judge the fairness of a pension system, because 'fairness' can mean different things. It can mean ensuring that everyone has enough to meet their needs or that they get exactly the same as everyone else. These are the principles embedded in flat-rate systems that guarantee a minimum income or pay just a basic pension. If contributions are earnings-related, then a flat-rate system tends to redistribute income from better-off people to poorer people, with higher earners paying in more but drawing only the same level pension as everyone else. These systems benefit most those on lower incomes. The risk is that higher earners might think these systems are unfair to them and be unwilling to carry on paying in. Another way to think of fairness is as a system that lets people take out in proportion to what they pay in. An earnings-related system does this because, although contributions are higher for people with higher earnings, they are also able to draw out higher pensions. Many state systems, like the example of Sweden in Box 10.3, combine a mix of features that aim to protect the poorest citizens while still retaining higher earners' support.

Fairness also riddles decisions about increasing state pension age. For some people, fairness means that everyone should be able to retire at exactly the same age, even if over time people of that age can expect to live progressively longer. Another view is that, to be fair, each generation should expect to spend roughly the same proportion of their adult life in retirement. This might be one-third, in which case, you might expect to work for 40 years and spend 20 in retirement or work for 50 years and spend 25 in retirement, depending on the average life expectancy of your generation. Looking at the average over whole generations raises another aspect of fairness: should people who have lower-than-average life expectancy be allowed to retire earlier and how can they be identified? You might think back to the example of China in Box 10.4, where the normal pension age for female manual workers is lower than for other workers.

10.2.2 Private pensions

If you want to retire on more than just your country's state pension, you will need to build up some additional savings for retirement. One way to do this is to use a private pension scheme. Private pension schemes are organised for you by your employer or arranged by you, yourself, with an insurance company or investment firm. The reason for choosing a pension scheme rather than other ways to save is that pension schemes typically benefit from tax concessions. These vary in different countries, but may include some or all of the following:

- Tax relief on contributions;
- The return from invested contributions might be tax-free;
- You may be able to draw out some or all of the proceeds tax-free.

For example, in the UK, pension scheme savers get tax relief on contributions (within limits), invested contributions grow largely tax-free and a quarter of the savings can be taken (currently from age 55 onwards, or up to ten years before state pension age from 2028) tax-free, but the rest is taxed. However, UK savers under 40 can choose a different, more flexible way to save for retirement, as outlined in Box 10.5.

If you save using a pension scheme at work, your employer usually pays towards your pension too. Together, tax relief and employer contributions cut the cost to you of saving for retirement.

❖ **BOX 10.5 THE UK LIFETIME INDIVIDUAL SAVINGS ACCOUNT**

From 2017, UK savers aged 18 to 39 can pay up to £4,000 each year into a new savings scheme, the Lifetime Individual Savings Account (ISA) (HMT, 2016). It is expected that these will be offered by banks, building societies and investment firms. The savings can be invested in a variety of ways, including cash, bonds and shares (see Chapter 9). Up to age 50, the government will add a bonus equal to 25 per cent of the money paid in plus the interest and investment returns that it has earned.

The savings can be withdrawn fully or partially tax-free from age 60 onwards, or withdrawn tax-free before then to use as deposit on first home. Although you can draw the savings out before 60 for any other reason, you then lose the government bonus and have to pay a penalty charge of 5 per cent.

The Lifetime ISA has some similarity to the New Zealand KiwiSaver (Inland Revenue, 2014), which is a retirement savings scheme that also allows early withdrawal for first-time home purchase. However, there are no arrangements for employers to pay into your Lifetime ISA.

There are two main types of private pension: **defined-benefit** and **defined-contribution**. With a defined-benefit scheme, you are promised a particular level of pension, often worked out according to some formula. You have already seen some examples in Section 10.2.1 above because nearly all state pensions are defined-benefit schemes. The distinguishing feature of a defined-benefit scheme is that you can predict in advance roughly what retirement income it will provide.

Some (particularly larger) employers in a few countries, like the UK and Sweden, offer their employees membership of defined-benefit schemes. Typically, these are salary related, promising a fraction of pay for each year you have been in the scheme. The fraction might be, say, one-sixtieth, one-eightieth or one-hundredth. The definition of pay might be 'final salary' (your pay close to retirement) or, more commonly, 'career average revalued earnings' (CARE) which means the average of your pay during all your years of membership, with the earlier years' pay revalued up to the date of retirement so that your pension keeps pace with inflation while it is building up.

❖ **CASE STUDY 10.1 A DEFINED-BENEFIT PENSION**

Kara has been in her pension scheme for five years. She pays 5 per cent of her earnings (£2,400 this year) into the pension scheme and her employer pays in a further 15 per cent of salary. The scheme pays one-eightieth of her career average revalued earnings for each year. The average of her pay over the past five years is £40,000. The pension she has built up so far is 5 × 1/80 × £40,000 = £2,500 a year.

Table 10.2 Examples of the impact of charges on your pension pot

This table shows how much your pension pot might be worth in future after charges if the total paid in was £100 a month in today's money and charges were at the different levels shown. Amounts shown are in today's money.

Level of charges	Value of your pension pot* after this many years:			
	20	30	40	50
No charges	£36,700	£68,700	£114,600	£179,500
0.3%	£35,600	£65,500	£107,400	£165,300
0.5%	£34,800	£63,500	£102,900	£156,600
0.75%	£33,900	£61,100	£97,700	£146,600
1.0%	£33,100	£58,800	£92,800	£137,400
1.5%	£31,500	£54,500	£84,000	£121,200
2%	£30,000	£50,700	£76,200	£107,500

* Assumes contributions start at £100 a month and rise each year in line with earnings at 3.5 per cent a year, investment growth is 5 per cent a year and inflation 2 per cent a year.

The majority of private pensions, including all personal pension schemes, are defined-contribution schemes. With these, the contributions paid in are invested to form your own personal pension pot. The amount in your pot at retirement depends on: the amount you – and your employer, if it is a workplace scheme – pay in and this might be boosted by tax relief; how well the invested contributions grow; and the amount deducted in charges. It is impossible to predict future investment performance especially when retirement is decades away or how inflation will affect the buying power of your savings. Therefore, unlike a defined-benefit scheme, with a defined-contribution, you are exposed to both **investment risk** and **inflation risk**. Chapter 9 suggests how you might manage investment risk, but you will need to review your savings regularly to see how your pension is building up and arrange to save extra if necessary. Finally, do not underestimate the impact of charges – see Table 10.2.

ACTIVITY 10.5

Suppose you are comparing two personal pension schemes, one with charges of 0.5 per cent a year and the other 1.5 per cent a year. Use Table 10.2 to estimate what your pension pot might be worth after 40 years if you start saving £100 a month. How much of your savings do you lose if you choose the higher-charging scheme?

In the cheaper scheme (charging 0.5 per cent a year), your pension pot might be worth £102,900 in today's money after 40 years of saving. With the more expensive scheme (charging 1.5 per cent a year), it could be worth £84,000 – that's around one-fifth less than the cheaper scheme. Choosing the more expensive scheme means you lose an additional £18,900 of your savings in charges. This does not mean you should always go for the cheapest scheme, but you should be clear in your own mind what extra you are getting if you decide to pay more.

10.2.3 Converting savings to income

With any defined-contribution scheme, you reach retirement with a pot of money and need to decide how you will use it to support yourself during retirement.

One option is to leave the money invested and draw out income and lump sums as and when you need them – often called **drawdown**. There are uncertainties involved in this. The biggest one is that you do not know how long your money will have to last. Look back to Figure 10.2 in Section 10.1.2. Where on those curves do you think that you will lie? Will you be someone who dies earlier than average or might you be one of the growing proportion who make it to 100 and beyond? Most people cannot know or even guess and so are exposed to **longevity risk**, the risk of outliving their savings. You will also continue to be exposed to investment risk and inflation risk.

You could avoid longevity risk by just drawing off the **natural income**, leaving your capital untouched. However, this means living on a lower income that might not be enough to meet your needs. Ideally, you would draw an income each year that, taking into account expected investment returns, would make your money last as long as you expect to live (Scenario A in Figure 10.4). Each year, you would need to review your savings. If investment returns have been lower than expected, you could consider cutting your income (Scenario B in Figure 10.4). Alternatively, you might keep the income constant and just accept that your money will not last as long (Scenario C in Figure 10.4). Box 10.6 gives an insight into how pensioners experience this dilemma in practice.

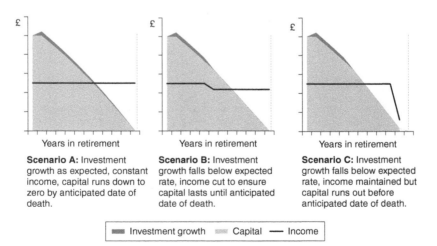

Scenario A: Investment growth as expected, constant income, capital runs down to zero by anticipated date of death.

Scenario B: Investment growth falls below expected rate, income cut to ensure capital lasts until anticipated date of death.

Scenario C: Investment growth falls below expected rate, income maintained but capital runs out before anticipated date of death.

▬▬ Investment growth ░ Capital —— Income

Figure 10.4 Drawdown options

❖ BOX 10.6 DRAWDOWN EXPERIENCE IN AUSTRALIA

...a significant portion of superannuation savings are being depleted before reaching Age Pension age. On average, around one-third of superannuation assets are withdrawn by the time an individual reaches the Age Pension eligibility age. Around one-quarter of people with a superannuation balance at age 55 have depleted their balance by age 70.

(Financial System Inquiry, 2014a, pp.120–1)

Evidence suggests that the major worry among retirees and pre-retirees is exhausting their assets in retirement. An individual with an account-based pension can reduce the risk of outliving their wealth by living more frugally in retirement and drawing down benefits at the minimum allowable rates. This is what the majority of retirees with account-based pensions do, which reduces their standard of living. The difficulty in managing this risk is also exacerbated by the uncertainty as to how long a retiree will live.

(Financial System Inquiry, 2014b, pp.120–1)

The alternative to drawdown is some kind of **annuity**. This is a type of insurance where in exchange for a lump sum (your pension pot) you get an income that is guaranteed to be paid for the rest of your life, however long you live. Like all insurance, annuities work by placing you in a pool with other similar people. Although you do not know how long you personally are likely to live and need an income for, the average life expectancy for the pool can be predicted. Everyone in the pool is offered the same income and it is pitched to run the capital of everyone in the pool down to zero by the time they all die. The left-over capital from people who die early is used to pay for the continuing income for the people who live longer than average. It follows that the income an annuity offers depends on the factors that affect your life expectancy, such as your age (the older you are when you buy an annuity, the higher the income you'll get). Although women tend to live longer than men (think back to Activity 10.2), legislation requires that men and women in European Union member states are offered the same 'unisex' annuity rates.

Not all countries have an annuity market and several that do not, such as Australia, New Zealand and the USA, are looking at how they might develop one. The UK market offers a particularly rich range of annuity products, for example:

- **Level annuities.** These pay the same income in pounds year after year, but the buying power of your income falls over time as prices rise due to inflation.
- **Inflation-linked annuities.** The starting income is lower than for a level annuity but increases each year in line with price inflation to maintain the original buying power of your income.

- **Enhanced and impaired life annuities** that pay a higher than normal income if your life expectancy is reduced because of health or lifestyle factors.

ACTIVITY 10.6

Which provides the more secure income: drawdown or an annuity?

The drawback of annuities is that the income they offer can look low compared with the income you might get from drawdown. However, you need to compare like with like. An annuity provider will invest the money you pay in low-risk assets, such as government bonds, so that it can be certain to provide the income it has promised. By contrast, you are likely to choose higher-risk investments, such as equities, to improve your chance of a higher return from drawdown. So this is a very standard investment trade-off: do you go for the lower-risk, lower-return secure income an annuity provides or the higher-risk, potentially higher-return and more flexible drawdown option? Often, a solution will be to mix and match the different options.

10.3 How much is enough?

Now you know the range of retirement saving products open to you, but how much do you need to save and why are you being pushed to start saving so early in life?

The amount you need to save depends, in part, on how much retirement income you think you'll need. As a rough rule of thumb, some experts suggest aiming for half or two-thirds of your current income (and you can recalculate this over time as your income and lifestyle change), but you might consider talking to any retired people you know to see how much they think is enough. In the UK, two surveys (NEST, 2014: CRSP, 2015) suggested that around £15,000 a year (at 2014/15 prices) was the minimum a pensioner would want.

How much to save also depends on what secure income you can already expect from the state pension system and any employer defined-benefit pensions you've built up, and when you expect to start drawing a pension. The later you start to draw out an income from a defined-contribution pension, the less you will have to save each month to reach your target. In addition, the amount you need to save depends on investment returns, inflation, charges and, if you opt for an annuity at retirement, how much it costs – these are all future unknowns, so you'll have to make assumptions and review your planning regularly.

Table 10.3 brings together all these factors to suggest the amount of retirement income that each £100 a month paid into your pension pot might provide. Bear in mind that some of the money paid in might come from your employer and tax relief, so the cost to you could be less. Even so, you can see from the table and Case Study 10.2 that pensions are expensive, which is one reason why you are encouraged to start saving early in life. If you leave starting to save too late, the retirement income you want may have become unaffordable.

Table 10.3 Examples of the pension £100 a month of savings might provide

This table shows how much retirement income you might get in future if the total paid in was £100 a month in today's money. Income is shown in today's money.

Level of charges	Assuming you retire after saving for this many years:			
	20	30	40	50
Value of pension pot*	£33,900	£61,100	£97,700	£146,600
Age at which you retire	Yearly pension**			
66	£1,288	£2,322	£3,713	£5,571
67	£1,342	£2,420	£3,869	£5,805
68	£1,383	£2,493	£3,986	£5,981
69	£1,437	£2,591	£4,142	£6,216
70	£1,546	£2,786	£4,455	£6,685

* Assumes contributions start at £100 a month and rise each year in line with earnings at 3.5 per cent a year, investment growth is 5 per cent a year, charges 0.75 per cent a year and inflation 2 per cent a year.

** Based on rates in March 2016 for an annuity where income increases each year in line with prices.

❖ CASE STUDY 10.2 A DEFINED-CONTRIBUTION PENSION

Rasheed currently earns £30,000. He pays 4 per cent of this into a defined-contribution pension scheme. The government adds a further 1 per cent in tax relief and Rasheed's employer pays in a contribution equal to 3 per cent. This means that Rasheed's own contribution of 4% × £30,000 = £1,200 is doubled so that, in total, £2,400 is paid into his pension pot this year, or £200 a month. Using Table 9.3, Rasheed estimates that every £100 a month he saves over the next 30 years would provide a pension of £2,493 a year assuming he retires at age 68. Therefore saving £200 a month could produce twice this amount which is £4,986 a year. Over the 30 years, Rasheed personally will have paid half the cost – about £46,000 in today's money – to get this pension of just under £5,000 a year.

ACTIVITY 10.7

Leonard and Sheldon both take out the personal pension illustrated in Table 10.3. Leonard saves for 20 years and ends up with a pension pot of £33,900. Sheldon saves for 40 years and ends up with a pension pot of £97,700. Suggest why Sheldon, saving for twice as long, has *more than twice* as much in his pension pot as Leonard.

A term of 40 years is twice a term of 20 years or 100 per cent bigger, so twice as much will have been paid in as contributions. Yet, the increase in pot size is

(£97,700 − £33,900)/£33,900 × 100 = 188 per cent bigger. The pot size is so much bigger because of **compounding** (which you looked at in Chapter 5) and this is a second reason why you should start saving for retirement as early as you can. When you pay in contributions, they are invested and earn a return. The return is reinvested and so, in the next time period, you earn a return not just on the contributions paid in but the previous returns as well. The earlier you start to save, the bigger this compounding effect is, and the less you will have to save in total to achieve the same retirement income goal.

10.4 Behavioural traits – going with the grain

Many governments are concerned that their citizens are not saving enough for retirement and are starting to save too late. There could be all sorts of rational reasons for this: other priorities, such as paying off student debt and buying a home; or a lack of awareness about just how expensive retirement is likely to be. On the other hand, do you feel that retirement is a bit dull, a long way off, you will get round to thinking about it but not quite yet? If so, you are falling prey to your innate behavioural biases – you're not alone! We all have them!

You considered in Chapter 2 how behavioural scientists (for example, Kahnemann, 2011; Thaler and Sunstein, 2009) explain that we have two ways of thinking: rationally and emotionally. Rational thought takes effort and, in many situations, we rely instead on our emotional side, which is quick, intuitive but also prone to biases. Some of these biases get in the way of long-term financial planning for distant events like retirement, in particular:

- **Myopia.** A tendency to give most attention to what is happening today and to assume that more distant issues will resolve themselves.
- **Hyperbolic discounting.** A tendency to place a much greater value on money today than money tomorrow, even though when tomorrow arrives we are likely to regret this.
- **Status quo bias.** A tendency to stick with the current situation rather than make changes.
- **Herd behaviour.** A tendency to base what we do on what the people around us are doing rather than rationally think through our own decision.

When it comes to pensions, some governments override our biases by making additional retirement saving compulsory – an example is Australia, where employers must pay into a workplace pension scheme on behalf of their employees. Some others, in particular New Zealand and the UK, have come up with a different solution that exploits our behavioural biases: **automatic enrolment**.

ACTIVITY 10.8

If you, along with most other employees, are automatically put into a pension scheme shortly after starting a new job, which of the behavioural biases mentioned in this section are likely to improve the chances that you will save for retirement?

The status quo bias is responsible for your putting off the decision to start saving for retirement. On the other hand, if someone else puts you into a pension scheme, the status quo bias means you tend to go with the flow and stay in the scheme. Even if you think you might opt out, you are likely to put off that decision until later, some day, one day. If, because of automatic enrolment, nearly everyone you know is in a pension scheme, herd behaviour suggests you will prefer to do the same. In these ways, automatic enrolment uses your behavioural biases to nudge you into saving.

10.5 Conclusion

In this chapter you've seen how saving for retirement is likely to be a relevant part of your financial planning even if you are only at the beginning of your working life. Starting to save early makes it more likely that you can achieve your eventual retirement goals, especially in the face of state pension systems that are being reformed and cut back.

You've also considered the various risks involved in saving over the long term and providing income throughout retirement and how some pension schemes, including state systems, can shield you from those risks.

Finally, you've looked at a few of the behavioural biases that can influence our decisions about long-term saving and how some governments have found ways to harness these biases to get us saving more and earlier.

End of chapter test

1. Explain how increasing life expectancy puts pressure on a pay-as-you-go pension system.
2. Use an example to show how a defined-benefit pension scheme can aid financial planning for retirement.
3. Describe the three major risks that individuals face when saving for retirement through a defined-contribution scheme.
4. Discuss two reasons why starting to save for retirement early in life can reduce the total cost of saving.
5. Describe three ways in which governments may aim to ensure their citizens have an income in retirement.

References

Centre for Research in Social Policy (CRSP) (2015) *A minimum income standard for the UK* [online] www.lboro.ac.uk/research/crsp/mis/ (Accessed 29 March 2016).
Department for Work and Pensions (DWP) (2011) *Number of future centenarians by age group* [online] https://www.gov.uk/government/uploads/system/uploads/attachment_data/file/223173/centenarians_by_age_groups.pdf (Accessed 26 March 2016).

Financial System Inquiry (2014a) *Interim Report* [online] http://fsi.gov.au/publications/
final-report/ (Accessed 29 March 2016).

Financial System Inquiry (2014b) *Final Report* [online] http://fsi.gov.au/publications/
final-report/ (Accessed 29 March 2016).

HM Treasury (HMT) (2016) *The new Lifetime ISA* [online] https://www.gov.uk/
government/uploads/system/uploads/attachment_data/file/508176/Lifetime_
ISA_final.pdf (Accessed 28 March 2016).

Inland Revenue (2014) *KiwiSaver: Retirement saving made easy* [online] www.kiwisaver.
govt.nz/ (Accessed 28 March 2016).

Kahnemann, D. (2011) *Thinking Fast and Slow* London, Penguin.

National Employment Savings Trust (NEST) (2014) *Retirement realities: Tomorrow's
worth saving for* [online] www.nestpensions.org.uk/schemeweb/NestWeb/
includes/public/docs/NEST_Retirement_Realities_2014,pdf.pdf (Accessed 29
March 2016).

Office for Budget Responsibility (OBR) (2016a) *Economic and fiscal outlook – March 2016*
[online] http://budgetresponsibility.org.uk/efo/economic-fiscal-outlook-march-
2016/ (Accessed 27 March 2016).

OBR (2016b) *Public finances databank* [online] http://budgetresponsibility.org.uk/data/
(Accessed 27 March 2016).

Office for National Statistics (ONS) (2015) *Expectation of life, principal projection, Great
Britain, 2014-based* [online] www.ons.gov.uk/peoplepopulationandcommunity/
birthsdeathsandmarriages/lifeexpectancies/datasets/
expectationoflifeprincipalprojectiongreatbritain (Accessed 26 March 2016).

Organisation for Economic Co-operation and Development (OECD) (2014) 'Old age
support ratios' in *Society at a glance 2014* [online] http://dx.doi.org/10.1787/
888932966352 (Accessed 26 March 2016).

OECD (2015a) 'Life expectancy at birth, 1970 and 2013' in *Health Statistics 2015* [online]
http://dx.doi.org/10.1787/health-data-en (Accessed 26 March 2016).

OECD (2015b) *Pensions at a glance 2015* [online] http://dx.doi.org/10.1787/pension_
glance-2015-en (Accessed 6 March 2016).

Pierson, C., Castles, F.G. and Naumann, I.K. (2014) *The Welfare State Reader*, 3rd edn,
Cambridge, Polity Press.

Thaler, R. and Sunstein, C. (2009) *Nudge* London, Penguin.

World Bank (2008) *The World Bank Pension Conceptual Framework* [online] http://
siteresources.worldbank.org/INTPENSIONS/Resources/395443-1121194657824/
PRPNoteConcept_Sept2008.pdf (Accessed 27 March 2016).

Chapter 11

Help from your family

Jonquil Lowe

In this chapter, we are going to look at ways that family might be able to support you in laying the foundations of your future financial wealth. The focus here is mainly on the UK and, as you work through the chapter, you may want to consider what similar or contrasting systems and support mechanisms exist in any other countries you are familiar with.

Learning outcomes

By the end of this chapter you will:

- be able to discuss the aims and features of some savings and investments for younger people;
- be aware of a range of ways in which families can help with buying a home;
- understand how gifts and inheritances are taxed in the UK;
- have a basic understanding of trusts and how they may be used.

11.1 Teaching you to fish!

There is a proverb: 'Give a man a fish and he eats for a day; teach him to fish and you feed him for a lifetime' (attributed to Ritchie, 1885). In a similar way, parents and other family members can sometimes provide (very welcome) help through gifts and loans, but the greatest gift is often introducing you to sound money habits, such as day-to-day money management, saving and how to make risk work for you. This teaching starts very early – when you are taken along on shopping trips or receive your first pocket money – and you may be unaware of just how much understanding of money and wealth seeps into you this way.

11.1.1 The cash flow game

Fundamental to the ability to build up wealth is the capability to control your spending. Not all parents give their children pocket money and they may have many reasons for doing so, but if yours did, they were doing you a big favour by providing you with an income. However small that income was, it had the potential to sow the seeds of the skills you learned about in Chapter 5: living within your means and even holding back a little to save for some big item you had set your heart on.

This sort of cash flow management becomes ever more important as you get older, enabling you to avoid distressed borrowing and creating a surplus that you can start to save and invest as the foundation for building your wealth. Figure 11.1 shows an example of what an ideal cash flow might look like over your working life. It tracks the relationship between three items, all of which are shown in today's money (in other words, after adjusting for inflation):

- **Income** (the solid black line and measured against the left-hand scale). If you are studying, you probably have little or no income in the early years, but once you get a job hopefully your income will build up steadily. It may peak in mid to later life and maybe there will be a time when you decide you'd rather work part-time,

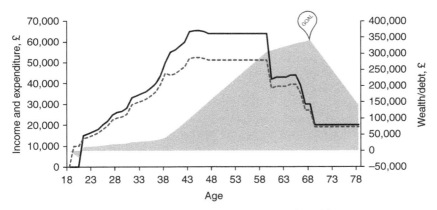

Figure 11.1 An example of cash flow during your working life

sacrificing some income for a better work-life balance. Somewhere towards age 70, you might decide to retire at which point income might again fall.

● **Expenditure** (the dashed grey line, also measured against the left-hand scale). During early years of study, you are most likely spending more than you have coming in as income (with the shortfall met by student loans). However, once you start working, the aim is to keep total expenditure below income. The gap between the (higher) income line and the (lower) expenditure line is the amount you are saving.

● **Wealth/debt** (the grey shaded area and measured on the right-hand scale). In the early years, spending exceeds income with the gap being met by debt, so the shaded area is below zero on the right-hand axis. Once income starts to come in you can pay off the debts and, provided you don't spend all your income, you can then start accumulating some wealth. This can take any of the forms we have looked at in earlier chapters, such as savings, investments, pensions and property. Whatever happens to income, provided you can adjust spending to keep in step, wealth continues to build. Wealth falls once you start to draw on it to pay for something – in Figure 11.1, it starts to fall around age 70 when it's assumed you start to use the stock of wealth to provide retirement income. However, your cash flow planning might include other goals as well, which may be short term – say, saving for a holiday – or long term, maybe building up savings for your own children.

ACTIVITY 11.1

Figure 11.1 is a very simple example of cash flow over the lifecycle but, using the same principles, you could create more complicated examples that included, say, breaks from work and periods of running up debt.

1. See if you can construct a cash flow chart for Andrew who is described below:

Andrew started an apprenticeship at age 18, enabling him to study while earning a wage. Once he completed this, he was hired and had worked up through the firm until a competitor offered him a better job on a much higher salary. A couple of years later he married Aisha. Up to then, Andrew had always saved some of his money and, when he met Aisha, he set a goal to use a big chunk of his savings on their wedding and honeymoon. When their first child was born, Andrew became a house-husband and the couple relied on Aisha's income. After five years Andrew returned to work, initially part-time, but getting back to full-time work a few years later and, at that point, he was able to start saving again. The period of child-caring prevented Andrew building up as much pension as he would have liked and so he carried on working full-time until 75 and part-time into his mid-80s.

2. Comment on how realistic you think the example of Andrew might be.

[Answers to this Activity are at the end of the chapter.]

If you find cash flow management difficult, don't despair! There are loads of resources and tricks you can use to make the task easier:

- Set up standing orders and direct debits to pay essential bills automatically as they fall due.
- Keep track of how much money you have and where it is going, for example by downloading a cash flow app to your phone.
- Be ruthless about cutting non-essential spending, especially clubs and memberships you sign up for but rarely use.
- Check your balance before you indulge in any impulse buys!
- When you can, save up for things rather than borrowing.
- Only borrow to finance activities that you expect to increase your future income or wealth (for example a student loan to increase your future earnings power, a car loan so you have transport to get you to work).

11.1.2 The saving habit

Another 'fishing' gift from your parents may have been a savings account where they encouraged you to put some of your pocket money and birthday gifts so that you could save up and buy the toys and gadgets that you especially wanted. In the UK, from the age of seven, you would have been able to manage this account yourself, helping you develop a sense of the value of money, the saving habit and confidence in dealing with financial firms. Many banks and building societies have special accounts for children, so these early lessons may have been sweetened with a piggy bank, magazine, young savers club or other goodies. Hopefully these days you are more motivated by the prospect of a good rate of interest!

Some schools have also been involved in initiatives to encourage the saving habit, for example running a school savings bank, which basically works as a branch of whatever commercial bank the school links up with. Between 2005 and 2011, the UK government promoted a scheme called the Child Trust Fund (CTF) (see Section 11.2.2 below) which was originally intended to act as a springboard for financial education sessions in schools to stimulate interest in long-term saving. While the CTF was abolished, personal finance education in schools more generally continues, not just in the UK but across many countries of the OECD (2012).

Whether you started young or not, it's a good idea to get the saving habit and these tips may help:

- Pay yourself first. Treat saving, however small the amount, as essential spending and set aside that amount from your income before you pay for anything else.
- Set up standing orders so part of your money goes direct to your savings account each pay day.
- Turn savings goals into concrete targets by working out how much you need and can afford to save (size) over a specified period (timescale) – Table 11.1 may help you to do this.
- To make achieving a saving goal easier, set yourself mini-targets and small rewards each time you hit one of these milestones.
- Tell someone close to you about your goal or try challenging a friend or family member to see who can meet their saving targets first. This helps you to stay committed.
- Check regularly to make sure you are getting the best return on your savings and, if not, switch to a new account. Price comparison websites (see Box 11.1) can help you do this.

ACTIVITY 11.2

Using Table 11.1, answer the following questions:

1. If Sajid wants to save £100 over a period of two years and can get 1 per cent a year on his savings, how much does he need to save each month?
2. If Paula wants to build up £800 to pay for a holiday in 12 months' time and can get 2 per cent a year tax-free on her savings, how much does she need to save each month?
3. If George and Em set aside £10 a month to build up some savings for their new baby, how much will the savings be worth after 18 years if the return on the savings averaged 4 per cent a year over the whole period?

Table 11.1 shows the monthly savings required to build up each £100 of savings given the rate of return and timescale. For Sajid, you need to find the column headed '1%' and run down to the cell that corresponds to the row headed '2'. Since he wants to save up £100, you can just read off the answer in the cell which is: he needs to save £4.12 a month. The example of Paula is slightly more complex. You need to find the cell corresponding to '2%' and '1' year, giving you a figure of £8.24. Since she needs to save up £800, she will need to save eight times the amount in the cell: £65.92 per month. With George and Em, you need to find the cell corresponding to '4%' and '18' years: £0.32, in other words the monthly saving that will produce a pot of £100. Dividing the amount they save which is £10 by £0.32 gives 31.25. Multiply this by £100 to find the answer which is that their savings will produce a pot of £3,125 after 18 years. However, when looking at long-term saving goals, bear in mind that inflation will reduce the buying power of the savings pot you build up.

Table 11.1 Giving size and timescale to a saving goal

Timescale (years)	How much you need to save each month to build up each £100 of your saving goal if you can save at this interest rate (%pa):										
	0%	1%	2%	3%	4%	5%	6%	7%	8%	9%	10%
1	£8.33	£8.29	£8.24	£8.20	£8.16	£8.12	£8.07	£8.03	£7.99	£7.95	£7.91
2	£4.17	£4.12	£4.08	£4.04	£4.00	£3.96	£3.92	£3.88	£3.84	£3.80	£3.77
3	£2.78	£2.74	£2.69	£2.65	£2.61	£2.57	£2.54	£2.50	£2.46	£2.43	£2.39
4	£2.08	£2.04	£2.00	£1.96	£1.92	£1.88	£1.85	£1.81	£1.77	£1.74	£1.70
5	£1.67	£1.62	£1.58	£1.54	£1.51	£1.47	£1.43	£1.40	£1.36	£1.33	£1.30
6	£1.39	£1.35	£1.31	£1.27	£1.23	£1.19	£1.16	£1.12	£1.09	£1.06	£1.03
7	£1.19	£1.15	£1.11	£1.07	£1.03	£1.00	£0.96	£0.93	£0.90	£0.86	£0.83
8	£1.04	£1.00	£0.96	£0.92	£0.89	£0.85	£0.82	£0.78	£0.75	£0.72	£0.69
9	£0.93	£0.88	£0.85	£0.81	£0.77	£0.74	£0.70	£0.67	£0.64	£0.61	£0.58
10	£0.83	£0.79	£0.75	£0.72	£0.68	£0.65	£0.61	£0.58	£0.55	£0.52	£0.50
11	£0.76	£0.72	£0.68	£0.64	£0.60	£0.57	£0.54	£0.51	£0.48	£0.45	£0.43
12	£0.69	£0.65	£0.61	£0.58	£0.54	£0.51	£0.48	£0.45	£0.42	£0.39	£0.37
13	£0.64	£0.60	£0.56	£0.53	£0.49	£0.46	£0.43	£0.40	£0.37	£0.35	£0.32
14	£0.60	£0.55	£0.52	£0.48	£0.45	£0.41	£0.38	£0.36	£0.33	£0.31	£0.28
15	£0.56	£0.51	£0.48	£0.44	£0.41	£0.38	£0.35	£0.32	£0.29	£0.27	£0.25
16	£0.52	£0.48	£0.44	£0.41	£0.37	£0.34	£0.31	£0.29	£0.26	£0.24	£0.22
17	£0.49	£0.45	£0.41	£0.38	£0.34	£0.31	£0.29	£0.26	£0.24	£0.22	£0.20
18	£0.46	£0.42	£0.39	£0.35	£0.32	£0.29	£0.26	£0.24	£0.21	£0.19	£0.17
19	£0.44	£0.40	£0.36	£0.33	£0.29	£0.27	£0.24	£0.21	£0.19	£0.17	£0.15
20	£0.42	£0.38	£0.34	£0.31	£0.27	£0.25	£0.22	£0.20	£0.17	£0.16	£0.14

❖ BOX 11.1 PRICE COMPARISON WEBSITES

Price comparison websites (PCWs) are mostly run by commercial firms. They bring together information about many different products in a market, presenting it in a way that lets you filter and search for the particular products that suit you and your needs. PCWs cover a multitude of different products, for example car insurance, possessions and home insurance, savings accounts, loans, credit cards, broadband services and energy suppliers. They do not usually cover every supplier in the market because most PCWs earn money when you click through to take out a product, so suppliers who do not pay commission are unlikely to be represented. Different PCWs include different providers, so it usually makes sense to search using two or three PCWs before making a decision. While the focus is on price, don't forget that other factors, such as how easily you can get your money back from a savings account, may be just as important.

11.1.3 Budding entrepreneurs

A quick glance at the Forbes (2016) list of the world's billionaires show that most very rich people's wealth comes from businesses that they or their families have started and built up. There is no age limit on becoming an entrepreneur. Zuckerberg famously started Facebook while at university and schoolchildren, like India's Kumaran brothers, are busy building mobile app businesses in their early teens (Quora, n.d.). It's no coincidence that these examples are digital entrepreneurs. The internet and mobile technology have opened the way for young people to start businesses without encountering some of the drawbacks that a conventional business may involve. For example, obvious youth may undermine your credibility when meeting clients face-to-face but is invisible online and a digital business can be conducted during unusual hours that do not interfere with school.

The UK is a particularly good environment for young entrepreneurs who, although when below age 16 are too young to run their own formal company, can nevertheless set up as 'sole traders'. This is a less formal business structure that merely requires registration with HM Revenue & Customs, the UK tax authority, if any tax will be due. Section 11.2.1 below looks at how young people are taxed, but many running just a small business will have too little income to worry about this and, under age 16, are too young to be liable for National Insurance contributions (a tax on earnings that pays for social insurance benefits, such as the state pension).

Encouraged by government and industry, schools may themselves foster young entrepreneurship through, for example, the Fiver Challenge (Young Enterprise, 2016) in which 5 to 11 year olds set up a mini-business for a fiver and engineering design contests for older children. These sorts of initiatives can attune you from an early age to the opportunities to build wealth through your own business or, if you are less hands on, by investing in the businesses of others – and investing, too, can start as early as you like.

11.2 Investments for children in the UK

Section 11.1 considered how savings products can be useful for laying the early foundations of the saving habit, money management and general financial capability. However, you may be lucky enough to have a pot of savings that your parents or others have been setting aside for you to use once you reach adult life. The aim of these savings is not so much developing good financial habits as increasing your financial opportunities later on. For example, you might use your savings pot to help fund learning to drive, continuing your education, broadening your horizons through travel or buying a first home. Far-sighted parents might even be thinking ahead to your retirement by starting a pension scheme for you!

In the UK, there are a number of savings products and investments specifically designed for building up children's savings for use later on. As with any savings and investments, in deciding how suitable they are, you need to think about factors such as access, risk, charges and tax. So, before considering each of the products in turn, we will first take a quick look at how young people are taxed in the UK. Be aware that UK tax legislation is complex, so only a broad overview is given here and the rules described are those that applied in mid-2016.

11.2.1 Tax when you are young

There are four main personal taxes in the UK: Income Tax, National Insurance contributions, Capital Gains Tax and Inheritance Tax (see Box 11.2). With the exception of National Insurance, these taxes apply however young you are, so even a baby could have an Income Tax bill! However, most children have too little income, gains or assets to have to pay tax. The upshot is that investments promoted as tax-free for children are not necessarily that special. However, if you will be drawing out the savings as a young adult, you might by then be working and so liable for Income Tax, which could then make tax-free savings and investments an advantage.

In addition, parents need to be aware of a tax anti-avoidance rule that means income generated by gifts they make to their children is usually taxed as income of the parent, not the child, whether the income is paid out or reinvested (Income Tax (Trading and Other income) Act 2005, ss629 and 631). This applies to the whole income where it exceeds £100 a year, but to each parent separately, so a couple could together give gifts that generate up to £200 a year. For larger gifts, it may be best to choose investments that are specifically exempt from the avoidance rule and these are: Junior Individual Savings Account (JISA), Child Trust Fund (CTF), National Savings & Investments (NS&I) Children's Bonus Bonds and Premium Bonds, tax-free friendly society plans and personal pension schemes. Gains (rather than income) are not caught by the anti-avoidance rule.

> ### ❖ BOX 11.2 MAIN PERSONAL TAXES IN THE UK
>
> **Income Tax** Tax on most forms of income, for example from work (as an employee or self-employment), pensions, rents, savings and investments. Some types of income are specifically tax-free. In addition, most people have tax allowances that mean they can have a certain amount of otherwise taxable

income tax-free each year. In the 2016–17 **tax year**, the main allowances were a personal allowance (set against any type of income for most people), Personal Savings Allowance (making up to £1,000 or £500 of interest tax-free for most people) and Dividend Tax Allowance (making up to £5,000 of dividends tax free for everyone).

National Insurance contributions Also a tax on income but only from work. Payable between age 16 and state pension age, paying or being credited with these contributions builds up an entitlement to certain benefits, including the state pension (see Chapter 10, Box 10.1).

Capital Gains Tax Tax on gains you make when you sell or give away something for more than it was worth when you started to own it. Some gains are specifically tax-free (for example, when you sell your only or main home – see Chapter 8, Section 8.2.3) and everyone has an allowance that lets them have a certain amount of otherwise taxable gains each year tax-free (£11,100 in 2016–17).

Inheritance Tax Tax paid by the giver on gifts and bequests. However, some are specifically tax-free and everyone has a 'nil-rate band' which means that a first slice (£325,000 in 2016–17) of otherwise taxable gifts and bequests are tax-free. As a result, there is no Inheritance Tax on most lifetime gifts to people and the majority of **estates** left on death are too small to pay tax.

11.2.2 Junior Individual Savings Account and Child Trust Fund

An Individual Savings Account (ISA) is a **tax wrapper** which ensures that the savings and investments you put inside it get special tax treatment – typically the return (income and gains) builds up tax-free and there is no tax when you draw your money out.

There are several different types of ISA. You can have an adult ISA from age 16 onwards, but there is also a Junior ISA (JISA) designed for under-18s. There are limits (called the ISA allowance) on how much can be invested in ISAs each year. In 2016–17, these were £15,240 for an adult ISA and £4,080 for a JISA.

It's up to parents whether they open a JISA for their child. Typically, the parent runs it and pays in money from themselves and anyone else (such as grandparents and family friends) who wants to make gifts to the child. If you have a JISA, the money inside it belongs to you but cannot normally be drawn out until you reach age 18. If you don't want to take the money then, you can instead roll it over into an adult ISA without it using any of that year's ISA allowance.

Only children born from 3 January 2011 onwards can start a JISA. However, if you were born after 1 September 2002, you may instead have a Child Trust Fund (CTF) or your CTF may have been converted to a JISA. CTFs are similar to JISAs in that they are a scheme designed to build up tax-free savings for a child that they can access from age 18. However, CTFs had some additional features because they were part of a social policy, sometimes called **asset-based welfare**, that aimed to change financial behaviour to increase **social mobility** and so improve financial opportunities and outcomes. To do this:

- A CTF was opened for every child born between 2 September 2001 and 2 January 2011 and the government paid in a starter amount (usually £250). Originally it was intended that a further government gift would be paid in at age seven, but this was scrapped. Parents and others could also pay in up to the annual allowance (now set at the same level as the JISA allowance), but even if parents paid in nothing, every child would still have a small lump sum available at age 18 because of the government payments.
- Around age seven and periodically after that, school children would have lessons in financial capability centred around their CTF and the importance of long-term saving.

Following the 2008 global financial crisis and a change of the UK government to one with a different ideology, the CTF was scrapped. It was replaced by the JISA that is optional rather than compulsory for all children, has no government payments and no associated financial education. However, children who already had a CTF kept them and they can now be transferred to a JISA if preferred.

Both CTFs and JISAs can be invested in a choice of ways, including cash (a bank or building society account) and/or investment funds (typically investing in shares or a range of assets).

ACTIVITY 11.3

Statistics show that, by both volume (number of JISAs) and value (sum paid in) over two-thirds of JISAs taken out by parents each year for their children are invested in cash and less than a third in stocks and shares. Drawing on what you learned in Chapter 9, comment on this behaviour.

These statistics suggest that parents are overly risk averse. As you saw in Chapter 9, when saving or investing over a long time horizon, higher risk investments such as equities are likely to produce a higher return than cash and give a better chance of beating inflation.

11.2.3 Other savings and investments for children

National Savings & Investments (NS&I) is a government agency whose remit is to raise money to help meet the UK government's Public Sector Borrowing Requirement (PSBR). To do this, it markets a range of savings products, including a Children's Bonus Bond.

NS&I Children's Bonus Bonds, which can be bought by parents and grandparents for children under 16, are five-year bonds offering a tax-free fixed interest rate. At the end of each five-year term, the bonds can be rolled over for a further five years until the child reaches age 21.

Table 11.2 Expected average number of Premium Bonds per year, June 2016

Size of holding:	£1,000	£5,000	£10,000	£25,000	£50,000 (Maximum holding)
From June 2016	0.4	2.0	4.0	10.1	20.1

Another popular choice for children's savings is NS&I Premium Bonds. These are intended mainly for adults but can be bought by parents and grandparents for children. Premium Bonds are an example of an **interest lottery**. Instead of paying interest directly on the sum invested, the interest goes into a prize fund and each £1 invested counts as a separate bond that takes part in a prize draw each month. In 2016, prizes ranged from £25 to £1 million. Table 11.2 shows the average number of prizes you might then have expected to win given the size of your holding, but most of these would be low-value prizes and the chance of a single bond winning a £1 million jackpot was 1 in 30 billion!

As highlighted in Activity 11.3, savings products are not usually the most suitable choice for long-term investment. Generally, below age 16, you are too young to enter into binding contracts, but parents can hold any investments on behalf of their child, for example, using trusts (see Section 11.4 below). However, parents need to bear in mind the £100-tax-avoidance rule described in Section 11.2.1 above which may make it more tax-efficient to invest through a JISA. Alternatively, friendly societies (similar to insurance companies) can offer small tax-free investment plans that are often marketed for children in the form of 'Baby bonds'. These also are exempt from the £100-tax-avoidance rule but limit the sum that can be invested to £270 a year (or £300 if money is paid in more frequently than once a year) and charges are sometimes relatively high.

Also outside the £100-tax-avoidance rule are pension schemes. Anyone can pay into a pension scheme for someone else and there is no minimum age limit for starting a pension, so a parent can pay into a personal pension for a child. This type of support has the following features:

- Assuming the child has no UK earnings, the maximum that can go into their pension scheme in any tax year is £3,600, including tax relief.
- With a personal pension, tax relief is given 'at source'. This means that the person paying into the scheme is treated as having deducted tax relief at the basic rate from the payment. The scheme provider then claims the tax relief from HM Revenue & Customs and adds it to the plan. Case Study 11.1 shows how this works.
- The savings build up tax-free. When they are withdrawn or converted into retirement income, a quarter of the savings pot can be taken tax-free but the rest is taxable.
- The child cannot usually draw money out of the scheme until 10 years before state pension age. The money can then be used for any purpose, not just retirement.
- The child can take over the scheme, usually from age 16, and make their own contributions to it.

> ### ❖ CASE STUDY 11.1
>
> George and Em decide to pay £10 a month into a personal pension scheme for their new baby. This is treated as a contribution from which tax relief at the basic rate has already been deducted (a 'net' contribution). The scheme provider then claims tax relief from HM Revenue & Customs and adds it to the baby's scheme. In 2016–17, the basic rate is 20 per cent, so tax relief on each contribution is £2.50. This means that the 'gross' contribution paid into scheme is £10 + £2.50 = £12.50. The £2.50 tax relief is 20 per cent of £12.50. You can convert a net contribution to a gross contribution by dividing the net amount by (1 – tax rate); in this example: £10 / (1 – 0.20) = £12.50.
>
> Over a whole year, George and Em pay in £120, so, with tax relief, £150 goes into the baby's scheme. This is well below the maximum allowed which is gross contributions of £3,600 a year equivalent to £2,880 in net contributions.

11.3 Buying your first home

As you saw in Chapter 8, when buying a home, you will normally need to pay at least 10 per cent of the purchase price yourself and find a mortgage for the rest. If you have a pot of savings as described in Section 11.2 above, you might be able to put it towards the deposit, but there are other ways your family might help too.

11.3.1 Help with the deposit

In 2016, around half of first-time buyers in the UK had help from the 'bank of mum and dad' (CML, 2015). This might take the form of:

- **A gift of a lump sum.** This is the most straightforward form of help. Usually, there are no tax implications, provided this is a gift of cash (see Section 11.4 below).
- **Loan of a lump sum.** If parents lend you money, the lender will want to know what the repayment arrangements are because these need to be factored in as part of your committed expenditure when deciding whether you can afford the mortgage (see Chapter 8, Section 8.3.4). A loan could be structured to help your parents meet their goals too, for example by starting repayments at the point when they will need retirement income.
- **Regular gifts to help you build up the deposit.** For example, regular gifts from parents could be paid into a Help-to-Buy ISA or, from 2017, a Lifetime ISA (see Chapter 8, Box 8.3), where they would be boosted by the help from the government.

With any family arrangement, you need to be very clear at the outset whether money is a gift or a loan and, if the latter, how you will all deal with a failure to pay the loan as agreed. Parents need to take care not to give or lend money they cannot afford to do without.

11.3.2 Help with the mortgage

If your income is not enough to convince lenders that you can afford your mortgage repayments, your parents (or other family member) may be able to help if they agree to act as **guarantor**. This means that if you cannot keep up your mortgage payments, then your parents will agree that they will take over making the payments for you. The lender will carry out an affordability check including a stress test (see Chapter 8, Section 8.3.4) on your parents as well as you to make sure that their guarantee is sound.

A variation on the usual repayment mortgage is an **offset mortgage** (which you looked at briefly in Chapter 8). With these, as well as borrowing from the mortgage lender, you also have your current account and or a savings account with the same firm. With a normal mortgage, interest each month is based on the amount of mortgage that you still owe. With an offset mortgage, interest is based on the mortgage debt less the balance in your current account and/or savings accounts. A further variation is a **family offset mortgage** where your mortgage is combined with the savings accounts of other family members. In effect, your family are transferring the interest they could have earned on their savings to you in order to reduce the amount of interest you are charged on your mortgage. This reduces your mortgage payments.

A further option for helping, offered by at least one mortgage lender (Barclays, 2016), allows first-time buyers to take out a 100 per-cent loan-to-value mortgage, provided family members deposit savings of at least a specified amount with the lender. The family get the savings back with interest after a few years, as long as you have kept up your mortgage payments. In this case, the aim is not so much to reduce your monthly payments, but to remove the need for a deposit.

11.3.3 Joint ownership

Another way that family might help is to buy a property jointly with you. For example, if you had equal shares with your parents, you would need only half the deposit and half the mortgage that you would need to buy the whole property. Points to bear in mind are:

- Will all the owners be living together? How well do you think you will get on?
- If just you will live in the property, will you have to pay some rent for the part owned by your parents? If so, your parents will need to declare the rent as income and pay tax on it. The mortgage lender will take the rent into account in deciding whether you can afford the mortgage (Chapter 8, Section 8.3.4).
- What happens if you want to move and your parents don't want to sell or they need to sell (say, to pay for care costs) and you don't want to move?
- When you sell, if the house has risen in value, there will normally be no Capital Gains Tax for you to pay because the property has been your home, but your

parents will have to pay tax on their share if they have never lived there (see Chapter 8, Section 8.2.3 and the Appendix).

ACTIVITY 11.4

Outline one advantage and one disadvantage for you of the following ways in which your family might help you buy a home:

1. An interest-free loan.
2. A family offset mortgage.
3. Buying the home jointly with your parents, but they will continue to live elsewhere.

[Answers to this Activity are at the end of the chapter.]

11.4 Gifts and bequests

Parents and others can help you directly by making gifts to you either during their lifetime or in their wills when they die. They – and sometimes you – need to watch out for tax, in particular Inheritance Tax (IHT) and Capital Gains Tax (CGT), but there are many ways to arrange gifts tax efficiently. This section highlights the main points and you'll find more details in the Appendix.

11.4.1 Capital Gains Tax and gifts to children

CGT is a tax on the gain a person makes when they dispose of something that has a higher value now than it did when they first started to own it. 'Dispose of' has a wide meaning and includes making gifts. The tax is paid by the giver.

There is no CGT on gifts of cash, so CGT issues arise only if your parents (or other family members) want to give you a physical asset, like a house or a painting, investments, or some other asset that has a value. However, these tax rules in particular may help:

- There is no CGT on 'tangible moveable property', in other words physical assets other than land and property, whose value does not exceed £6,000 and special rules may reduce the CGT on these items if they are worth more than that. Note that, if giving a set of things, they count as a single asset, so each part cannot be valued separately.
- Everyone has an annual CGT allowance (£11,100 in 2016–17) which means they can give away assets with gains up to that amount tax-free.

11.4.2 Inheritance Tax on gifts and bequests

IHT may be payable whenever someone gives away money or assets and is (in most cases) paid by the giver. However, many gifts and bequests are tax-free and everyone has a **nil-rate band** (NRB), which is a first slice of gifts that are tax-free (£325,000 in 2016–17).

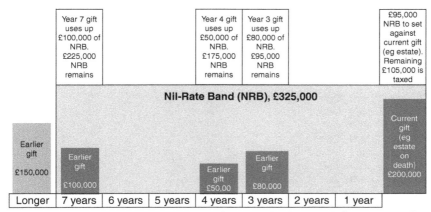

Figure 11.2 Example of how Inheritance Tax works

IHT is an unusual tax, because, instead of applying to a transaction in isolation, tax is calculated by looking at the record of gifts the seven years up to the latest gift (see Figure 11.2). Earlier gifts are set against the NRB first to determine how much NRB is available to set against the current gift. Tax-free gifts and any gifts longer than seven years ago drop out of the calculation and so are ignored. This process applies to lifetime gifts and also to bequests on death when the passing on of their estate is treated as the final gift a person makes.

Table 11.3 outlines the main gifts that are always free of Inheritance Tax and so would never be part of the calculation shown in Figure 11.2. Many of these tax-free gifts could be used by family members wanting to make you a gift. For example, provided the giver still had enough income left to support their usual lifestyle, many gifts to children could be covered by the 'normal expenditure out of income' exemption. This is a particularly useful exemption because there is no upper limit on the value of the gifts made. To qualify, there must be some element of regularity to the gifts, for example a parent could make regular payments into a savings account, investment or pension scheme for a particular child, or a grandparent could make a regular habit of always giving every grandchild a substantial gift at Christmas or on reaching their eighteenth birthday. It will be important for the giver to keep careful records of these gifts to demonstrate the regularity and of their budget to show that the gifts were made out of income without impacting on lifestyle.

Gifts for the maintenance of family is another useful unlimited exemption that could enable your parents, say, to give you help with living expenses while you study.

Gifts that are not tax-free will usually be Potentially Exempt Transfers (PETs). A PET is treated as tax-free for now and will be confirmed as tax-free provided the giver survives for seven years after making it. If they die within seven years, the gifts are deemed to be taxable after all, in which case there could be some tax to pay on the gift – and you as the recipient of the gift might be asked to pay the tax, but if you cannot or will not, the estate will pay it instead. Failed PETs may also cause some extra tax on the giver's estate because some of the nil-rate band will have been used up on the PET leaving less to set against the estate.

Table 11.3 Gifts that are free of Inheritance Tax, 2016–17

When the gift is made	Limit on the amount you can give this way
Tax-free in lifetime and on death	
■ Gifts between husband and wife or civil partners	Usually unlimited, but £325,000 if the recipient's permanent home is outside the UK
■ Gifts to charities and some similar bodies	Unlimited
■ Gifts of national heritage property	Unlimited
■ Gifts to political parties	Unlimited
■ Gifts to housing associations	Unlimited
Tax-free lifetime gifts	
■ Normal expenditure out of income	Unlimited
■ Gifts for the maintenance of your family	Unlimited
■ Lottery syndicates and similar arrangements	Unlimited, provided prior agreement (preferably in writing) to share wins
■ Yearly tax-free exemption	£3,000. Unused part can be carried forward but one year only
■ Small gifts	£250 per person per year. Cannot be combined with any other exemption
■ Wedding gifts	£5,000 if you are a parent, £2,500 if you are a grandparent, £1,000 anyone else
■ PETs if you survive seven years	Unlimited

Gifts that are neither tax-free nor PETs are taxable and there might be tax to pay at the time they are made. There may also be extra tax to pay if the giver dies within seven years. Very few types of gift are taxable, mostly just gifts to trusts, which we will look at in Section 11.5.

In 2016–17, where Inheritance Tax is due, the rate is 20 per cent on lifetime gifts and 40 per cent for any tax that becomes due on death. However, most gifts from family members will be tax-free provided the giver:

● makes use of the exemptions for tax-free lifetime gifts;
● makes sure any other gifts are covered by their nil-rate band.

11.5 Using trusts

A **trust** is a legal arrangement, used mainly in the UK, where money and/or assets are set aside to benefit one or more people but are legally held and looked after by someone else. It's a way that, say, family members can make you a gift but keep some control over how you use that gift.

The people involved in a trust have special names as follows:

● **The settlor.** This is the person (or people) who sets up the trust and gives money and/or assets to it. The settlor may have IHT to pay on the gift to the trust and possibly CGT too (but bear in mind there is no CGT on gifts of money).
● **The trustees.** These are the people (usually more than one) who look after the money and/or assets owned by the trust. There are restrictions on how they

do this and when and to whom they can pay out the money and assets. These restrictions are set out in a document called the trust deed.

- **The beneficiaries**. These are the people who the trust is designed to help. This could be one or more named people or a whole group, such as the settlor's grandchildren even if some are not yet born. (Trusts can also be set up to benefit others, such as investors on a unit trust (see Chapter 9) or charities.)

Trusts can be extremely flexible and allow families to help you in a very wide range of ways. For example, you might be the beneficiary of a trust that allows you to receive income, money or assets automatically at a specified age, say 21, or allows the trustees to decide whether to advance you money or assets at their discretion if you are in need. A trust might allow you to use assets, for example living in a house owned by the trust, rather than take ownership of the assets yourself. Families may also set up trusts to ensure that financial support is available for, say, a child with a disability even after the parents have passed away. A trust might be used to skip generations, where passing assets on to grandchildren rather than children is more tax-efficient.

As a beneficiary, you may have to pay tax on any income you receive from a trust. Tax might already have been deducted, in which case, if you are a non-taxpayer, you will need to claim it back. The taxation of trusts is complicated and outside the scope of this book – you can find an introduction on the UK government website (Gov.uk, 2016).

It is important to be precise, clear and accurate when setting up a trust, so it is usually best to get professional help – for example from a member of the Society of Trust and Estate Practitioners (STEP, 2016).

❖ BOX 11.3 BARE TRUST

There is one type of trust that does not require a formal trust deed and legal advice: a bare trust. This describes an arrangement where one person holds assets on behalf of another – for example, a parent holding investments on behalf of a child. The investments or other assets in a bare trust are taxed as those of the beneficiary, not the trustee (unless the £100-tax-avoidance rule applies – see Section 11.2.1 above). The beneficiary can take control of the investments (or other assets) at any time once they have reached age 18 (16 in Scotland).

ACTIVITY 11.5

1. Ruth's aged grandmother wants to give her £20,000 to help towards buying a home. Explain how CGT and IHT might affect these different ways of making the gift:
   a. Giving Ruth a collection of silver heirlooms that Ruth can sell
   b. Giving Ruth £20,000 cash
2. Gian and Beth want to set aside £30,000 to help their son, Alec (currently aged 16), when he reaches adulthood, but are worried that he might not

have the maturity to use the money wisely before, say, his 20s. Which of
the following options might be most suitable for Gian and Beth (choose all
that apply):

a.   A Junior ISA

b.   A savings account opened by Beth on Alec's behalf

c.   A trust

[Answers to this Activity are at the end of the chapter.]

11.6 Conclusion

This chapter has invited you to consider the many ways in which family might be
able to help you to start building up your own wealth. They range from foster-
ing your development of knowledge and skills to generating your own wealth
to a variety of gifts and loans that transfer wealth to you, either permanently
or temporarily and outright or with some strings attached. The chapter considers key advantages and disadvantages of each option, including some of the tax
implications.

Answers to Activity 11.1

Figure 11.1 is a very simple example of cash flow over the lifecycle but, using the same
principles, you could create more complicated examples that included, say, breaks
from work and periods of running up debt.

1. See if you can construct a cash flow chart for Andrew who is described below:

Andrew started an apprenticeship at age 18, enabling him to study while earning a
wage. Once he completed this, he was hired and had worked up through the firm

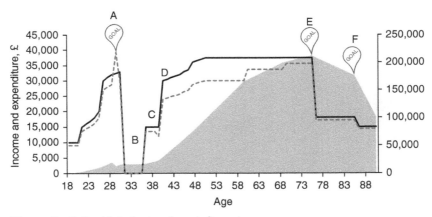

Figure Activity 11.1 Andrew's cash flow chart

until a competitor offered him a better job on a much higher salary. A couple of years later he married Aisha. Up to then, Andrew had always saved some of his money and, when he met Aisha, he set a goal to use a big chunk of his savings on their wedding and honeymoon. When their first child was born, Andrew became a house-husband and the couple relied on Aisha's income. After five years Andrew returned to work, initially part-time, but getting back to full-time work a few years later and, at that point, he was able to start saving again. The period of child-caring prevented Andrew building up as much pension as he would have liked and so he carried on working full-time until 75 and part-time into his mid-80s.

There is no single, correct answer to this Activity, but your chart may have looked something like the one above. Using the same key as before:

- **Income** (solid black line) starts from age 18 with earnings while an apprentice and continues to climb as Andrew is hired and then poached by another firm. It falls to zero when he becomes a house husband (B) but resumes when he returns to work part-time (C) and then full-time (D). In his mid-70s, income falls when he decides to cut back to part-time working (E) and again when he retires completely (F).
- **Expenditure** (dashed grey line). Andrew is by nature a saver and so spending is typically below the income line. The only time it definitely is not is when he splashes out, as intended, on the wedding and honeymoon (A) and when spending falls to zero, matching his income, during the period when the family rely on Aisha's earnings.
- **Wealth** (shaded grey area). Because Andrew is normally careful to spend less than his income, he starts to accumulate wealth early in life. Wealth drops a bit after point A because of the savings he has used on the wedding and honeymoon and stops growing during his time as a house husband. Once he gets back to work, his wealth starts growing again until he reaches partial retirement E. This chart assumes he supplements his part-time working after E with some drawing down of his savings and this increases from F onwards when Andrew stops work completely.

2. Comment on how realistic you think the example of Andrew might be.

In the UK, it is still unusual for a man to stop work to care for children, so the cash flow diagram you have drawn for Q1 may not be so common for a man, but might be a fairly typical profile for any woman who combines working with having a family.

Answers to Activity 11.4

Outline one advantage and one disadvantage for you of the following ways in which your family might help you buy a home:

1. An interest-free loan. Advantages: helps to pay the deposit; cheaper than a loan from any other source because interest-free. Disadvantages: depending on the repayments required may reduce the amount of mortgage because of the affordability test; might not be able to afford the required repayments; family might need the money back unexpectedly.

2. A family offset mortgage. Advantages: helps you get a higher mortgage and/or may reduce your monthly payments. Disadvantage: family might want their savings back and you might not be able to afford the resulting rise in mortgage payments.
3. Buying the home jointly with your parents, but they will continue to live elsewhere. Advantages: you need less deposit and a lower mortgage; parents might let you live in their half rent-free. Disadvantages: parents might need to sell when you don't want to move; you might want to sell but parents don't want to.

Answers to Activity 11.5

1. Ruth's aged grandmother wants to give her £20,000 to help towards buying a home. Explain how CGT and IHT might affect these different ways of making the gift:
   a. Giving Ruth a collection of silver heirlooms that Ruth can sell. If the silver has increased in price since she started to own it, the grandmother may have CGT to pay (since this tangible moveable property is worth more than £6,000). There should be no CGT for Ruth to pay unless she delays selling and the price increases in the meantime. The gift is likely to be a PET for IHT purposes (although the first £3,000 might be tax-free if the grandmother has not used her annual exemption for lifetime gifts). The PET is tax-free provided the grandmother survives seven years. However, the grandmother sounds very old, so might die sooner. In that case, whether any IHT is due depends on whether the grandmother had enough nil-rate band to cover the gift. If not, Ruth may be asked to pay some IHT but if she cannot do this the estate would be charged instead.
   b. Giving Ruth £20,000 cash. There is no CGT on gifts of cash. The IHT position is the same as for (a) above.
2. Gian and Beth want to set aside £30,000 to help their son, Alec (currently aged 16), when he reaches adulthood, but are worried that he might not have the maturity to use the money wisely before, say, his 20s. Which of the following options might be most suitable for Gian and Beth (choose all that apply):
   a. A Junior ISA. Unlikely to be suitable because Alec takes control at age 18.
   b. A savings account opened by Beth on Alec's behalf. Unlikely to be suitable because Alec takes control at age 18.
   c. A trust. Most likely to be suitable because the trust deed can specify that Alec does not receive any benefit until, say, age 25, or until the trustees believe he is ready. (However, a point not discussed in the chapter, is that the costs of setting up the trust might be uneconomic if the only gift is this one to Alec.)

End of chapter test

1. Discuss the role of families in helping their children to develop financial capability.

2. Select and compare two ways in which a family might help a son or daughter to buy his or her first home.
3. Explain why there might be Inheritance Tax to pay when a parent dies and leaves the family home to a child.

References

Barclays (2016) *Family Springboard Mortgage* [online] www.barclays.co.uk/mortgages/family-springboard-mortgage (Accessed 14 May 2016).

Council of Mortgage Lenders (CML) (2015) *New CML data shows nearly half of first-time buyers didn't use the 'bank of mum and dad'* [online] https://www.cml.org.uk/news/news-and-views/712/ (Accessed 14 May 2016).

Forbes (2016) *The World's Billionaires* [online] www.forbes.com/billionaires/list/4/#version:static (Accessed 13 May 2016).

Gov.uk (2016) *Trusts and taxes* [online] https://www.gov.uk/trusts-taxes/overview (Accessed 14 May 2016).

Organisation of Economic Co-operation and Development (OECD) (2012) *PISA 2012 Results: Students and Money. Financial Literacy Skills for the 21st Century* [online] https://www.oecd.org/pisa/keyfindings/pisa-2012-results-volume-vi.htm (Accessed 13 May 2016).

Quora (n.d.) *Who are the most successful youngest entrepreneurs in India?* [online] https://www.quora.com/Who-are-the-most-successful-youngest-entrepreneurs-in-India (Accessed 13 May 2016).

Ritchie, A. I. (1885) *Mrs Dymond* [online] https://archive.org/details/mrsdymond00ritcgoog (Accessed 13 May 2016).

Society of Tax and Estate Practitioners (STEP) (2016) *Member directory* [online] www.step.org/member-directory (Accessed 14 May 2016).

Young Enterprise (2016) *Fiver Challenge. What could you do with £5?* [online] www.fiverchallenge.org.uk/ (Accessed 13 May 2016).

Part IV

The next steps

Chapter 12

Take action

Lien Luu

When you establish a destination by defining what you want, then take physical action by making choices that move you towards that destination, the possibility for success is limitless and arrival at the destination is inevitable.

Dr Steve Maraboli (*Life, the Truth, and Being Free*, 2009)

Planning is bringing the future into the present so that you can do something about it now.

Alan Lakein (*How to Get Control of Your Time and Your Life*, 1973)

Our society is rapidly changing. Increasing longevity means you are likely to have a much longer life than earlier generations, but this poses challenges for you, governments and societies as a whole. You are also more likely than earlier generations to go to university but also to start your working life with student debt. High house prices are making it harder for you to buy your own home and start the process of acquiring property wealth. On the other hand, living standards are higher than in the past and you are more likely to aspire to travel and experiences. Whatever your goals and the challenges you face, equipping yourself with some financial literacy, a saving habit and control of your natural behavioural biases will take you a long way. Like it or not, you are now expected to take full responsibility for your financial well-being throughout your life cycle. As Jim Rohn, America's business philosopher has aptly remarked: 'you must take personal responsibility. You cannot change the circumstances, the seasons, or the wind, but you can change yourself. That is something you have charge of.'

The first step in taking control is defining the life that you want to have. Ben Stein, actor and author, has observed: 'the indispensable first step to getting the things you want out of life is decide what you want'. You need to decide on what you want to do, be and have. What do you want to accomplish? What do you want to experience? What possessions do you want to have? One reason why most people do not get what they want is because they do not know what they want now and in the future. To help you clarify your vision of your ideal life, it is worthwhile to reflect on where are you now and where do you want to get to. To create a balanced life, your vision should include seven key areas: work and career, finances, recreation and free time, health and fitness, relationships, personal goals, and contribution to the larger community (Canfield, 2005).

Research into the life experiences of older generations gives us valuable insights into the important areas to focus on in life. In a pioneering study of nearly 1,500 elders aged between 70 and 100 years old, Professor Karl Pillemer (2011) asked them to share the most important lessons they would like to pass on to younger people. Ten lessons stand out, and these offer a recipe for success and happiness:

1. **Choose a career for the intrinsic rewards, not the financial ones:** The biggest career mistake people make is choosing a profession based only on potential earnings. However, having a sense of purpose and passion for one's work is much more important than just a big salary. You should therefore choose a career you enjoy and avoid the jobs you hate.
2. **Act now like you will need your body for a hundred years:** You need to look after your health and body and avoid bad health habits such as smoking, drinking, poor eating habits and inactivity, to avoid years or decades of chronic disease.
3. **Say 'yes' to opportunities:** When offered a new opportunity or challenge, you should take a risk and grab opportunities when they come. Otherwise, you will regret saying 'no', rather than saying 'yes'.
4. **Choose a mate with extreme care:** The key is not to rush the decision, taking all the time needed to get to know the prospective partner and to determine your compatibility with them. This is important so that you can avoid the problem of divorce and all the associated headaches and heartaches.
5. **Travel more:** Travel while you can, sacrificing other things if necessary to do so. Most people look back on their travel adventures (big and small) as highlights of their lives and regret not having travelled more. As one elder told the researcher: 'If you have to make a decision whether you want to remodel your kitchen or take a trip – well, I say, choose the trip!'
6. **Say it now:** Many people express regrets for failing to express themselves before it's too late, such as telling someone how much you love them. The only time you can share your deepest feelings is while people are still alive. According to an elder interviewed: 'If you have a grudge against someone, why not make it right, now? Make it right because there may not be another opportunity, who knows? So do what you can do now.'
7. **Time is of the essence:** Life is short. We should not be depressed by this knowledge but we need to act on it, making sure to do important things now.
8. **Happiness is a choice, not a condition:** Happiness is not a condition that occurs when circumstances are perfect or nearly so. Happiness is a choice we make, in spite of challenges and difficulties. One elder said: 'My single best piece of advice is to take responsibility for your own happiness throughout your life.'
9. **Time spent worrying is time wasted:** Stop worrying or cut it down as it is a colossal waste of your precious lifetime. Indeed, one of the major regrets expressed by the elders was time wasted worrying about things that never happened.
10. **Think small:** When it comes to making the most of your life, think small. Enjoy the simple daily pleasures (e.g. nice cup of coffee in morning) and learn to savour them now.

Some of these sentiments are also echoed in Bronnie Ware's (2012) article on *5 Regrets of the Dying*. Ware was a nurse looking after patients at the end of their life, and she found that her patients shared five common sorrows. First, they regret not living the life they wanted and so they lie on their deathbed with many dreams unfulfilled due to the choices they had made, or not made. Second, they wish they had not worked so hard, and that they had spent more time with their children and family, and not spent so much time at work. By simplifying our lifestyle, it is possible that we may not need the income we think we do, and so face less financial pressure, and have more time to do things that make us happy. Third, they wish they had expressed their feelings more, both in relation to positive and negative feelings (e.g. anger and love). Some people suppress their feelings to keep the peace, and as a consequence, may develop illnesses relating to the bitterness and resentment they carry. This is not healthy. In addition, it is also not healthy not to tell the people we love how much we care and love them. Being honest with other people about our feelings, whether negative or positive, may raise the relationship to a new and healthier level. Fourth, they regret not staying in touch with friends, and letting friendship falter, as a result of a busy lifestyle or a lack of effort. Fifth, they wish they had allowed themselves to experience more happiness. Many did not realise until the end that happiness is a choice.

The research described above provides the clues for developing your own happiness, including being honest with yourself, making time to nurture friendship and relationships, taking charge of your happiness and living your dreams.

It is worth remembering that wealth is only a means to an end, and has many dimensions. Financial wealth constitutes only one aspect. Lee Brower (cited in Canfield, 2005, p.386), the founder of Empowered Wealth, adds intellectual and civic assets to human and financial assets, as shown by the four quadrants in Table 12.1.

When Brower (2009) asks wealthy families which quadrants they would pick if they could pass on assets from only two of the four quadrants, they unanimously choose human assets and intellectual assets. This is because they know that if their children have those, they can always make more money.

Table 12.1 Different types of assets

Human Assets		Intellectual Assets	
Enrich/Love		**Capture/ Learn**	
Family	Character	Wisdom	Relationships
Health	Values	Formal education	Ideas
Spirituality	Unique ability	Life experiences	Traditions
Happiness	Relationships	Reputation	Skills
Well-being	Habits	Systems	Talents
Ethics	Future		
Morals	Heritage		
Financial Assets		**Civic Assets**	
Capitalise/ Earn		**Contribute/ Give**	
Cash		Taxes (e.g. taxes directed to charities through Gift Aid)	
Stocks & bonds			
Pension funds		Private foundations	
Businesses		Charitable foundations of financial assets	
Property			
Things – your financial & material possessions		Charitable contributions of financial assets, human capital and intellectual assets	

Source: Canfield (2005), p.387.

Brower (2009) also makes a distinction between wealth and true wealth. True wealth is different from wealth because financial abundance is enjoyed without neglecting other important areas in our life: relationships, communities or personal searches for meaning. True wealth encompasses all things that money does not. To achieve happiness, Brower categorises assets in four areas: 1) *Our Core Assets* (the essence of who we are); 2) *Our Experience Assets* (the sum of our physical, emotional, mental and spiritual experiences); 3) *Our Contribution Assets* (our effect on others); 4) *Our Financial Assets* (our net worth). True wealth comprises all of these assets and there should not be a domination of one over another.

In order to achieve your goals and dreams, there are six steps you need to follow, as illustrated in Figure 12.1:

1. **Determine your dreams and goals**: Success begins with a fundamental question: where are you going (Hill, 2004)? As the definiteness of purpose is the start of all achievements, you need to establish what dreams and goals you want to achieve, and how much will these cost (Eisenberg, 2006). In order to achieve wealth, you need to eliminate any limiting beliefs about money you have, develop a desire to be wealthy, as well as a strong faith in its accomplishment (Hill, 2009). As Dr John Demartini (cited in Canfield, 2005, p.381), self-made multi-millionare and consultant on financial and life mastery, has observed: 'If no burning desire for wealth arises within you, no wealth will arise around you. Having definiteness of purpose for acquiring wealth is essential for its acquisition.'

    After establishing your dreams, you need to design practical steps or SMART goals to achieve these – as discussed in Chapter 4 (see also Tracy, 2004). As Andrew Carnegie said: 'if you want to be happy, set a goal that commands

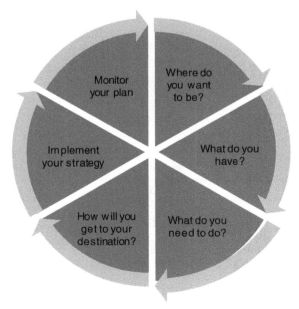

Figure 12.1 Six steps of financial planning
Source: adapted from http://margohess.weebly.com/financial-planning-process.html.

your thoughts, liberates your energy, and inspires your hopes'. One way to get clarity is to write your goals down in detail and visualise the future with these goals complete, and 'begin to live as if you have succeeded in your goal'. Visualisation is regarded as a powerful tool because it accelerates success by activating creative powers of your subconscious mind, programming your brain to notice available resources previously unnoticed, and attracting people, resources and opportunities you need to achieve your goal. Albert Einstein declared that: 'imagination is everything. It is the preview of life's coming attractions'.

2. **Evaluate your current situation**: the next step is to establish where you are now by analysing your current financial situation. You need to understand two key areas – your net-worth and your cashflow. You need to calculate your net-worth and determine your cashflow position. Do you have resources and surplus income to achieve your goals? This 'auditing' exercise is empowering as it will put you in control of your finances. In addition, it is also important to understand whether your most valuable assets (e.g. human capital) are protected.

   As discussed in Chapters 5 and 7, it is important to establish your attitude to risk, your credit profile and the amount of debt you may have. Fear of taking risk, bad credit and the existence of debt will hinder your effort to build wealth, while leverage (in a wide sense) and compound interest can assist you in this endeavour (see Figure 12.2).

3. **Analyse shortfalls or gaps**: after establishing your financial situation, you need to calculate the gap between what you *have* and what you *want*. For example, how much wealth do you want and how much have you got at the moment? How much income do you want and how much are you currently earning? Simplifying your lifestyle will reduce the need to take massive steps.

4. **Strategies**: after calculating the shortfall, you will need to think of strategies: what do you need to do to get to where you want to be? You need to consider your options and ways to reach your goals. Here you need to consider your strengths and your passions. What do you enjoy doing? How can you exploit your passions and skills?

5. **Act**: after deciding on the strategies, you need to take action and implement your strategies. For example, if you decide that you need to build residual income through property investment, you need to do something about it (e.g. research

Figure 12.2 Negative and positive forces of wealth

the property market and take action). As John Ruskin, English author, art critic, has remarked: 'What we think or what we know or what we believe is, in the end, of little consequence. The only consequence is what we do.' (Canfield, 2005, p.98). Abraham Lincoln, president of the United States, once observed: 'Things may come to those who wait, but only the things left by those who hustle.'

6.   **Monitor**: your goals and needs may change as well as the market conditions. New opportunities may present themselves. It is important to monitor your progress regularly to make sure that you are on track to achieve your goals.

ACTIVITY 12.1

Read the four case studies below and, in each case, try to match the life histories to the ideas about happiness and principles of financial planning discussed in this chapter. In each case, what would you pick out as the key motivations to succeed? What decisions seem to have played a major part in the case studies life outcomes? Are there any common themes running through the case studies?

[You will find some indicative answers at the end of the chapter.]

❖ CASE STUDY 12.1

I was born and raised, with my two older brothers and younger sister, in a tiny terraced house in South East London through the 1970s and 1980s. We had no bathroom and only an outside toilet until I was 8! My parents divorced when I was 6 and my mum remarried when I was 9. We were always poor and never had foreign holidays or luxuries. One of my most vivid memories is the debt collector coming round each week to collect repayments of what today would be classed as pay day lending. My parents never had any money and were always in debt. That made a big impression on me and I vowed never to be poor or end up with 'bad debt'.

My brothers and I were entrepreneurial and hardworking from when we were quite young. We all did part-time work when we were at school because my mum couldn't afford to give us pocket money. I worked with my brothers when I was a teenager doing a range of things from running a toy stall at various markets, managing a small team of lads doing gardening work for rich people (the homes were amazing), car repairs and decorating.

My education was appallingly bad and I went to a very rough and large state comprehensive, where the only thing I had any aptitude for was public speaking, music and English. I knew then that I was going to be successful and run a business. I never went to university and after a series of dead end jobs I stumbled into financial services when I was 20 selling life insurance for a large company. From there I buckled down and took every financial services qualification I could find as I liked dealing with people and problem solving. I eventually started my own firm and sold it after 17 years at the helm.

I lost £17,000 on my first property as I bought this in the late 1980s just before a property slump. However, over the past 20 years I've developed a simple approach to building wealth through regularly saving 25 per cent of my income and investing in an index portfolio, some property and various businesses. I now have income from a range of earned and unearned sources and shareholdings in several trading businesses managed by other people. I know I have more money than many people but I don't view myself as rich. Instead I feel that I have achieved what I call 'true wealth' because I now only do things which I am good at, which have positive impacts on others and which I enjoy. I hope to continue working on my portfolio of activities until I die and I have no aspirations to ever retire in the conventional sense.

❖ CASE STUDY 12.2

I came to England as a refugee at the age of 13, after spending one year in a refugee camp in Hong Kong where I had to grow up quickly, looking after my 6-year-old sister, doing all the domestic chores (cooking, cleaning and shopping) and running a small business to earn extra money while my parents were at work. We arrived in England with savings of less than £200, no command of English, no friends and no social networks. Having grown up with my grandmothers, aunties, uncles and cousins, it was painful to be separated from them, and we felt lonely, isolated and dislocated in our new life, despite the kindness we received.

We were given a council house and all the basic necessities such as second-hand clothes, furniture, white goods and beds. For everything else, we had to buy through Littlewoods and Freemans catalogues where we would pay weekly. In their early 40s, my parents had to learn English and start a new career, and it was hard for them as they had financial pressures. We lived on income support and had to save very hard as this money had to support our extended family and relatives back home as well. Without language proficiency, life at school was difficult and queuing for free school meals was particularly humiliating.

I knew that a good education was the only way for me to progress and I was determined to go to university. I obtained the necessary A-level grades to go to a good university and received a grant to support me. Knowing that my parents worked very hard to earn very little, I made sure that I saved so that I was not a burden to them. After finishing my first degree, I was very lucky to be awarded a scholarship, funded by a very wealthy entrepreneur, to pursue a PhD as part of an international project investigating the sources of human achievement. This amazing opportunity allowed me to meet many famous academics around the world, and experience a good life as many of our conferences (funded by the entrepreneur) were held in luxurious settings in the UK and Europe. Seeing how wealth was used to promote research, I began to appreciate its power. I then went on to pursue an enjoyable career as an academic teaching world history.

However, things became financially more difficult when I had children and wanted a big family. I wanted to give my children a good life but was frustrated by my salary. It was then that I went to see a financial adviser to help me create extra income. In the meeting, the adviser asked me what I wanted to achieve and what my current financial situation was. He showed me how I could achieve my goals. The session made me feel empowered and inspired. I realised that financial planners had a very powerful role to play as they could change lives, and so I decided to pursue a new career as a financial planner. I studied hard and greatly enjoyed acquiring financial knowledge and professional qualifications, and improving my financial literacy. I also took the opportunity to build wealth for myself and loved helping clients achieve their goals. Now with residual income and professional qualifications in financial planning, I have the means to support my children and extended family, and the privilege of different career openings. I choose to work at university, as I love learning and being part of a vibrant and global intellectual community, and relish the opportunity to help students and young people achieve their potential in life.

❖ CASE STUDY 12.3

I was born and bred in the East End of London. My parents were blue-collar workers. We were quite poor. My parents, my sister and I shared one bedroom until I was 10 and my sister 14. I lived in council houses until I was 27. I know what it's like to have little or no money.

Due to my parents' influence I went to a grammar school, got a decent education and left school with good grades for three A levels. I declined an offer to attend Durham University and decided to go to work instead. My first career was as an accountant and tax adviser. Eventually I got bored with recording history for a job and decided to change career to become a financial planner and make history instead! I much prefer planning for the future than recording the past!

Because of my childhood experiences with a lack of money I have always enjoyed helping people to become financially free. There is nothing more satisfying than helping others.

I have constantly worked on my business, Wealth & Tax Management, by providing the best possible service to our clients, selecting the best suppliers and recruiting staff with a great attitude. The whole philosophy of our business is win-win with all of our stakeholders. The key to my success in business is doing what I love. It's never been solely about making money. It's always been about offering great service and enjoying running a successful business.

I have now achieved financial independence but I continue to work. Why? Because I love what I do. Why would anyone want to stop doing what they love?

❖ CASE STUDY 12.4

My older sister was born while my parents were still living with Dad's parents – that was the norm back then. By the time I came along, we had a council house, but Dad studied for a degree in the evenings after work which led to a better job and, when I was 7, my parents bought their own home. That must have inspired me! I saw how education could be a route out of pretty humble beginnings.

I studied economics at university – and was lucky to do that in an era when the state paid for tuition – and went straight into stockbroking. That was a great foundation for understanding finance and markets, and had the potential to make me very wealthy I suppose, but it was not the career to make me happy. I wanted to do something where I could feel I was more directly helping people, so I moved into personal finance, working with a consumer organisation for some years before starting my own freelance business.

Like everyone, I've had ups and downs in life, including raising my two children as a single parent. But education, including putting myself through professional exams, the experience of working with many and varied clients, an insatiable thirst to know and understand and a can-do attitude, have enabled me to enjoy a successful business, to pay off my mortgage early in life and build up a good pot of savings and investments. Perhaps a rarity these days, I have to admit that the only item I have borrowed to buy is my home. I've always tailored every other purchase, even cars, to what I could afford out of my own resources. The only downside of being self-employed for much of my working life is that I've had to build up most of my pensions without help from employers.

More recently, I've found my intellectual home in a university, where I teach and research. It is an enormous privilege to be paid to do the work I love. Financially, I am in a position to retire in a few years' time, but I would miss the buzz and the challenges. Spending my days doing what I enjoy is probably my greatest achievement in life!

Success requires a strong focus on your goals and the ability to prioritise, as well as discipline, commitment and short-term sacrifice. However, the peace of mind afforded by knowing that you are on track to achieve your goals makes this worthwhile. The journey to achieving financial security is exciting, and you should enjoy the process and make friends on the way.

The key to success is to apply what you have learned. In this book, we have shown you the importance of taking greater responsibility for your life and finances, understanding your goals and values and the relationship between money and happiness, planning your future, budgeting and saving, insuring your risks, creating residual income, making wise investments, buying a place to live, saving for later life, and getting help from your family. To achieve your goals, you must invest in yourself and in your continuous education (Schwartz, 1995). Although you cannot do everything at once, you can begin the process, and as Lao Tzu, a Chinese philosopher, once said: 'A journey of 1,000 miles must begin with one step.'

Activity 12.1: Suggested answers

Life does not follow set paths or conform strictly to theories – how dull it would be if it did! – so you may have come up with different answers from the ones we are suggesting here.

Case study 12.1: Ben Stein (p. 257) stresses the importance of defining what you want and, in this case study, a key driver is never to be in debt. You might apply Lee Brower's ideas of the dimensions of wealth relevant (p. 259): the case study has a particular focus on intellectual assets, realising early on his/her innate skills for entrepreneurship and later on building these assets by taking *'every financial services qualification I could find'*. By adopting a financial plan (p. 260) that involves saving regularly and investing in a diversified portfolio, this case study has achieved the 'True Wealth' that Brower advocates (p. 260).

Case Study 12.2: Throughout this case study, there is a strong sense of the importance of family, a theme that is common to the work of Bronnie Ware (pp. 258–9) and Lee Brower (p. 259). There is also evidence of planning (p. 260) from an early age with education identified as the 'how to get there' way to meet his/her goals and this use of planning becomes more embedded and powerful as the case study moves into different stages of life.

Case study 12.3: There is a sense in this case study of saying 'Yes' to opportunities as advocated by the respondents in Karl Pillemer's study (pp. 257–8): it must have been quite brave to take a decision early in life to turn down the university place and go into business instead and then later to start a business. Again, Lee Brower's dimensions of wealth (p. 259) come into play with human assets in the form of happiness and helping others being just as important as financial assets.

Case study 12.4: As with Case study 12.2, investing in human capital (see Schwartz, above) through education was identified early on as a means of achieving goals. There is evidence in this case study of financial planning (p. 260) through the saving for retirement, paying off the mortgage early and (like Case Study 12.1) an aversion to debt. It is clear that human and intellectual assets are at least or even more important than financial assets, once again chiming with Lee Brower's theory (p. 259).

Common themes running through all the case studies are that:

- All four had humble starts in life so had to build up whatever financial assets they now have from scratch.
- All seem to have succeeded in building financial assets.
- However, they all find their happiness and satisfaction in other aspects of life, albeit that a sound financial base enables the pursuit of these other goals.

Now you have completed this Activity, we will admit that the case studies are ourselves, the four authors of this book. We hope our experiences will demonstrate that the ideas and theories we have presented in this book can really work and inspire you to achieve your own goals.

References

Brower, L. (2009), *The Brower Quadrant: Live Life Deliberately* – a sample chapter is available at http://empoweredwealth.ca/thebrowerquadrant_sample.pdf (Accessed 19 October 2016).

Canfield, J. (2005), *The Success Principles: How to Get from Where You Are to Where You Want to Be* (New York: Element).

Eisenberg, L. (2006), *The Number: What Do You Need for the Rest of Your Life, and What Will It Cost?* (New York: Free Press).

Hill, N. (2004), *Napoleon Hill's Keys to Success* (London: Piatkus Books).

Hill, N. (2009), *Think and Grow Rich* (West Sussex: Capstone).

Pillemer, K. (2011), 'Top 10 Lessons for Living from the Wisest Americans', 12 July, available at www.huffingtonpost.com/karl-a-pillemer-phd/top-10-lessons-for-living_b_1133585.html (Accessed 19 October 2016).

Schwartz, D.J. (1995), *The Magic of Thinking Big* (London: Pocket Books).

Tracy, B. (2004), *Goals: How to Get Everything You Want – Faster Than You Ever Thought Possible* (San Francisco: Berrett-Koehler Publishers).

Ware, B. (2012), 'Top 5 regrets of the dying', available at www.dmcc.cc/pdf/kalina%20 handouts/regretsOfTheDying.pdf (Accessed 19 October 2016).

Appendix

UK tax and tax planning

Throughout this book, we have tried to emphasise the universal rules of personal finance and wealth planning that apply across most developed economies and many other countries as well. However, personal finance decisions always take place within the context of the tax system of whatever country you find yourself in.

Since many readers will be residents of the UK, in this appendix we outline the main features of the UK tax system as it applies to individuals and suggest some tax planning angles you might want to consider.

However, the UK tax system is complex, so the information in this appendix can only be a brief introduction. In addition, be aware that there are changes to the tax system every year. The main changes have previously been announced in an Autumn Financial Statement and a Budget (typically mid-March but due to move to the Autumn) – details are published on the government website, GOV.UK.

A.1 Why tax planning matters

Tax planning is the skill of arranging your affairs in ways that legally reduce or postpone the amount of tax you must pay by taking advantage of tax allowances, reliefs and exemptions. Through effective tax planning, you can have more money to save and invest or to spend.

With UK tax legislation growing ever more complex, the benefits of sound tax planning are increasingly important too. However, your financial behaviour and decisions should not be driven purely to avoid taxes. Don't let the tax tail wag the investment dog! For example, investing solely to save tax would be a poor decision if the underlying investment is bad or unsuitably risky and all of your money could be lost.

A.1.1 Tax avoidance vs tax evasion

Denis Healey, a former Labour Chancellor of the Exchequer, once said: *'The difference between tax avoidance and tax evasion is the thickness of a prison wall'* (Healey cited in Bishop, 2000, p.80). Tax evasion is the general term for efforts by individuals, companies, trusts and other structures to reduce their taxes by illegal means. Tax avoidance, on the other hand, is the legal use of the tax regime to reduce the amount of tax that is payable.

However, official attitudes towards tax avoidance have shifted since Lord Clyde deemed in 1929 that: *'No man in this country is under the smallest obligation, moral or other, so as to arrange his legal relations to his business or to his property as to enable the Inland Revenue to put the largest possible shovel into his stores'* (Ayrshire Pullman Motor Services v Commissioners of Inland Revenue, 1929). HM Revenue & Customs (HMRC), the UK's tax authority, has long waged a cat-and-mouse game of plugging loopholes in the tax legislation to scupper tax-saving schemes.

In 2013 the UK government went further with the introduction of a General Anti-Abuse Regulation (GAAR), following the path of several other countries, including the USA. As HMRC put it, the aim of the GAAR is to nullify any tax gain from arrangements where *'action taken by the taxpayer aims to achieve a favourable tax result that Parliament did not anticipate ... and, critically, where that course of action cannot reasonably be regarded as reasonable'* (HMRC, 2015). This was underscored by Chancellor

George Osborne (2012) who, announcing the GAAR, said he regarded: *'aggressive tax avoidance as morally repugnant'*.

Therefore, you should be wary if your tax planning becomes too imaginative and takes you beyond the tax breaks Parliament clearly intended and into areas that, while technically legal, violate the spirit of the tax legislation. But don't despair! There are more than a thousand tax reliefs in the UK (NAO, 2014) and many tax allowances too. Quite literally, billions of pounds of tax are overpaid each year because people do not use and claim these legitimate tax breaks (Unbiased.co.uk, 2016).

A.2 Direct taxation

There are four main **direct taxes** that individuals in the UK have to pay: Income Tax, National Insurance contributions, Capital Gains Tax and Inheritance Tax.

A.2.1 Income Tax

Income Tax, as the name suggests, is a tax on income you receive. Everyone, regardless of age, may have to pay Income Tax. The bill is based on the total income received during a tax year.

Unless the income is specifically tax-free (see Table A.1), the tax applies to all types of income – for example, earnings from a job, profits from self-employment, rental income, interest on savings, dividends from shares, and so on.

However, most people have a Personal Allowance, which is an amount of otherwise taxable income that you can have without having to pay any Income Tax on it. In addition, from April 2016, many people have a Personal Savings Allowance, which allows you to have a certain amount of income from savings tax-free, and everyone has a Dividend Tax Allowance. See Table A.2 for the amounts in 2016–17. Allowances for other tax years can be found on the government website, GOV.UK.

If you are married or in a civil partnership and neither you nor your partner pay tax above the basic rate, you can opt to transfer up to 10 per cent of your Personal Allowance (£1,100 in 2016–17) to your partner. This is called Marriage Allowance.

Table A.1 Examples of tax-free income

Income from:
Up to a quarter of the value of your pension savings
Individual Savings Account (ISA)
National Savings & Investments (NS&I) Savings Certificates
National Savings & Investments Premium Bonds
Junior ISA and Child Trust Fund
NS&I Children's Bonus Bonds
First £7,500 of rent from a lodger
Drawing down a loan, such as a student loan
Some expenses and benefits in kind from a job, such as mileage allowance (within limits)
Up to £30,000 of redundancy pay
Some state benefits, such as Tax Credits, Universal Credit and Pension Credit

Table A.2 Main Income Tax Allowances, 2016–17

Allowance	Amount
Personal Allowance [1]	£11,000
Income threshold for Personal Allowance [1]	£100,000
Personal Savings Allowance	£1,000 for basic-rate taxpayers
	£500 for higher-rate taxpayers
Dividend Tax Allowance	£5,000

[1] Personal Allowance is reduced by £1 for every £2 of taxable income in excess of £100,000.

Table A.3 Tax bands and rates, 2016–17

		Type of income and tax rate		
Tax band	Amount [1]	Earnings, profits, pensions, rents, and so on	Savings income (e.g. from bank and building society accounts)	Dividends (e.g. from shares and share-based investment funds)
Starting-rate band	£0 to £5,000	20%	0%	7.5% or 0% [4]
Basic-rate band	£5,001 to £32,000 or £0 to £32,000 [2]	20%	20% or 0% [3]	7.5% or 0% [4]
Higher-rate band	£32,001 to £150,000	40%	40% or 0% [3]	32.5% or 0% [4]
Additional-rate band	Over £150,000	45%	45%	38.1% or 0% [4]

[1] Amount of taxable income after deducting Personal Allowance.

[2] Because the starting-rate band applies only to savings income and affects relatively few people, the basic-rate band is usually described as £0 to £32,000.

[3] 0% on interest covered by the Personal Savings Allowance.

[4] 0% on dividends covered by the Dividend Tax Allowance.

The transferred allowance reduces the amount of tax your partner has to pay by up to 20 per cent of the amount transferred (maximum saving of £220 in 2016–17).

You can also reduce the income liable for tax if you make payments that qualify for tax relief, for example contributions to a pension scheme (see Chapter 10, Section 10.2.2).

Income Tax is a progressive tax, meaning that the average tax rate increases with income. This is achieved by dividing income into bands with a higher tax rate applying to each band. The tax rate charged on income in each band varies depending on the type of income. See Table A.3 for bands and rates for 2016–17. Again, figures for other years can be found on GOV.UK. The Personal Allowance and each tax band are applied to income in a strict sequence, being set first against earnings, profits from self-employment, pensions, rents and so on; next against savings income; and next against dividends.

❖ CASE STUDY A.1 WORKING OUT INCOME TAX

In 2016–17, Hayley has annual earnings from her job of £30,000, £1,300 of interest from savings and £500 of dividends. Her Personal Allowance of £11,000 is set against her earnings leaving £19,000 (£30,000 – £11,000) of earnings to be taxed at the basic rate of 20 per cent. Tax on her earnings comes to £3,800 (20% × £19,000). The £1,300 of interest also falls within the basic rate band, but (since Hayley is a basic-rate taxpayer) the first £1,000 is covered by her Personal Savings Allowance and so tax-free. The remaining £300 of interest is taxed at 20 per cent, so tax on that is £60 (20% × £300). The £500 of dividends also fall within the basic-rate band but are completely tax-free because they are covered by Hayley's Dividend Tax Allowance. Hayley's total Income Tax bill for the year is £3,860 (£3,800 + £60).

From 2016–17, income from savings and dividends are paid without any tax deducted, as are profits from self-employment, and you might have to pay tax through **self-assessment**. However, earnings from a job are paid after deduction of tax – and National Insurance (see below). If a taxpayer thinks too much Income Tax has been taken from his or her earnings in error, this can be claimed back. Details of how to do this are on the GOV.UK website.

❖ BOX A.1 INCOME TAX PLANNING

- Make the most of tax reliefs, for example by saving through a pension scheme.
- Make efficient use of your allowances – for example, building up just enough savings so that the interest is covered by your Personal Savings Allowance.
- Make the most of tax-free income – for example, once your main allowances are used up, save through ISAs.
- If married or in a civil partnership and one of you is a non-taxpayer, you may be able to transfer Marriage Allowance to the taxpayer saving up to £220 tax.
- Always check your tax bill to make sure you have paid the right amount.
- If you have paid too much Income Tax, claim it back.

A.2.2 National Insurance

You only pay National Insurance contributions on income from work – this might be wages or salary from a job or earnings from self-employment. Not everyone pays them – only working people aged between 16 and State Pension age. This means a young person starting a business in their early teens does not have to pay this tax.

Table A.4 Main National Insurance contributions, 2016–17

Paid by	Type of contribution	Income band	Rate	Counts towards state benefits?
Employees	Class 1	Up to the Primary Threshold, £155 a week	0%	Yes [1]
		Over £155 up to Upper Earnings Limit, £827 a week	12%	Yes
		Over £827 a week	2%	No
Self-employed	Class 2	Above £5,965 [2]	£2.80	Yes
	Class 4	Up to Lower Profits Limit, £8,060 a year	0%	No
		Over £8,060 up to Upper Profits Limit, £43,000 a year	9%	No
		Over £43,000 a year	2%	No

[1] Provided your income is at least £112 a week (called the Lower Earnings Limit).

[2] Below £5,965, Class 2 contributions are optional.

Unlike Income Tax, National Insurance is worked out separately for each pay period, for example each month if you are paid monthly, not over a whole year.

With some types of National Insurance contributions, you are building up an entitlement to claim certain state benefits, such as State Pension, Jobseeker's Allowance (payable to employees who become unemployed) and Maternity Allowance (for new mums).

In some situations when you are not paying National Insurance, you will instead receive National Insurance credits that count towards your entitlement to state benefits. For example, this applies if you cannot work (for example, because of illness or unemployment) or you are claiming certain state benefits because your income is low.

Table A.4 shows the main rates of National Insurance contributions payable in 2016–17. Figures for other tax years can be found on the GOV.UK website. Employers also have to pay National Insurance, so this would be relevant to you if you started your own business and employed someone.

If you are an employee, National Insurance is deducted from your pay before you get it. If you are self-employed you pay National Insurance through **self assessment**.

❖ CASE STUDY A.2 WORKING OUT NATIONAL INSURANCE

In 2016–17, Hayley has annual earnings from her job of £30,000, £1,300 of interest from savings and £500 of dividends. National Insurance is charged only on income from work. Hayley is paid monthly, getting gross pay of £2,500 a month (£30,000 / 12). The first £672 a month is below the Primary Threshold (the monthly equivalent of £155 a week). National Insurance on the remainder comes to £219.36 a month (12% × [£2,500 – £672]).

❖ **BOX A.2 NATIONAL INSURANCE PLANNING**

- If you are self-employed and earning less than £5,965, it's often worth paying Class 2 contributions because they are a cheap way to build up State Pension entitlement.
- Always check the National Insurance deductions from your wages or salary to make sure you have paid the right amount.
- If you have paid too much National Insurance, ask your employer to correct it.

A.2.3 Capital Gains Tax (CGT)

CGT is charged on any profits (the 'gains') you make when you sell or give away something and it has increased in value since the time you started to own it. It can apply to anyone, regardless of age.

Unless a gain is specifically tax-free – see Table A.5 – CGT applies to gains from any type of asset, for example shares, investment funds, a second home, buy-to-let property, jewellery, paintings, antiques, and so on.

If the total of any gains made in a tax year, less any losses made that year or brought forward from earlier years exceeds an annual allowance, the excess is liable to CGT. The annual allowance in 2016–17 is £11,100.

Gains on which tax is due are added to your taxable income for the tax year. Any part of the gains that falls within the basic-rate band is taxed at a lower CGT rate and any gains above that are charged at a higher rate. The rates depend on the type of asset and are shown in Table A.6.

Table A.5 Examples of tax-free gains

Type of asset or gift
Gifts to your husband, wife or civil partner
Gifts to charity
Whatever you leave on death
Your only or main home
Investments held in pensions
Investments held in ISAs
Junior ISA and Child Trust Fund
Gilts and many corporate bonds
Tangible personal belongings, such as paintings and antiques, sold for less than £6,000
Private cars
'Wasting assets' (things with a predictable life of less than 50 years)
British money, including sovereigns dated after 1837
Foreign currency for your personal use

Table A.6 CGT rates, 2016–17

Type of asset	Lower CGT rate	Upper CGT rate
Residential property	18%	28%
Any other asset	10%	20%

❖ CASE STUDY A.3 WORKING OUT CGT

In 2016–17, Hayley has annual earnings from her job of £30,000, £1,300 of interest from savings and £500 of dividends (£31,800 of income in total). The first £11,000 is covered by her Personal Allowance and the remaining £20,800 (£31,800 – £11,000) falls into the basic-rate band. The standard basic-rate band in 2016–17 is £32,000 (see Table A.2 above), so Hayley has £11,200 (£32,000 – £20,800) of unused basic-rate band.

In 2016–17, Hayley also sells a house that she inherited from her uncle. Hayley has never lived in the house and, during the time she has owned it, it has increased in value and she has a gain of £40,000. After deducting the annual allowance, the taxable gain is £28,900 (£40,000 – £11,100). This is added to her taxable income and the first £11,200 of the gain falls into the basic-rate band where it is taxed at 18 per cent. The rest is taxed at 28 per cent. Her CGT bill is £6,972 ([18% × £11,200] + [28% × £17,700]).

❖ BOX A.3 CGT PLANNING

- Consider investments that are CGT-free, such as ISAs.
- Where possible, stagger sales and gifts of assets so that your gains do not exceed your annual allowance.
- If you are married or in a civil partnership, making CGT-free gifts to your partner may help them to use their Income Tax and CGT allowances and reliefs more effectively.

A.2.4 Inheritance Tax (IHT)

IHT may be payable whenever someone gives away money or assets in their lifetime or when they pass on their estate on death. It is (in most cases) paid by the giver. However, many gifts and bequests are tax-free – see Table A.7 – and everyone has a nil-rate band (NRB), which is a first slice of gifts that are tax-free (£325,000 in 2016–17).

From April 2017, an extra slice of NRB is due to be introduced. It will start at £100,000, increasing each year until it reaches £175,000. It can only be set against a

Table A.7 Main gifts that are free of Inheritance Tax

When the gift is made	Limit on the amount you can give this way
Tax-free in lifetime and on death	
■ Gifts between husband and wife or civil partners	Usually unlimited, but £325,000 if the recipient's permanent home is outside the UK
■ Gifts to charities and some similar bodies	Unlimited
■ Gifts of national heritage property	Unlimited
■ Gifts to political parties	Unlimited
■ Gifts to housing associations	Unlimited
Tax-free lifetime gifts	
■ Normal expenditure out of income	Unlimited
■ Gifts for the maintenance of your family	Unlimited
■ Lottery syndicates and similar arrangements	Unlimited, provided prior agreement (preferably in writing) to share wins
■ Yearly tax-free exemption	£3,000. Unused part can be carried forward but one year only
■ Small gifts	£250 per person per year. Cannot be combined with any other exemption
■ Wedding gifts	£5,000 if you are a parent, £2,500 if you are a grandparent, £1,000 anyone else
■ PETs if you survive seven years	Unlimited

family home (or other assets if the giver has downsized their home) passed on to children or other direct descendants.

With married couples and civil partners, where the first to die does not fully use their NRB, the surviving partner can inherit the unused proportion to increase the NRB available against their own estate.

IHT is an unusual tax, because, instead of applying to a transaction in isolation, tax is calculated by looking at the record of gifts over the seven years up to the latest gift (see Figure 11.2 in Chapter 11). Earlier gifts are set against the NRB first to determine how much NRB is left to set against the current gift. Tax-free gifts and any gifts longer than seven years ago drop out of the calculation and so are ignored. This process applies to lifetime gifts and also to bequests on death when the passing on of their estate is treated as the final gift a person makes.

Lifetime gifts that are not tax-free will usually be Potentially Exempt Transfers (PETs). A PET is treated as tax-free for now and will be confirmed as tax-free provided the giver survives for seven years after making it. If they die within seven years, the gift is deemed to be taxable after all, in which case there could be some tax to pay on the gift – and you as the recipient of the gift might be asked to pay the tax, but if you cannot or will not, the estate will pay it instead. Failed PETs may also cause some extra tax on the giver's estate because some of the nil-rate band will have been used up on the PET leaving less to set against the estate.

Gifts that are neither tax-free nor PETs are taxable and there might be tax to pay at the time they are made. There may also be extra tax to pay if the giver dies within seven years. Very few types of gift are taxable, mostly just gifts to trusts (see Chapter 11, Section 11.5).

Where Inheritance Tax is due, the rate is 20 per cent on lifetime gifts and 40 per cent for any tax that becomes due on death. Where at least 10 per cent of the taxable estate on death is left to charity, the tax rate on the remainder is reduced to 36 per cent.

> ### ❖ BOX A.4 IHT PLANNING
>
> - Provided you can afford to give money away, making tax-free lifetime gifts can be a way to reduce tax on your estate.
> - Chapter 11 suggests ways that family may be able to help you tax-efficiently.

A.3 Indirect taxes

In addition to the direct taxes described in Section A.2, there are a variety of **indirect taxes** that are levied on your money when you spend it.

Indirect taxes that are particularly relevant to personal financial planning include, for example:

- **Value Added Tax (VAT).** This is charged at a rate of 20 per cent on most goods and services that you buy. However, there is no VAT on some items, such as food, children's clothing, books, postage and most financial services, but not financial advice (which has VAT added at the standard 20 per cent rate). A reduced rate of 5 per cent is charged on domestic fuel.
- **Insurance Premium Tax (IPT).** This adds 10 per cent to the cost of many types of insurance in 2016–17. However, where insurance is bundled with other goods, such as travel cover sold as part of a package holiday, the rate is higher at 20 per cent. Some types of insurance, such as life cover, are IPT-free.
- **Stamp Duty Land Tax** (or **Land and Buildings Transaction Tax** in Scotland) when you buy a property. You can find information about this in Chapter 8, Section 8.3.1.
- **Stamp Duty Reserve Tax** when you buy shares. In most cases, this is 0.5 per cent of the price you pay.

There is very little you can do to avoid indirect taxes apart from reducing or avoiding spending on taxed items.

References

Ayrshire Pullman Motor Services v *Commissioners of Inland Revenue*, 1929, 14 TC 754.

Bishop, M. (2000) 'The mystery of the vanishing taxpayer' in *The Economist*, Issue 8155, 29 January.

HM Revenue & Customs (HMRC) (2015) *General Anti-Abuse Rule (GAAR) guidance Parts A-C* [online] https://www.gov.uk/government/publications/tax-avoidance-general-anti-abuse-rules (Accessed 12 April 2016).

National Audit Office (NAO) (2014) *Tax reliefs* [online] https://www.nao.org.uk/wp-content/uploads/2014/03/Tax-reliefs.pdf (Accessed 2 June 2016).

Osborne, G. (2012) *Budget speech* [online] www.publications.parliament.uk/pa/cm201212/cmhansrd/cm120321/debtext/120321-0001.htm (Accessed 12 April 2016).

Unbiased.co.uk (2016) *Tax action 2016* [online] https://www.unbiased.co.uk/tax-action (Accessed 2 June 2016).

Glossary

Active income
Income that requires continuous effort through work if it is to be sustained.

Active investing
Selecting individual investments ('stock picking') and choosing the timing of purchases and sales ('market timing') in the belief that this can produce superior returns.

Ageing population
A population where the proportion of people in older age cohorts is rising relative to younger age cohorts.

Annuity
An insurance product where you give up a lump sum in return for an income. In the case of a 'lifetime annuity' the income is payable for the rest of your life and so provides protection from longevity risk.

Asset allocation
Combining different asset classes within a portfolio in specified proportions in order to manage risk and return.

Asset-based welfare
An approach to relieving poverty and increasing social mobility that relies on helping people to build up wealth through transfers and incentives. This contrasts with most welfare policies that aim to top up the income of people with low means.

Asset class
A group of assets that have broadly the same characteristics, for example in terms of risk and how they are affected by economic events.

Attitude to risk
The degree to which you are comfortable taking investment risk, particularly capital risk.

Automatic enrolment
A requirement that employers automatically put most employees into a workplace pension scheme. Employees can opt out if they want to.

Automatic (System 1) thinking
Rapid, intuitive, non-conscious, effortless processing that relies on emotions and short-cuts.

Average
The central point of a set of data. Unless otherwise stated, this typically is the sum of all the values in the set divided by the number of items in the set. Technically, this is called the 'mean'.

Bonds	(also called Fixed interest) Loans to a company, government, local council or other body. Typically, the loans will be repaid on a set future date and, in the meantime, may pay interest. However, the loans can also be bought and sold on a stock market.
Budget	This is a statement of intended spending, i.e. a tool for control.
Budget constraint	The maximum goods and services an individual can buy at current prices given their current income.
Capacity for loss	The degree to which you can absorb a loss of capital or income without jeopardising your financial independence.
Capital risk	The risk of losing some or all of your original investment (your 'capital') or returns you have built up but not yet cashed in.
Cashflow statement	What you start out with when you first list income and spending to see if you have a surplus or deficit is a cashflow statement.
Closet trackers	Investment funds that are marketed as actively managed (and have the higher charges associated with active investing) but in reality track their benchmark closely and so behave like passive funds.
Compounding	The process by which the return on savings and investments is reinvested and so itself earns future returns.
Correlation	A statistical term that describes how well changes in one item are matched to changes in another item. If both change in exactly the same way, the correlation is called 'perfect'.
Credit reference agency	Firm that specialises in collecting data about individuals (and businesses) that can be used to predict how likely a borrower is to default on a loan.
Defined-benefit	This describes a pension scheme where you are promised a certain level of future pension (often linked to your salary while working).
Defined-contribution	This describes a pension scheme where you cannot know in advance how much pension you will get because it depends on the amount paid in, investment returns, charges and investment conditions when you retire.
Direct taxes	Taxes on income or wealth.
Diversification	Reducing risk by investing in a range of different investments.

Drawdown	An arrangement where a pension pot is left invested after retirement and income and lump sums are provided by cashing in investments when needed or drawing off the 'natural income' (the return from the investments).
Earnings-related pension	Arrangement where those who pay more in tax get higher levels of pension with both linked to earnings.
Efficient frontier	The set of portfolios that offer the highest return for a given level of risk, or the lowest risk for a given level of return.
Equities	Shares in a company. Buying shares, in effect, makes you a part owner of the company along with all the other shareholders.
Estate	The value of everything you own less everything you owe.
Extrinsic motivation	External factors that drive behaviour and actions. Closely related to 'Push factors'.
Family offset mortgage	An offset mortgage that combines one person's mortgage with the savings of other people.
Financial capital	Assets that have a monetary value.
Financial independence	The ability to fund your desired lifestyle throughout any stage of life regardless of your ability or desire to work.
Financial planning	'The process of determining whether and how an individual can meet life goals through the proper management of financial resources' (cfp.net, 2016).
Flat-rate pension	Arrangement where everyone who qualifies receives the same level of pension even if they have paid in different amounts in tax.
Flow	The amount of something *over a period of time*. For example, income is an inflow and expenditure an outflow.
Funded	A method of financing where contributions to a pension scheme are invested. The investments can be cashed in later to provide an income and/or lump sums during retirement.
Gross Domestic Product (GDP)	The value of all the goods and services produced by a country over a specified period, such as a year. Often used as an indicator of a country's wealth or economic health.
Guarantor	A person who gives a guarantee, for example guaranteeing to take over a borrower's mortgage payments if they can no longer make the payments.

Hierarchy of needs	A theory in psychology that identifies the types of needs, and their relative importance, in motivating human behaviour.
Human capital	The skills, knowledge and experience a person possesses.
Imputed rent	The financial benefit you are deemed to get as a result of living rent-free in your own home. This is offset by loan repayments for as long as you are paying a mortgage.
Indirect taxes	Taxes on spending.
Inflation	A sustained rise in prices.
Inflation risk	The risk that the buying power of your money will fall, or be less than expected, because of rising prices.
Interest lottery	Savings product that is a form of gambling where the stake you put up is the interest you would otherwise have earned. You are not gambling with your capital (the sum you originally paid in) which remains intact.
Intertemporal choice	Decisions about shifting consumption through time. For example, deferring consumption from today until the future is achieved by saving. Bringing consumption forward from the future to today is achieved by borrowing.
Intrinsic motivation	Internal reasons that drive behaviour and actions. Closely related to 'Pull factors'.
Investment	An asset whose value can go up and down. This may be a 'tangible' asset (sometimes called a 'real' asset), such as a house, a gold bar or a case of fine wine or an 'intangible' asset, such as equities (shares in a company).
Investment fund	(called mutual funds in the USA). A ready-made portfolio of investments run by a professional investment manager.
Investment risk	Typically interpreted as capital risk, in other words the risk that the value of your savings will be worth less (or more) than you had expected because of lower (higher) investment returns.
Leverage (also called 'gearing')	Using borrowed money to increase the amount you invest in an asset.
Life cycle	Different stages of life that an individual passes through. Financial planning focuses particularly on the stages from young adult through to end of life.

Life Cycle Hypothesis	An economic model that aims to explain consumption patterns over the life cycle.
Life expectancy	The average number of years that someone may expect to live. This can be measured at birth to give the expected total life span or at a later age, in which case, it is a measure of expected remaining life.
Life planning	A process by which an individual takes stock of their life now, identifies their goals and works out the steps needed to achieve them.
Liquidity	The ability to turn savings and investments into cash quickly and with a high degree of certainty about the amount of money you will get back.
Loan-to-value ratio (LTV)	The maximum amount of mortgage you can have expressed as a percentage of the property valuation.
Longevity risk	The risk of living longer than expected. For individuals, this is the risk of living longer than their savings last. For firms, it is the risk of paying out more to customers than had been anticipated and costed.
Market timing	Choosing the best time to buy and sell stock-market investments in the belief that it is possible to identify when the market will peak or a trough has been reached.
Markowitz-efficient portfolio	A portfolio lying on the efficient frontier.
Means-tested	Describes state benefits which are payable only to people whose income and savings are below a specified threshold.
Median	A way of measuring an average (the central point of a set of data). All the values in a data set are ranked from lowest to highest and the median is the middle value. This will usually give a different average from other measures, such as the 'mean'.
Modern Portfolio Theory (MPT)	Economic theories that aim to explain how risk-averse investors construct portfolios that maximise return for a given level of risk or minimise risk for a given level of return.
Mortgage	A loan taken out to finance buying a property and 'secured' against the property. 'Secured' means that, if the borrower fails to make the agreed repayments, the lender can sell the property in order to recover the money it has lent.

Natural income	The income (yield) produced by an investment that can, if required, be drawn off leaving the capital untouched.
Nil-rate band (NRB)	A first slice of otherwise taxable gifts made over a seven-year period on which there is no Inheritance Tax to pay.
Nominal return	The rate of return from savings or investments without taking account of inflation.
Nominal value	The amount of money you have considering just the number of pound notes, say, without any reference to what that money can buy.
Offset mortgage	Type of mortgage that is combined with one or more savings accounts and/or a current account and where the interest charged is calculated on the combined balance of the mortgage and these accounts. Where the mortgage is combined with just a current account, it may be referred to as a 'current account mortgage' (CAM).
Ongoing charges	(previously called 'total expense ratio' or TER) A single figure that expresses the operating costs of an investment fund.
Passive investing	Investing in the market as a whole with the aim of maximising returns by keeping cost low. It is underpinned by the belief that it is not possible to consistently beat the market through stock picking and market timing.
Pay-as-you-go	A method of financing where the pensions paid to today's pensioners are paid for out of the taxes paid by today's workers.
Platform	An online service that allows investors and/or their advisers to buy, sell, value and manage their investments. Platforms often include additional services, for example share and fund information and interactive tools.
Portfolio	A collection of different investments.
Pound-cost averaging	Investing through regular fixed sums (as opposed to a single lump sum) in order to remove the risks associated with market timing.
Present value	The lump sum today that is equivalent to a future sum or future stream of payments. It involves reducing (discounting) the amount of future sums to reflect the fact that we tend to value money today more highly than money in future because of the effect of factors such as inflation, risk, the desire for instant gratification and ability to earn interest.

Propensity to consume	The proportion of any increase in income that is expected to be used to buy further goods and services.
Pull factor	An internal reason that motivates a decision or action. Pull factors are often positive in nature.
Push factor	An external force that motivates a decision or action. Push factors are often negative in nature.
Rational behaviour	Making reasoned choices that aim to maximise satisfaction.
Real return	The return from savings or investments after adjusting for the effect of inflation.
Real value	The buying power of a sum of money taking into account the change in prices (up in the case of inflation) since some specified base year. When the base year is today, the real value may be referred to as a value in 'today's money'.
Reflective (System 2) thinking	Slow, logical processing that requires effort.
Residual income	Income that is sustained without the need for continuous effort – for example, income from investment in property and financial assets.
Risk premium	The expected extra return from a riskier asset required to persuade an investor to hold that asset rather than one which is risk-free (where 'risk' is defined as capital risk).
Self assessment	A process for collecting tax in the UK that involves you completing a tax return once a year and paying tax due in one, two or more lump sums during the year.
Shortfall risk	The risk of being unable to reach your goal because the return on your savings or investments is too low.
SMART goals	Financial planning goals that are Specific, Measurable, Attainable, Relevant and Timely.
Social capital	There is no single definition, but social capital can be thought of as the connections, shared values and trust that enable groups of individuals to work together and provide mutual support.
Social mobility	Movement of people during their lifetime to different levels in a social hierarchy typically linked to income and wealth.
Stock	The amount of something *at a point in time* – for example, wealth.

Stock picking — Choosing the best shares or other investments in the belief that it is possible to identify which ones will perform better in future than the market as a whole.

Support ratio — This is often defined as the number of people of working age divided by the number of people over retirement age, sometimes called the 'old-age support ratio'.

Tax wrapper — An arrangement through which you can save or invest that gives special tax treatment to the savings and investments that you choose.

Tax year — The 12-month period over which many tax calculations are made. It runs from 6 April one year to the following 5 April.

Tenure — The way land or buildings are occupied, in particular as an owner or as a tenant (someone who rents).

Term — The time period over which you borrow or invest a sum of money.

Trust — A legal arrangement, where money and/or assets are set aside to be used for the benefit of one or more people but are legally held and looked after by someone else.

Index

Page numbers relating to figures will be in italics followed by the letter 'f', and page numbers relating to tables will be in italics followed by the letter 't'.

Taylor & Francis eBooks

Helping you to choose the right eBooks for your Library

Add Routledge titles to your library's digital collection today. Taylor and Francis ebooks contains over 50,000 titles in the Humanities, Social Sciences, Behavioural Sciences, Built Environment and Law.

Choose from a range of subject packages or create your own!

Benefits for you

» Free MARC records
» COUNTER-compliant usage statistics
» Flexible purchase and pricing options
» All titles DRM-free.

Benefits for your user

» Off-site, anytime access via Athens or referring URL
» Print or copy pages or chapters
» Full content search
» Bookmark, highlight and annotate text
» Access to thousands of pages of quality research at the click of a button.

 REQUEST YOUR **FREE** INSTITUTIONAL TRIAL TODAY | **Free Trials Available** We offer free trials to qualifying academic, corporate and government customers.

eCollections – Choose from over 30 subject eCollections, including:

Archaeology	Language Learning
Architecture	Law
Asian Studies	Literature
Business & Management	Media & Communication
Classical Studies	Middle East Studies
Construction	Music
Creative & Media Arts	Philosophy
Criminology & Criminal Justice	Planning
Economics	Politics
Education	Psychology & Mental Health
Energy	Religion
Engineering	Security
English Language & Linguistics	Social Work
Environment & Sustainability	Sociology
Geography	Sport
Health Studies	Theatre & Performance
History	Tourism, Hospitality & Events

For more information, pricing enquiries or to order a free trial, please contact your local sales team:
www.tandfebooks.com/page/sales

 Routledge Taylor & Francis Group | The home of Routledge books | **www.tandfebooks.com**